THE AUSTRALIAN DREAM

Housing Experiences of Older Australians

Alan Morris

For all those people, young and old, struggling to cope with everyday life because of government's failure to provide affordable, adequate and secure housing

THE AUSTRALIAN DREAM

Housing Experiences of Older Australians

Alan Morris

© Alan Morris 2016

All rights reserved. Except under the conditions described in the *Australian Copyright Act 1968* and subsequent amendments, no part of this publication may be reproduced, stored in a retrieval system or transmitted in any form or by any means, electronic, mechanical, photocopying, recording, duplicating or otherwise, without the prior permission of the copyright owner. Contact CSIRO Publishing for all permission requests.

National Library of Australia Cataloguing-in-Publication entry

>   Morris, Alan, author.
>
>   The Australian dream : housing experiences of older Australians / Alan Morris.
>
>   9781486301454 (paperback)
>   9781486301461 (epdf)
>   9781486301478 (epub)
>
>   Includes bibliographical references and index.
>
>   Older people – Housing – Australia.
>   Older people – Housing – Australia – Case studies.
>   Home ownership – Australia.
>   Rental housing – Australia.
>
>   363.59460994

Published by

CSIRO Publishing
36 Gardiner Road, Clayton VIC 3168
Private Bag 10, Clayton South VIC 3169
Australia

Telephone: [+613] 9545 8555
Email: csiropublishing@csiro.au
Website: www.publishing.csiro.au

Front cover: © Mr Aesthetics/Shutterstock

Set in Set in 12/15 Adobe Garamond Pro and Myriad Pro
Edited by Peter Storer Editorial Services
Cover design by Andrew Weatherill
Typeset by Desktop Concepts Pty Ltd, Melbourne
Index by Bruce Gillespie
Printed by Ingram Lightning Source

CSIRO Publishing publishes and distributes scientific, technical and health science books and journals from Australia to a worldwide audience and conducts these activities autonomously from the research activities of the Commonwealth Scientific and Industrial Research Organisation (CSIRO). The views expressed in this publication are those of the author(s) and do not necessarily represent those of, and should not be attributed to, the publisher or CSIRO. The copyright owner shall not be liable for technical or other errors or omissions contained herein. The reader/user accepts all risks and responsibility for losses, damages, costs and other consequences resulting directly or indirectly from using this information.

Jan26_RP_ILS

Contents

	Preface	vi
	About the author	ix
	Acknowledgements	x
1	Housing tenure and an ageing society	1
2	The growing divide: housing policy and older Australians	17
3	'You cannot live on that … It's a joke': housing tenure and the capacity to pay for accommodation	29
4	'You go past the shops and you look and you can't buy': the cost of accommodation and the ability to lead a decent life on the Age Pension	47
5	'Exceedingly miserable and bloody cold': accommodation and housing tenure	85
6	'My social life is down the drain': housing tenure, social ties and leisure	117
7	'I really have thought this can't go on': housing tenure and health	147
8	'I won't be here that long because they are waiting for the right price': landlord–tenant relations	179
9	The increasing residualisation[49] of social housing and its implications for older tenants	211
10	Conclusions: where to from here?	227
	Appendix A: methodology employed in the study	235
	Appendix B: profile of interviewees	239
	Endnotes	244
	References	249
	Index	270

Preface

George Ritzer, the distinguished Professor of Sociology at Maryland University noted,

> There is a great need for theorists and sociologists more generally to do work that can be read by a more general, literate audience. Sociology should be of interest and relevance to such a readership and should inform public dialogues on a wide range of substantive issues. (Ritzer 2001: 1)

This book is written in this spirit. I attempt to present a complex story in an accessible fashion, because the significance of the topic extends far beyond the academy. The book is based primarily on ~125 in-depth semi-structured interviews with older private renters, outright homeowners[1] and social housing tenants who are solely or primarily dependent on the Age Pension for their income. It is premised on the argument that an older person's housing tenure potentially plays a fundamental role in shaping their capacity to live a decent life. The book begins by sketching the situation of older Australians and discusses the particular challenges faced by older people in regards to housing. Chapter 2 examines housing policy and its impacts on and implications for older Australians. The crucial argument in this chapter is that, although historically most older Australians have been able to become outright homeowners by the time they retire, housing policy over the last two decades in the context of increasing casualisation and unemployment means that it is inevitable that the proportion of older Australians who are dependent on the private rental sector for their accommodation will continue to increase. Chapter 3 examines the capacity of older Australians to pay for their accommodation and how they view the costs thereof. What emerges is that older social housing tenants and homeowners are generally able to cope with accommodation costs. However, the cost of accommodation is an enormous burden for many of the older private renters. Chapter 4 investigates how the cost of accommodation impacts on older Australians' ability to consume and lead a decent life on the Age Pension. The interviews suggested that, as long as older homeowners and social housing tenants do not smoke or drink in excess and do not have constant substantial out of the ordinary expenses, they are able to consume adequately. However, many of the older private renters interviewed were battling to purchase everyday necessities and the high cost of their accommodation meant that some were running out of money for food before the next pension payout. Chapter 5 reviews the accommodation of the different tenure groups. Noteworthy is that many of the older private renters had managed to secure decent accommodation. However, a proportion were living in dire circumstances. The social housing tenants were generally happy with their accommodation and felt that they had the ability to age in place. The accommodation of the older homeowners varied significantly. What was evident was that most were deeply attached to their homes. Chapter 6 discusses the social ties and leisure activities of the interviewees. Again, it was evident that the housing tenure of interviewees was influential. Many of the social housing tenants had strong social ties. Their length of residence, the composition of their accommodation complex (most lived in complexes that had a large number of older people) and the proximity of fellow tenants/friends, facilitated the forming of strong ties. Most had enough disposable income to partake in some leisure activities. Many of the older homeowners had a circle of friends and close family connections. The older private renters generally struggled to maintain social connections, and their parlous financial situation meant that their capacity to engage in leisure activities was usually negligible. The private renters who did not have family connections were particularly prone to social isolation. The impact of housing tenure on the health of interviewees is explored in Chapter 7. Although it was difficult to draw definitive links between the housing tenure of interviewees and physical and mental health, the interviews indicated that the mental health of the older private renters was often compromised by their situation. Those in precarious and expensive rental situations spoke of the enormous stress they endured as a result. The affordability of their accommodation, combined with guaranteed security of tenancy, created the basis for most of the older social housing tenants and homeowners having a positive disposition. The landlord–tenant relationship in the private rental sector and social housing is considered in Chapter 8. The latter group were generally happy with their landlord, although there was some concern about maintenance. The landlords and real estate agents in the private rental sector varied. A small number of interviewees had been fortunate and had found themselves in situations where the landlord was empathetic and kept the rent manageable. However, the majority of tenants were in situations where they felt their landlord was unpredictable and they could be confronted with an untenable rent increase or be asked to vacate at any time. The final empirical chapter focuses on the increasing marginalisation/residualisation of social housing and its implications for older tenants. What is shown is that the enormous shortage of social housing has resulted in a proportion of newer entrants into social housing being difficult and challenging neighbours. The chapter analyses how older residents view this influx, its impact and how they cope.

Although the study was conducted in Sydney and regional New South Wales, I am confident that if the research was repeated in other parts of Australia similar results would be obtained. The issues facing older private renters, social housing tenants and homeowners are similar in all of Australia.

About the author

Alan Morris is a research professor in the Institute for Public Policy and Governance at the University of Technology Sydney. His most recent book, *A Practical Introduction to In-depth Interviewing* (2015) is published by SAGE. He has held academic positions in the Department of Sociology at the University of the Witwatersrand in Johannesburg and the School of Social Sciences at the University of New South Wales in Sydney.

Acknowledgements

This book would not have been possible without the participation of the 125 interviewees who were prepared to talk about their lives, concerns and challenges to a total stranger who they will probably never see again. To all the interviewees I am extremely grateful. Any book requires ample quality time. Roberta Ryan, the Director of the Institute for Public Policy and Governance at the University of Technology Sydney, provided a context that allowed me to focus on the book with minimal disruptions. Sasindu Gamage did an excellent job organising the interview material using NVivo software. Jo Milner's transcribing of the interviews was of the highest quality. The assistance of Council on the Ageing (COTA) NSW with the recruitment of interviewees was invaluable. Robert Mowbray gave excellent input and ensured that my interpretation of the law in relation to private renting was accurate. Peter Marincowitz's reading of the manuscript was reassuring and much appreciated. Sue, Sophia and Jeremy were always supportive. I want to thank Ted Hamilton who made the initial decision that CSIRO Publishing should publish the study. Lauren Webb at CSIRO Publishing was always encouraging. In the early stages of this research, funding was provided by the Faculty of Arts and Social Sciences at the University of New South Wales.

1
Housing tenure and an ageing society

Introduction

Australia, like all developed economies, is experiencing a significant demographic shift. The proportion of the population that is aged 65 years and older has increased substantially and is continuing to do so. However, it is doing so in the context of one of the world's most expensive housing markets (Cox and Pavletich 2016; Janda 2015; Scatigna *et al.* 2014). The demographic shift, combined with the nature of Australia's housing market, potentially has major ramifications. In 1971, 8.3% of Australia's population was 65 years and older, which had risen to 11.8% by 1994 and to 14.7% by June 2014 (ABS 2012a, 2014; AIHW 2014). If current trends continue, it is estimated that, by 2034–35, 19.5% of the population will be 65 and over (Australian Government 2015: 12). Globally, there is much debate about the implications of an ageing society and the capacity of governments to sustain the Age Pension and the capacity of the health system (Australian Government 2015; Biggs *et al.* 2007; Productivity Commission 2013). At the end of 2013, the influential think tank, The Grattan Institute, issued a report that advocated the Australian Government increase the age of access to the Age Pension and superannuation (the legislated private pension scheme to which all employers and employees have to contribute) to 70. The report argued that this measure 'is one of the most economically attractive choices to improve budgets in the medium term' (Daley *et al.* 2013: 29). At the same time, a report titled *An Ageing Australia: Preparing for the Future*, was released by the government advisory research body, the Productivity Commission. It too presented the ageing society as a major concern concluding, 'The main sources of such pressures over the next 50 years are likely to be rising obligations for publicly funded health care, aged care and retirement' (Productivity Commission 2013: 11). The Commission also suggested that raising the eligibility age of the Age Pension to 70 should be considered: '… increasing the eligibility age [for the Age Pension] in line with increases in life expectancy would *prima facie* have some benefits' (Productivity Commission 2013: 15). The 2015 Intergeneration Report argues that population ageing will slow down economic growth and put greater pressure on the health services (Australian Government 2015). Noteworthy, is that there is no discussion of the housing concerns of older Australians in these reports.

The presentation of the demographic shift as a major problem is certainly contestable. Mullan (2002) argues that the construction of the ageing society as a burden on developed economies is a myth and helps detract from the general crisis of advanced capitalist economies. In the Australian context, Johnstone and Kanitsaki (2009) argue 'that the 'demographic time-bomb' portrayal of population ageing in Australia is misleading and incorrect'. They draw on the HSBC Future of Retirement Study (2007) of 21 000 people from 21 countries, which concludes that, contrary to the portrayal of older people by governments as a drain and a burden, 'older people contribute billions of dollars to their nation's economies through taxation, volunteer work and the provision of care for family members …'. The debate around the implications of an ageing society is being played out in the context of a continuing weakening of the welfare state, minimal or no economic growth in the developed economies and a dominant neoliberal discourse and policy framework that emphasises minimising government expenditure and regulation and maximising the role of the market (Harvey 2007). In this context, the housing of older Australians and the general population has been given little attention by government.[2]

What this book argues is that housing tenure and the related affordability, adequacy, location and security of occupancy (see Hulse and Milligan 2014 for an extended discussion of secure occupancy in rental housing) of their housing, fundamentally shape the lived experience of older people, their social in/exclusion and wellbeing, their ability to age in place and live a decent life (Colic-Peisker *et al.* 2015; Jones *et al.* 2007; Oswald *et al.* 2007; Windle *et al.* 2006). The main focus is to illustrate and explain the impact of housing tenure on the lives of older Australians primarily by using their articulations of their perspectives and concerns (see Appendix A for a detailed discussion of the methodology). Are older homeowners who are solely dependent on the single Age Pension managing financially? Are they able to maintain their homes and engage in social activity? How are older private renters who have to pay market rents faring in comparison with older homeowners and social housing tenants and how do they cope with minimal security of occupancy? What are the implications of subsidised rents and legally guaranteed security of tenure for older social housing tenants?[3] These are some of the key questions considered.

The study is located within a critical gerontology approach. This approach takes cognisance of the political economy and the significance of inequality through the life course: '… social processes allow the accumulation of advantages over the life course for some but the accretion of disadvantages for others' (Phillipson and Baars 2007: 78). The impacts of globalisation on older people are also highlighted in this approach. It is argued that globalisation has disrupted the stability and predictability that characterised the period up until the early 1970s, deepened inequalities and also created new possibilities for a segment of the older population. Phillipson (2007: 328) concludes that within the older population in developed economies there is now:

> a much clearer division between, on the one hand, those able to choose and to identify with particular locations, which are viewed as consistent with and affirmative of their own biographies and life histories, and on the other hand, those who experience rejection or exclusion from their locality and who see neighbourhood change as incompatible with their own view of themselves and their peers.

Social class is central to this differentiation. Upper- and middle-income households are able to accumulate savings and assets over the life course and invariably in Australia are outright homeowners by the time they retire. Households whose members have historically experienced poorly paid employment and perhaps periods of unemployment or under-employment are less likely to be homeowners by the time they permanently leave the labour force, and their savings will be limited. However, the link between housing tenure and social class in Australia is not straightforward. Noteworthy is that in Australia historically most older working-class households have been able to become outright homeowners over the life course (see Table 1.1) and the guaranteed government Age Pension does give these households a reasonable amount of disposable income, providing their housing costs are low. As this study illustrates, for people who are primarily or solely dependent on the Age Pension for their income, housing tenure is often a more significant differentiator than class. The interviews illustrated that an older person who at the end of their working life was in adequate, secure and affordable housing was far more able to live a good life than an older person who was not in this situation. The guaranteed security of occupancy and the low accommodation costs of older homeowners and social housing tenants meant that they were able to live a decent, albeit frugal, life on the Age Pension, providing they did not have any substantial and constant extraordinary expenses. In contrast, the negligible security of occupancy of older private renters, who have to use a large proportion of their Age Pension to pay for their

Table 1.1. Housing tenure of older Australians and all households, 2011–2012

Housing circumstance	Couple only, reference person aged 65 and over	Lone person aged 65 and over	All households
	Proportion of households		
Owner	90.3	76.7	67.5
Owner without a mortgage	82.1	71.9	30.9
Owner with a mortgage	8.2	4.8	36.6
Renter	7.9	19.3	30.3
Renting from state or territory housing authority	2.6	7.2	3.9
Renting from private landlord	3.9	9.3	25.1

Source: AIHW (2013a: 37)

accommodation, meant that their situation was often grim. As will be shown, many were plagued by constant anxiety due to their high accommodation costs and the ever-present possibility that they may be subject to an untenable rent increase or be asked to vacate.

Defining older Australians

It is evident that ageing is partially a socio-cultural construction and that within the older population there are major variations as to how people see themselves, their health status and how they experience and participate in society (Phillipson 1998; Vincent 2006). In this study, an older person is anybody who is eligible for the Age Pension. For women and men in 2015 it was 65 years. When I first began this research in 2005, it was 63 years for women and 65 years for men. From 1 July 2013, women have had to be 65 to claim the Age Pension. On 1 July 2017, the qualifying age for the Age Pension will increase from 65 years to 65 and-a-half years. The qualifying age will rise by 6 months every 2 years, reaching 67 on 1 July 2023.

Why the focus on housing tenure?

Housing has rightly been called the 'wobbly pillar under the welfare state' (Torgersen 1987). Whereas the key components of the welfare state – education, health and social security – are, in varying degrees, accepted as the government's responsibility, there is little consensus as to what role governments should play in regards to the provision of housing (Kemeny 2001). Increasingly, individuals and families are expected to take responsibility for finding their accommodation in the private market (Harvey 2007). The policy shift around housing provision is bound up in a neoliberal ethos that citizens need to make their own way in the housing market (and increasingly in all other spheres) and cannot rely on government to protect them from risk (Beck 2009; Bourdieu 2003; Taylor-Gooby *et al.* 1999). This sentiment has been accompanied by an increasing emphasis by governments globally on home ownership, the selling off of existing social housing stock, cutting back on the provision of new social housing and growing deregulation of the private rental market (Hulse *et al.* 2011; Scanlon *et al.* 2014; Watt 2013).

The minimal involvement historically of Australian governments in the provision of housing has meant that most older Australians have always had to rely on the private market for their accommodation. Table 1.1 shows that the majority have succeeded in securing outright home ownership, although lone-person households were far less likely to be outright homeowners. In 2011–12, 82% of couple-only households, reference person 65 and over, owned their home outright, as did 72% of lone-person households aged 65 and over. An important trend is that the proportion of older private renter households, the most vulnerable group, is growing and the proportion in the social housing sector is declining. In 2011–12, about one in 11 lone-person older households were in the private rental sector (PRS), as were 4% of older couple households. In contrast, only 2.6% of older couple households and about one in 14 lone-person older households were in social housing. The changing proportions are discussed further in Chapter 2.

The housing tenure of a household does not necessarily have an impact on their everyday life and wellbeing when its members are employed. However, when they are no longer in the labour force it can be enormously significant. If they are totally dependent on government benefits for their income, their income will be fixed and almost certainly considerably less than when employed. Older homeowners who are dependent on the Age Pension will usually have far lower accommodation costs than their counterparts in the PRS and social housing, and thus more disposable income (ABS 2013a, 2015). As Yates and Bradbury (2010: 194) argue, 'older households who miss out on home ownership are multiply disadvantaged in that they also have lower non-housing wealth, lower disposable incomes and higher housing costs in retirement'. They concluded that older homeowners had almost twice as much disposable income after accounting for housing costs.

The issue of accommodation costs is not straightforward and within these different tenures there will be substantial variations. Thus, the proportion of their income an older person living by her or himself requires for accommodation will invariably be a lot higher than that of a couple. Older homeowners who live in apartment blocks may have to pay crippling strata fees and older private renters who reside in metropolitan areas will generally have higher accommodation costs than their counterparts in regional locations. Accommodation costs and their myriad impacts for people dependent on the Age Pension are discussed in detail in Chapters 3, 4, 5, 6 and 7.

The other key issue in relation to housing tenure is security of occupancy. Older homeowners who own their homes outright and tenants in social housing usually have guaranteed security of occupancy. There is little or no possibility that they will lose access to their accommodation. Older private renters are in a different position. The limited regulation of the PRS in Australia means that almost all private renters have minimal legal security of tenure once their written agreement ends after 6 or 12 months (Hulse *et al.* 2012).[4] The impacts of having or not having security of occupancy are profound and is a central theme of the book. The regulation of the PRS is discussed in more detail in Chapters 2 and 8.

The scarcity of affordable and secure private rental accommodation, combined with the shortage and stigmatisation of social housing, makes the pursuit of home ownership a sensible option in Australia. Kemeny (2001: 67) has effectively summarised this situation:

> If open access to public renting is denied as a realistic alternative housing to middle-income households while the profit dominated rental market only offers housing at high rents and with insecurity of tenure, the only remaining alternative will be owner occupation.

In those European countries with high levels of affordable and secure rental accommodation and with adequate Age Pension systems, home ownership, not surprisingly, is much lower than it is in Australia (Hulse *et al.* 2011; O'Sullivan and De Decker 2007). Home ownership in these contexts is not viewed as a necessary requirement for secure and affordable living in retirement (Castles 1998; Doling and Horsewood 2011). Probably the most outstanding example is Switzerland. In 2005, despite it being one of the world's wealthiest countries, ~65% of households lived in private rented accommodation (Lawson 2009: 47). In 2008, in Germany, ~60% of households were renters and in the Netherlands and Austria this proportion was ~40% (Hulse *et al.* 2011; O'Sullivan and De Decker 2007).

The high level of home ownership in Australia has important implications for the Age Pension payment rate. Kemeny (2001, 2005) argues that in countries with high levels of outright homeownership, there is less pressure on governments to introduce high Age Pensions because of the low housing costs of outright homeowners.

This study examines Kemeny's argument. Are older homeowners and social housing tenants able to live a decent life if they are solely or mainly dependent on the Age Pension and what are the implications for older private renters of being subject to market rents? These questions are examined in depth in Chapter 4.

Why the focus particularly on older Australians and housing?

Housing tenure is certainly important for all age groups in Australia. However, in the case of housing, older Australians do have particular issues and challenges. Besides the increasing size of this cohort absolutely and as a proportion of the population, there are several other distinctive features. The greater likelihood of ill health, disability, widowhood and living alone are all important features, as is the large-scale dependence on the Age Pension. Finally, the relatively extensive amount of time older people spend in their home means that their housing situation is usually a vital contributor to their wellbeing. These aspects are discussed in turn.

Older people, housing and health

There is consensus that poor housing and/or stress around one's housing circumstances is associated with reduced health and wellbeing (Libman et al. 2012; Smith et al. 2003) and that its impacts are more profound for older people (Allen 2008; Windle et al. 2006). Allen (2008: 34) concludes:

> Housing quality is highly significant for older people's emotional wellbeing. Poor housing contributes to depression, anxiety and stress and older people are most susceptible as they are more likely than other age groups to spend long periods of time at home.

The link becomes even more significant with the very old: 'In very old age in particular, the relationship between housing and health is significant, because older adults have an increased vulnerability to environmental challenges' (Oswald *et al.* 2007: 96). This is perhaps most pertinent in the case of indoor temperature. Older people are at more risk of 'accidental hypothermia' (Howden-Chapman *et al.* 1999). Global warming means that summers are becoming increasingly dangerous for older people living in houses without adequate ventilation or cooling systems (Abrahamson *et al.* 2008).

An individual's housing situation becomes far more significant when they have a disability or have poor health (Smith *et al.* 2008). The proportion of the population with a disability increases with age. In 2012, ~18.5% of the population had a disability compared with 39.5% of Australians between 65 and 69, 55.5% between the ages of 75 and 79, and ~80% of those 85 years and over (ABS 2013b).

Noteworthy is that housing tenure and the ability to age in place has been associated with variations in health status and mortality (Oswald *et al.* 2007; Petersen *et al.* 2014; Waters 2002). The potential impacts of housing tenure on health are discussed in detail in Chapter 7.

Large-scale dependence on the Age Pension
For the majority of older Australians, the Age Pension is their primary or sole source of income. In June 2012, 3.2 million Australians (14% of the population) were aged 65 and over and 76% received an Age Pension (AIHW 2013b). Of those receiving the Age Pension, 59% received a full-rate pension. Only 12% of older Australians were employed in 2012, mostly part-time. The Age Pension, introduced in 1909, and funded from general revenue, is income and asset tested. At the moment, the private home is not part of the asset test. In June 2015, the single Age Pension, if we include the 'maximum pension supplement' and the 'energy supplement', was $430.10 a week and couples received $648.40 a week or $324.20 each. Both payments are above the poverty line (including housing costs), which, in December 2014, was estimated at $414.90 a week for a single person who is not in the workforce and $585.70 for couples not in the workforce (MIAESR 2015). The poverty line after housing was estimated to be $403.70 for couples and $247.60 for a single person not in the workforce.

The widespread dependence on the Age Pension is highly significant as it means that for most older Australians the cost of their accommodation is a key factor determining their ability to live a decent life. If a substantial proportion of a person's Age Pension is used to pay for accommodation, it will obviously have negative implications for the person concerned. As will be illustrated, this is certainly the case for most older private renters, especially those living by themselves. Fortunately, at present, a large proportion of older Australians are outright homeowners. Yates and Bradbury (2010) found that Australia has one of the highest before-housing-poverty rates of older households in the OECD, 19.1%, which is higher than the USA. However, it has one of the lowest-after-housing poverty rates. This is due to the low housing costs of most older Australians. The cost of accommodation and its impacts are examined in detail in the next few chapters.

Gender, housing and living alone
Ageing and housing has a significant gender dimension (Darab and Hartman 2013; Watson 1988). In Australia, women constitute 54% of all people aged 65 and over and 66% of those aged 85 and over (ABS 2012a). In regards to housing, older women, because of greater life expectancy and the historical gender division in the workplace and the domestic realm, are more likely to be living by themselves and to be dependent solely or primarily on the Age Pension for their income (Darab and Hartman 2013). In 2011, 32% of older women and 17% of older men lived by themselves (ABS 2013c). Unsurprisingly, the older a person is, the more likely they are to be living by themselves – 20.3% of people aged between 65 and 74; 29.7% of people between 75 and 84 and 35.2% of people aged 85 years and older (ABS 2013c). An important trend is the growing incidence of divorce in retirement. In 1990, the average divorcee was 32 (for both females and males). In 2013, the average age was 42 for women and 44 for men (Jones 2015). Divorce while dependent on the Age Pension can have devastating consequences.

Living alone potentially has significant implications for an older person. Besides having to face everyday life alone, it can be financially crippling. The accommodation costs of a single person are not much lower than that of a couple. However, their income is much lower. For example, if widowed, the surviving partner's household income will drop by ~50%, but many of their expenses will remain constant or decrease marginally. This is especially pertinent in the case of older private renters; unless they relocate, their accommodation costs remain the same and can become untenable (see Wood *et al.* 2008). Petersen *et al.* (2014) reached a similar conclusion, noting that the death of a partner or relationship breakdown was particularly serious for older private renters and had the potential to precipitate homelessness.

The amount of time spent at home, length of residence and the meaning of home

Another important feature of housing and older people is the amount of time older people tend to spend in their homes. The United Nation's International Plan of Action on Ageing (2000) concludes, 'Suitable housing is even more important for the elderly, whose abodes are the centre of virtually all of their activities'. A German study found that people aged 64 and older spent ~80% of their time at home compared with less than 60% for younger age cohorts (Brasche and Bischof 2005). A survey of 419 older people in Wales found that respondents spent an average of 19.97 h per day in their homes (Windle *et al.* 2006). The amount of time spent in the home makes the quality, affordability and security of occupancy crucial for the wellbeing of older people (Dahlin-Ivanoff *et al.* 2007).

Research indicates that most older people have been in the same home for many years. A German survey of 4000 people aged between 70 and 85, found that the average length of residence in their present dwelling was 31.6 years (Motel *et al.* 2000 in Oswald and Wahl 2005). Length of residence does make the home a special place for many older people (Rubinstein 1989). Of course, the meaning people attach to their home is shaped by their experience of home life and the broader societal context. Thus, for people whose home life has been characterised by abuse, the home may be the repository of unhappy rather than happy memories (Dupuis and Thorns 1996; Easthope 2004).

Historically, in Australia and other countries where there has been a great deal of emphasis on the importance and virtues of home ownership, home has been 'synonymous with home ownership' (Dupuis and Thorns 1996: 486). Home ownership is viewed as a symbol of success through the life cycle: a housing tenure that offers financial security and a space where the homeowner can impose their identity. It is also viewed as an important part of the family's continuity. The importance of leaving the home to the children was given much prominence by the interviewees in the study by Dupuis and Thorns (1996). Home ownership in later life can also be made fraught by contemporary circumstances, especially for women who have lost their spouse. It is important not to view older homeowners as a homogenous group. Meaning of home may be heightened by an ability to choose. Thus, older homeowners who are able to choose a particular lifestyle and a home that accords with this lifestyle are more likely to feel at home (Phillipson 2007).

An important focus in this study is how interviewees in the respective housing tenures viewed their home. Thus, social housing tenants and private renters may feel as devoted to their homes as older homeowners if their homes are secure, pleasant and affordable.

Social inclusion/exclusion/wellbeing and housing

There is no doubt that an older person's housing tenure can be a major factor contributing to social exclusion and wellbeing. A defining feature of social exclusion is an inability to participate in key aspects of human activity. Burchardt *et al.* (2002) identify four features of social exclusion: consumption; production (the ability to participate in the labour market); political engagement (involvement in local decision making) and social interaction and social connections with family and friends. In the case of the older people I interviewed, the two crucial features of social exclusion are consumption and social interaction and connections. Political disengagement could be a voluntary activity, as could non-participation in the labour market. Of course, the latter is often a function of age discrimination.

A UK study on the social exclusion of older people found that older people who were most prone to social exclusion: lived alone; had no children they could rely on; were over 80; were in poor physical or mental health; and had low income and lived in rented accommodation (Barnes *et al.* 2006). The report found that older '[r]enters and part renters in the private and social rental sector have the highest proportion of individuals excluded on all dimensions' and that 'private renters are even more likely to be excluded from basic services, and are more likely to experience neighbourhood and financial exclusion' (Barnes *et al.* 2006). This finding is not surprising. As is discussed, the high cost of accommodation in the PRS and the limited security of occupancy have the potential to have several cumulative impacts. Older private renters are likely to suffer from exclusion in regards to consumption and their lack of security and high accommodation costs would make them more prone to poor physical and mental health and this in turn is likely to affect their capacity to maintain social connections. As Barnes *et al.* (2006: 9–10) argue, the more excluded an older person is, the more likely it is that their wellbeing will be poor:

> The aspects of quality of life defined in terms of self-realisation (optimism, life satisfaction, disposition, energy) appear to be most related to multiple exclusion. Multiply excluded older people are likely to report a lack of control over their lives.

An important aspect is the extent to which social exclusion is a chronic or temporary phenomenon. Like homelessness or unemployment, the longer social exclusion ensues, the more likely it is that the individual or household will remain permanently excluded and the intensity of the exclusion and its impacts may heighten (see Morris and Wilson 2014). In the case of an older person who is socially excluded, it is more likely to become a permanent phenomenon unless there is a major shift in their circumstances. Thus, the exclusion of an older private renter is likely to become more entrenched over time due to their savings being depleted (presuming they had some savings at the outset) and them living with the constant possibility that their rent could be increased and that they may be forced to move.

On the other side of the coin is social inclusion. Age-friendly cities are defined by older residents having the capacity to engage in all activities. Adequate, appropriate, secure and affordable housing is integral to an age-friendly city and social inclusion (Kneale 2012).

The capabilities approach and the capacity to live a decent life

The study draws on the capabilities approach of the Nobel prize-winning economist, Amartya Sen. The approach focuses on whether individuals have the capacity to do the things that they value in order to lead a decent life. It thus 'gives a central role to the evaluation of a person's achievements and freedoms in terms of his or her actual ability to do the different things a person has reason to value doing or being' (Sen 2009: 15). In summary, it refers to how much agency an individual has. A deprivation of basic capabilities denotes situations where an individual has minimal opportunities and choices and does not have the capability to lead a decent life – 'to pursue the objectives they have reason to value' (Dreze and Sen 2002: 36). A central finding of this study is that many of the older private renters interviewed were suffering from a deprivation of basic capabilities. They had minimal control and capacity to lead a decent life.

Central to the capability approach is the distinction between capabilities and 'functionings'. Functionings refer to what people actually achieve and do whereas capabilities refers to the capacity of people to achieve functionings if they so desire. Functionings range from elementary activities such as adequate nutrition to 'very complex activities or personal states, such as being able to take part in the life of the community and having self-respect' (Sen 1999: 75). A good example of capabilities impacting on functioning is literacy. If a person cannot read or write, it is evident that there will be a range of activities closed off to the individual in question.

For Sen, the aim of development is to extend the freedoms individuals have and to remove the 'unfreedoms from which the members of society may suffer' (Sen 1999: 33). Freedom for individuals would mean that they have the capabilities that gives them 'the ability to achieve valuable functionings and well being' and participate in the society with dignity (Sen 1988: 278). While recognising that income plays a central role in determining the opportunities a person has, Sen argues that there are 'various contingencies [that] can lead to variations in the 'conversion' of income into the capability to live a minimally acceptable life, and … there may be good reason to look beyond income poverty' (Sen 2002: 87). He gives the example of a person who has a reasonable income but who has an illness that costs a great deal to treat. He identifies the 'social climate' an individual resides in as significant;

thus, in a crime-ridden neighbourhood it is difficult for individuals to pursue opportunities. Although Sen does not explicitly refer to housing tenure as a factor shaping capabilities, what the following chapters illustrate is that the capabilities of Australians who are dependent primarily or solely on the Age Pension for their income are shaped fundamentally by their housing tenure.

2
The growing divide: housing policy and older Australians

Introduction
This chapter briefly examines past and current policies around housing and its impacts on older Australians. It first outlines the rise of home ownership post World War 2 and how government policy and the general economic and social climate encouraged and facilitated home ownership in the second part of the 20th century. It then looks at the fraying of home ownership and its implications for older Australians. Housing policy in the rental sector (social housing and the private rental sector) is then reviewed. The review of policy provides the context for the analysis that follows in the remaining chapters of the ways in which the present housing situation of older Australians shapes their everyday lives, dispositions and perspectives.

The rise and stagnation of home ownership
The notion that home ownership is an essential part of creating the basis for a good life has been part of the Australian ethos since the late 19th century and by 1947 just over half of Australians were homeowners (Beer 1993; Paris 1993). Prior to 1945, intervention by government to stimulate home ownership was minimal. However, post World War 2, the housing policy of successive Australian governments, combined with sustained and substantial economic growth and a shortage of rental accommodation, encouraged and facilitated the rapid expansion of home ownership (Bourassa *et al.* 1995; Kendig and Bridge 2007; Paris 1993). Government policy encouraging home ownership included: exempting the principal residence from capital gains tax; encouraging banks and other lending institutions to give low interest loans to

purchasers; the establishment of a specialist housing finance sector; selling government built homes at favourable rates; and first time home buyers' grants. In addition, home ownership was constructed and generally accepted as a fundamental part of the 'Australian dream' and an essential aspiration (Apps 1976). Also, the spread of home ownership to the working classes was viewed as an antidote to radicalisation (Kemeny 1977).

Although government policy certainly contributed to the surge of home ownership in the 1950s and 1960s, there is no doubt that the strong economy and the lack of alternatives to home ownership were crucial (Beer 1993; Bourassa *et al.* 1995; Paris 1993) The low levels of unemployment, substantial economic growth, high trade union membership and strong wage growth meant that many households, including working-class households, had the income required to save for a deposit and service a mortgage (Beer 1993: 152). In addition, rental housing after World War 2 was in short supply so households were forced to purchase or self-build. The PRS was not considered an attractive long-term option due to the 'insecurity of tenure, low maintenance standards, and considerable landlord interference in the private lives (as well as the initial 'selection') of tenants' (Kemeny 1977: 49).

Home ownership rates increased from 53% in 1947 to 71.4% in 1966: the high point of home ownership in Australia (Bourassa *et al.* 1995). In the ensuing decades, home ownership rates have declined and, in 2011–12, 67.5% of all Australian households were homeowners and only 30.9% were outright homeowners. Home ownership for older Australians has remained high. A key question is whether this situation will persist.

The future of home ownership for older Australians

Current data suggests that an increasing proportion of Australians will be retiring or leaving the workforce (not necessarily voluntarily) as mortgage holders or private renters rather than outright owners (see Colic-Peisker *et al.* 2015; Jones *et al.* 2007). Yates and Bradbury (2010: 207) estimate that by 2046 the rate of homeownership in the 65 and over age group will be 10 percentage points lower. This has significant implications:

Table 2.1. Housing tenure – occupied private dwellings, 1996–2011

Tenure type	1996	2001	2006	2011
Fully owned	40.9	39.8	32.6	32.1
Being purchased	25.5	26.5	32.2	34.9
Rented	28.7	27.6	27.2	29.6
Other tenure	1.0	1.4	0.9	0.9
Not stated	3.8	4.7	7.1	2.5
Total	**100**	**100**	**100**	**100**

Source: ABS (2007) Census of population and housing and ABS (2012a) housing tenure data in the Census

> As the post-1980s generations age, home ownership rates amongst the 65+ age group are projected to fall by about 10% points. This means that the proportion of older non-homeowners, half of whom currently are in after-housing poverty, will increase from 20% at present to 30% within two generations.

The data (see Tables 2.2 and 2.3) suggest that their projection may be an underestimation.

Table 2.1 indicates that, between 1996 and 2011, although the overall home ownership rate did not drop, there was a substantial drop in the number of homes owned outright. In 1996, 40.9% of homes were owned outright and 25.5% were being purchased (i.e. the owner had a mortgage). In 2011, only 32.1% were fully owned and 34.9% were being purchased.

The proportion of private renters has also increased, from 19% in 1995–96 to 25.1% in 2011–12, while the proportion of social housing tenants has dropped from ~6% in 1995–96 to 3.9% in 2011–12 (AIHW 2013a). These shifts are significant and suggest that in coming decades an increasing proportion of the 65-year-old and over grouping will be homeowners with a mortgage, or alternatively private renters. The strong possibility of an increased proportion of older Australians being located in these two potentially precarious housing tenures is given further credence by the housing tenure status of the 55–64-year-old group in 2011–12, as illustrated in Table 2.2.

In 2011–12, only 45% of households where the reference person was aged 55–64 years owned their home outright and over one in three

Table 2.2. Housing tenure by age, 2011–12

Housing tenure by age (2011–2012)		55–64	65–74	75 and over	All households
Owner	No mortgage	45.0	73.0	80.4	30.9
	Mortgage	35.1	9.8	4.8	36.6
Renter	State/territory housing authority	4.9	4.6	4.9	3.9
	Private landlord	11.9	9.0	5.3	25.1

Source: ABS (2013a) Housing occupancy and costs 2011–2012 (4130.0)

had a mortgage. A proportion of these mortgage holders would be investors with more than one property. For homeowners in this age cohort who are not investors, the size of their mortgage would be a crucial factor. Households with moderate mortgages will probably be able to sell their homes and downsize into situations where they do not have a mortgage. However, households with large mortgages may find themselves in a difficult situation and a proportion may not be in a position to downsize.

The sizeable proportion of private renters, 11.9%, in the 55–64-year-old group in 2011–12, is noteworthy. It is likely that most of these households will still be private renters when they retire. The possibility of being a private renter is far greater for single person households. In 2009–10, one in five lone-person households in the 55–64-year-old age group was in the PRS (ABS 2012b). We can safely assume that almost all of these households will continue to be in this position when they stop working, because few will be in a position to purchase a property and the decline in the social housing stock means that this housing tenure will not be available for most of these households.

Implications of the decline of public housing and limited supply of social housing

In Australia, the role of government in the direct provision of housing has always been modest. There have been periods when the Australian Government has viewed the provision of public housing as a priority, but these have not been sustained for any length of time or resulted in a fundamental shift in the housing tenure split. In November 1945 the Commonwealth State Housing Agreement (CSHA) was signed. In terms of the agreement the Australian Government provided low interest loans to the States for the building of public housing (Hayward 1996; Troy 2012). Post World War 2, there was much activity and between 1945–46 and 1955–56 a total of 96 138 homes were built under the CSHA, representing ~14.4% of all homes built (Troy 2012: 117). Post 1956, there was a renewed emphasis on home ownership and public housing construction slowed; between 1956–57 and 1983–84, 248 731 CSHA homes were built, representing 7.5% of all homes constructed. Noteworthy, is that 142 534 CSHA homes were sold in this period (Troy 2012).[5]

The coming into power of the Australian Labor Party (ALP) in 1983 saw a renewed government commitment to public housing. This was mainly in response to the substantial increase in the waiting list for public housing and the housing affordability crisis that had developed in the years following the recession and economic restructuring from the mid-1970s (Beer 1999). At the beginning of the 1983, there were 125 500 people on the waiting-list for public housing (Wilkinson 2005). The 1984 ALP platform stated:

> the Labor Party believes that every Australian resident regardless of age, sex, marital status, disability, race, religion, or life situation, has a right to adequate and appropriate accommodation at a price within his or her means.

It went on to declare, 'The public housing sector should be developed as a viable and positive housing sector for the community. It should not be a residual or stigmatised form of housing' (in Troy 2012: 192). The ALP's commitment led to a spurt in public housing construction and between 1985 and 1995, ~115 000 public housing dwellings were built and the number increased from 273 465 in 1985 to 337 736 in 1989 to 388 601 in 1995 (McIntosh 1997).

The early 1990s saw a waning of Labor's commitment to public housing and instead the private rental market in combination with rent assistance from the Australian Government was presented as the primary means to provide affordable housing for low-income families. The then Prime Minister, Paul Keating, captured this policy change when in 1995 he stated the way to 'reduce the public housing waiting lists [is] by improving the scope for people to choose private rental accommodation' (in Wilkinson 2005: 25).

The return to power of the conservative Coalition government under John Howard in March 1996 represented a further blow for public housing. During the tenure of the Coalition government (March 1996–September 2007), there was a virtual freeze on the building of public housing and a substantial part of the stock was sold off, and in some cases demolished. In less than a decade, the public housing stock declined by over 50 000, from just under 390 000 homes in 1995 to 335 259 in 2005. The Australian Council of Social Service (ACOSS) calculated that, in real terms, using 2000–01 dollars, funding for the CSHA, the fund responsible for providing funds to the States for the provision and maintenance of public housing, dropped from $1643.5 million in 1995–96 to $1229.6 million in 2002–03 (ACOSS 2002).

The decline in funding for public housing was accompanied by an intensification of the emphasis on the PRS rather than public housing as the preferred route for low-income households unable to access home ownership. Commonwealth Rent Assistance (CRA)[6] was meant to make the PRS affordable for low-income Australians. The policy change is reflected in the massive shift in government resources to CRA and a decline in funding for the CSHA. In 1984–85, only $234 million was budgeted for CRA and over a billion dollars was allocated to the CSHA. However, by 2006–07, the CRA budget had increased to $2.2 billion and the CSHA budget had fallen to $955 million (Biggs et al. 2008; Parliament of Australia 2007; Productivity Commission 1993; Wulff 2000). In the 9 years to 2007–08, federal funding for state housing authorities fell by 24% (Pawson and Gilmour 2010).

A major policy shift over the last decade has been the steady shifting of public housing to community housing providers (CHPs) (Audit Office of New South Wales 2013). The decline in public housing has been partially compensated for by an increase in community housing. Nationwide in 2000, 23 351 households were in community housing and in June 2014, this figure was 67 046 (ABS 2011; SCRGSP 2015). The proportion of social housing managed by CHPs increased from 10% in 2009 to 15% in 2013 (AIHW 2014). The target set by the Housing Ministers Council was for 35% of public housing stock to be transferred to CHPs by the end of 2014 (Audit Office of New South Wales 2013). The transfer of public housing to CHPs is premised on the state housing authorities being too large and as a result unduly bureaucratic, undemocratic and unresponsive to tenants (Pawson and Gilmour 2010). It is argued that CHPs, because they are smaller, are better able to respond to tenants' needs and they give tenants more choice. An important difference between public housing and community housing is that tenants in the latter are eligible for CRA. Their rent is 25% of their income plus 100% of their eligible CRA. The higher rent in community housing is to help CHPs operate at a profit.

The CHPs are now viewed as the key mechanism for growing social housing. CHPs can leverage their assets and through private finance borrow funds to enable the delivery of new supply. So far, the impact of CHPs has been modest and they have not helped resolve the major shortage of social housing in most parts of Australia.

From the late 2000s, the term 'affordable housing' emerged and has become an important focus of CHPs. CHPs own or manage affordable housing and these are allocated to people on very low, low or moderate incomes. Affordable housing is a different housing product to social housing and is underpinned by different policy and eligibility compliance and also has a lower government subsidy than social housing. When allocating these homes, CHPs need to ensure tenants are eligible under policy and program guidelines, as well as ensure the affordable housing is financially viable.[7] Some CHPs are more likely to rent out their properties to households with higher incomes than the Age Pension, because the higher rent obtained will give the CHP concerned greater capacity to maintain and extend its holdings over time and to be financially self-sustaining. The NSW Affordable Housing Guidelines state that affordable housing is defined by an ability to be not dependent on 'recurrent subsidies from the NSW

Government for meeting operational, financing and asset management costs...' (New South Wales Government 2013).

Despite the growth of community housing, the total number of occupied social housing dwellings fell from 404 992 in 2001 to 396 665 in 2012–13 (ABS 2011; SCRGSP 2015). The decline in social housing is mainly a result of inadequate government funding. In New South Wales (NSW) it has contributed to a substantial sell-off of public housing; between 2003–04 and 2011–12, the NSW Land and Housing Corporation (LAHC), the state government department that owns public housing in NSW, sold over 5500 dwellings (Audit Office of New South Wales 2013). The LAHC argued that the asset sales are necessary 'to support operating costs' and 'cover the annual funding gap' (Audit Office of New South Wales 2013: 22). Nationally, as a proportion of the total housing stock, social housing has declined from 5.5% of all dwellings in 1994–95 to 3.9% in 2011–2012 (ABS 2013a; AIHW 2013a). In June 2013 in NSW there were 290 000 people (140 000 households) living in social housing and ~20% were aged 65 and over (New South Wales Government 2014).

This brief history of public and community housing in Australia is a fundamental part of the context for this study. The minimal involvement of Australian governments historically in the direct provision of housing, and the stagnation of social housing in more recent times, has meant that most older Australians have generally had to rely on the private market for their accommodation. In 2011, ~6.3%[8] of older Australian households were in social housing, down from 6.8% in 1996 (ABS Census 1996 and 2011). The shortage of social housing has made it exceptionally difficult for older people to access it. In NSW, older people dependent on the Age Pension, 'may be approved for housing assistance as an elderly client' only when they turn 80 and if they are Indigenous Australians, when they turn 55 (New South Wales Government 2006). The difficulty in accessing social housing has serious implications for older renters. Social housing has enormous advantages when compared with private renting. In the former, rents are fixed at 25% of income and security of occupancy is virtually guaranteed. In contrast, private renters have to pay a market rent and they have minimal security of occupancy once their written lease ends. The shortage of social housing has meant that increasingly it has become a housing tenure reserved for highly disadvantaged people with complex needs. A proportion of the more recent entrants into social housing are challenging tenants and their presence has affected many older tenants. The respective situations of social housing tenants and renters in the private rental sector are examined in detail in Chapters 3, 4, 5, 6, 7 and 8. The impact of the increasing marginalisation/residualisation[9] of public housing on older residents is discussed in detail in Chapter 9.

The private rental sector and older Australians

Historically, the centrality of the PRS in Australia has varied. In 1945, it was Australia's largest housing tenure, accounting for 45% of all households (Beer 1999). In the 1950s, it declined dramatically in line with the phenomenal rise in home ownership and by the beginning of the 1960s the PRS accounted for ~20% of all households (Paris 1993; Stone *et al.* 2013). Up until the 1950s, being a private renter was viewed as a permanent, life-long situation by working-class households, but by the 1960s it was regarded as a transitional housing tenure: a stage in the life-cycle (Paris 1993). Once people married, it was expected that home ownership would follow. The small proportion of older Australians who were in the PRS tended to be from poor households 'who, whether by misfortune or choice, had not got onto the ladder of home ownership during the long post-war boom' (Paris 1993: 178).

Over the last two decades, the PRS has once more become substantial and at present accommodates about one in four households. A major shift is that, for many households, the PRS is no longer a transitional stage. It is estimated that about one in three households in the PRS are long-term private renters, defined as having been in the PRS for 10 years or longer (Stone *et al.* 2013).

The proportion of older Australian households in the PRS is low but is growing (Jones *et al.* 2007). Between 1996 and 2011, the number of aged 65 and over households in the PRS increased by 79%, from 64 211 households to 114 908 households. In 1996, 4.9% of older

Table 2.3. Housing tenure of older Australians (65 and over), 1996 and 2011

Tenure	1996	2011
Owners	76.8 $n = 1\ 007\ 599$	77.7 $n = 1\ 342\ 156$
Private renters	4.9 $n = 64\ 211$	6.7 $n = 114\ 908$
Public renters	6.8 $n = 89\ 895$	6.3 $n = 108\ 885$
Other	11.5 $n = 150\ 959$	9.3 $n = 160\ 350$
All households	100 $n = 1\ 312\ 664$	100 $n = 1\ 726\ 299$

Source: Customised ABS tabulations based on 1996 and 2011 Australian Census of population and housing data[11]

households were in the PRS; in 2011, this had risen to 6.7%. In the same period, the proportion of older households in the social housing sector dropped from 6.8 to 6.3%.[10] This is illustrated in Table 2.3.

As indicated in Chapter 1, about one in 11 aged 65 and over lone-person households are private renters. This group will be particularly vulnerable due to their dependence on the single person Age Pension. Unlike the situation that pertains in home ownership and social housing, the cost of accommodation and security of occupancy in the PRS are unpredictable. The regulation of the PRS is minimal and, once the written agreement ends, the landlord is able to increase the rent to whatever the market can bear (Mowbray and Boulton 2011). Besides the ever-present possibility of untenable rent increases, once the fixed term agreement ends tenants can be given notice at any time. In NSW under a 'periodic agreement' (the agreement post the fixed term agreement) no grounds for notice to vacate have to be provided by the landlord. All that is required is written notice of 90 days. If the landlord sells the property, only 30 days written notice is required. In NSW (the setting for this study), if the tenant feels that the grounds for notice are not fair or not legal they can appeal to the Consumer, Trader and Tenancy Tribunal. It would appear that the Tribunal is not necessarily sympathetic to older tenants (Mowbray 2010). The constant possibility of an untenable rent increase or being asked to vacate means that homelessness is an ever-present possibility for older private renters (Jones and Petersen 2014; Petersen and Parsell 2015). The landlord–tenant relationship in the PRS is examined in depth in Chapter 8.

Conclusions

There is no doubt that housing policy has and is contributing to a deepening divide within the aged 65 and over population. Most older homeowners are in a totally different position to that of an older private renter. The accommodation costs of the former will usually constitute a manageable proportion of their income and their security of occupancy will be great. In contrast, the minimal regulation of the PRS means that older private renters will often have to spend a considerable proportion of their income on rent. In addition their *de jure* security of tenure will be minimal. Some will be fortunate and acquire a property where their *de facto* security of tenure is significant, but there is a great deal of contingency and many will be in situations characterised by pervasive uncertainty. The dismal situation of many older private renters is accentuated by their knowing that social housing is not a likely or acceptable possibility. The decline in the social housing stock means that the possibility of an older private renter accessing social housing is minimal. As mentioned, the Australian Government's cuts to social housing have led to the increasing residualisation of this housing tenure. Many older social housing tenants have to contend with difficult and challenging neighbours. This has certainly affected the quality of life of these tenants. However, in most instances, older social housing tenants enjoy strong security of occupancy and a manageable rent. This gives them the capacity to live a decent life. The impacts of the variations in the cost of accommodation and security of tenure are discussed in detail in the proceeding chapters.

3
'You cannot live on that … It's a joke': housing tenure and the capacity to pay for accommodation

Introduction

The fixed income of older Australians dependent on the Age Pension means that the cost of their accommodation is a key determinant of their capacity to lead a decent life. This chapter examines how interviewees in the respective housing tenures perceive the cost of their accommodation and reviews their ability to pay for their present housing situation.

The chapter, to an extent, engages with and reinforces Jim Kemeny's important argument, first voiced in 1980 (Kemeny 1980, 2005, 2006) and subsequently supported by Frank Castles (1998, 2005) that housing has a fundamental impact on the welfare state. Kemeny argues that in countries such as Australia and the USA that have relatively high levels of home ownership and view home ownership as a key life pursuit, pension provision will be lower than in countries where renting is common and viewed as an acceptable and secure housing option. In high home owning societies, the citizenry is aware that in order to lead a decent life in retirement it is crucial to be an outright homeowner and eschew the private rental sector if at all possible. To quote Kemeny:

> … insecurity in old age which results from inadequate retirement provision will be an incentive for households to

buy accommodation, and in turn where a large proportion of retired persons are owner-occupiers the political pressure for more adequate retirement provision may be weakened. Equally, in a society where there is a high level of social security for the aged there will be both less incentive to become owner-occupiers in order to stave off poverty in old age and more pressure for higher levels of pension provision in a population where many aged are renting. (Kemeny 1980: 384)

Although we may question the generalisability of Kemeny's argument, what is evident is that in Australia the accommodation costs of an older person on the Age Pension are shaped fundamentally by their housing tenure and that this in turn lays the basis for the capacity of retirees to lead a decent life (see Chapters 4, 5, 6 and 7). The respective mean housing costs of older Australians in 2011–12, as calculated by the Australian Bureau of Statistics, are illustrated in Table 3.1.

Table 3.1 illustrates the dramatic differences in housing costs and how much better off older homeowners are. Drawing on the data from Table 3.1, and the maximum single Age Pension payable in 2011 ($365 a week) and the 2011–12 mean cost of accommodation for homeowners ($37 a week), after paying for accommodation older homeowners would have $328 a week to spend on other items besides housing; social housing tenants would have $245 a week; private renters aged between 65 and 74, $137.50 a week and private renters aged 75 and over, $217.50 a week. In the case of private renters, I have added the maximum Commonwealth Rent Assistance ($50.50 a week in June 2011) to the income they receive from the Age Pension ($365 a week). The after-

Table 3.1. Cost of accommodation by housing tenure, 2011–12

Mean housing cost per week by age	Age	
	65–74	75 and over
Owner without a mortgage	$37	$34
Renter, State/Territory	$120	$120
Private landlord	$283	$203

Source: ABS (2013a) Housing Occupancy and Costs 4130.0

accommodation incomes of older private renters aged between 65 and 74 years ($137.50 a week) is dramatically below the poverty line, which in December 2011 for a single person not in the labour force, the Melbourne Institute of Applied Economic and Social Research (MIAESR) calculated was $221 a week, after housing costs were taken into account (MIAESR 2012). If we present the cost of housing as a proportion of income, in 2011–12: older homeowners drawing the full Age Pension and paying the mean cost for their accommodation would have been using ~10% of their income for accommodation; older social housing tenants, 25% (the rent of all social housing tenants is a maximum of 25% of their income); older private renters aged 65 to 74 years, 67%, and older private renters aged 75 and over, 48%.

Table 3.2 illustrates the median rent for a one-bedroom dwelling in Sydney in relation to the Age Pension in March 2015. It illustrates what proportion of income a person living by themselves and couples would be using if they were paying the median rent in various parts of Sydney and whether they would be above or below the poverty line.

The table shows that a person on the Age Pension who is living by themselves in outer Sydney, where the rents are much lower than in middle or inner Sydney, and paying the median rent will be left with an income that is way below the poverty line of $247.58 a week after housing costs. Couples are in a far better position but only if they are living in the outer ring of Sydney will they have an income above the poverty line: $403.76 a week after housing costs.

This chapter first examines the capacity of social housing tenants to pay for their accommodation and their perceptions of their rent. It then explores the ability of older private renters to pay for their accommodation and how they view the cost thereof. The chapter concludes with an assessment of older homeowners' views around the costs of their accommodation.

'I've never had any problems with the rent': Social housing tenants' perceptions of the cost of their accommodation[12]

Almost all of the social housing tenant interviewed, thought that their rent was fair, modest and manageable. They were extremely appreciative

Table 3.2. Median rent in Sydney as a proportion of income of households dependent on the Age Pension, March 2015

Region	Median rent per week[a]	Rent as a proportion of income for a person living by themselves ($494.30 per week, $430.10 single Age Pension plus $64.20 rent assistance) for single Age Pensioner if paying the median rent[b]	Amount of money left per week after paying rent	Rent as a proportion of income for a couple ($708.80 per week, $648.40 couple Age Pension plus $60.40 rent assistance) for a couple on Age Pension if paying the median rent[b]	Amount of money left per week after paying rent
Greater Sydney	$460	93%	$34.30	65%	$248.80
Inner ring	$500	100%	–$5.30	71%	$208.80
Middle ring	$450	91%	$44.30	63%	$258.80
Outer ring	$303	61%	$191.30	43%	$405.80
Poverty line[c]			$247.58		$403.76

[a] The median rents are based on figures supplied by NSW Government Rent and Sales Reports for March 2015 (New South Wales Government 2015a).
[b] The income was calculated on the basis that the single person or couple was receiving the full pension and maximum rent assistance. Maximum income for a single person on the Age Pension in the private rental sector in July 2015 was $494.30 per week and for a couple, $708.80 per week.
[c] Poverty line is the other than housing requirement per week in December 2014 (MIAESR 2015).

and aware of the enormous impact the low cost of their housing had on their ability to lead a decent life:

> And the government did give us a pension that you can easily live off, and pay this rent. We do not pay big money. (Olga)

> Ah, yes. I think the rent is pretty fair. Yes. I mean I can manage. (Maureen)

> The rent is, what, 25% of your income, so that's 25% of my pension each fortnight. I think it's reasonable. I mean, like I was saying before, there is no way I could afford to live in private rental around here. I just couldn't afford it. The rents are just too high for me on a single pension. (Kay)

Social housing tenants were acutely aware that compared with the private rental sector the cost of their accommodation was modest:

> My rent's very good. I'm paying $80 a week. If I was out in private I'd be paying at least $200 and that'd be for a hole in the wall. (Betty)

> Let's put it this way. You wouldn't get the same private rental anywhere. You'd be paying a lot more and, I suppose, yes, 25% of your total income when you're a lone, single pensioner. It sounds a lot but by the same token if you do it the right way, direct debit, it's taken out of your pension, you don't see it, so you don't miss it. (Colin)

Joyce (85) had been in the same public housing apartment in inner-city Sydney for over 40 years:

> The rent's very good here. I pay $120 a fortnight but there's water in that ... I'm always ahead of me rent. Always 4 weeks ahead ... I'd never be able to live if I had to go out private. I look at it that way ... I know it's good you know. I never complained about the rent. Never, never complained about the rent since I came here.

A community housing tenant who was living in a spacious one-bedroom cottage reflected:

> I'm actually on $166 [a week]. Ten years ago I was paying $220 for a tiny little room [in the private rental sector] and here I'm paying $166. (Anne)

Asked whether she thought the rent was fair, Anne responded: 'Yes. I do think the rent's fair for this place. The rent is very fair'.

The knowledge that the rent would remain at 25% of income was immensely comforting and meant that social housing tenants felt that they could comfortably age in place:

> I wouldn't still be here if I had to pay that rent [the market rent]. I simply couldn't afford it. And now I'm paying $112 ... I write it every fortnight, $112 a fortnight. It is tremendously helpful. People here [the private renters in the apartment block] are paying at least $350 a week. (Rita)

There was consensus that if a social housing tenant dependent on the Age Pension was able to budget, did not smoke or drink in excess, and did not have a large ongoing expense (this was usually due to a medical condition), they were able to live a decent albeit careful life on the Age Pension. A long-term public housing tenant commented:

> In public housing you see, even if they've only got the old Age Pension, nothing else, because their rent is only a quarter [of their income], they manage. Most of them quite well. People who don't manage are the ones who drink, smoke a lot. ... or who have an illness that requires heavy expenditure on medication. (Betty)

An ex-smoker backed up Betty's observation:

> It was costing me between $70 and $80 per week and I was having to buy food on top of that. Paying my rent was difficult. (John)

A public housing tenant noted how the fixed and reasonable rent combined with her frugal living, created the basis for a decent and content life:

> Rent is 25% of our pension. Sometimes they add a little. Sometimes $3 ... I don't feel it because I cook. I don't go to cafes. I don't drink Vodka, nothing. So it's enough for me. I am happy. I am very happy. (Marina)

An 85 year-old tenant who at the time of the interview had been in the same two-bedroom apartment for 26 years, and whose rent was equivalent to only 18% of her income, was dismissive of the impact of the rent on her life:

> I have no problem cos I've got no rent. Well when I say no rent, that's no rent to me. I live very, very well. (Norma)

Only one interviewee in social housing expressed some dissatisfaction. Asked whether he thought the rent was fair, John responded:

> Not really. I know that the people renting privately would say we get cheap rent but when you work it out the CPI (consumer price index), you know we're not in front. We're behind. Every time we get a pension rise we get a rent rise ... and now we're paying for water.

'You cannot live on that ... It's a joke': Private renters' perceptions of the cost of their accommodation

The private renters were in a completely different situation to their social housing counterparts. Their rent was generally considerably higher than the amount charged for social housing and this meant that their disposable income after housing costs was often below the poverty line. This is not surprising. By 2004 it was established that 'Housing affordability problems, on any measure, are most profound for low-income households in the private rental market' (Burke and Ralston 2004: 1). Drawing on Census data, Wulff *et al.* (2011) found that, in 2005–06, 64% of low-income households in the private rental sector were in housing stress; that is, they were using more than 30% of their income to pay for accommodation. A more recent study by Wood *et al.* (2013) drawing on the Household, Income and Labour Dynamics in Australia (HILDA) survey, found that private renting has become steadily less affordable – the proportion of older private renters using more than 30% of their income for rent increased from 22% in 1982 to 31% in 2009.

The cost of their accommodation and negligible security of occupancy were primary concerns of the older private renters interviewed and fundamentally shaped their everyday lives and dispositions. Of course there was differentiation. Some of the older private renters interviewed had been fortunate and had managed to find reasonably priced accommodation. For example, Nellie had been extremely lucky. Her landlord had given her a 10-year lease and her rent, $125 a week (interviewed in 2015), was well below the market rate for the regional area she resided in: 'I manage that well and I do pay extra where it suits me to pay extra. It is just marvellous'. Nellie was certainly an exception. For most of the private renters, the cost of their housing was a considerable burden and provoked a great deal of stress (see Chapter 7).

The most vulnerable older private renters were those who lived by themselves and had minimal or no family support to fall back on. June fell into this category and was deeply troubled:

> At the moment I'm paying $190 per week. I've been here since March 2005 and this that was the fourth rental increase and on 1 December (2008) it is increasing to $210 per week, which I'm finding it very hard to afford ... As I say I've got nowhere to go. My family have got no room for me ... I've got all I need really but the uncertainty of what's going to happen. I've got nowhere to go.

Phyllis (interviewed in 2015) was in a similar position to June. She had recently separated from her partner:

> Last May I started back into the rental on my own and I have found it very difficult cos it is very expensive but it is very hard to get a place that's suitable for an older person especially if it is a female on her own ... So it [the apartment] is very tiny and I pay $270 a week for it and that's a lot of money even though you get a little bit of help, not very much, from Centrelink[13] and so you know you struggle.

Yvonne (interviewed in 2015) was in a studio apartment in Sydney. She was struggling:

> Well I get $981.76 a fortnight and my rental for the fortnight is $500 so it doesn't leave me with much.

Interviewees on the couple pension were in a better position, but were also battling. Interviewed in 2013, Raelene and her husband were living on the south coast of NSW. They had been homeowners but had unfortunately lost their home:

> But we could manage fine on it [the Age Pension] when we were in the house [and homeowners]. But it's a bit of a struggle now. We're paying $330 a week rent plus electricity, etcetera. We can only just manage to pay the rent and get by.

Paying the rent was especially difficult for interviewees who had been on the couple Age Pension, but due to their spouse passing away were now on the single Age Pension. Carmel was interviewed in 2015. Her husband had died 3 years earlier. Asked whether moving from the couple pension to the single pension had made a difference, she responded:

> Well it did cos my rents gone up three times since he died and it makes it very difficult because … I pay $685 a fortnight rent. Well that doesn't leave that much for all the other things that you've got to do.

Faye (interviewed in 2015) was in the Coffs Harbour area, 500 km north of Sydney:

> I was renting with my partner for $250 a week and he passed away and I'm just about to move into a smaller cheaper property next week but it has taken me from June till now [December] to find one. I'll move into a one-bedroom beach shack. The process of getting there has been terrible. A few different factors and one of the major ones was trying to find something that didn't take all my pension.

Although their research was not aimed specifically at people on the Age Pension, Wood *et al.* (2008: 2), drawing on 62 in-depth interviews with people aged over 50 who had lost a partner due to divorce or death, found that in terms of tenure groupings, older private renters were certainly the most affected by the loss of a partner:

> Private renters were the most disadvantaged among the group, with many unable to afford the most basic luxuries and also unable to meet unexpected expenses. Public renters tended to be somewhat cushioned, as their rents are a fixed percentage of their income. Home owners also had some financial concerns, with many being 'asset rich and income poor'.

It was not only older private renters in Sydney who could not find affordable accommodation. Carmel, Raelene and Faye were renting in regional areas, as was Gloria. Gloria was paying $320 a week (interviewed in 2013).[14] She considered herself fortunate: 'If I have to move out of there I'm looking at a minimum of about $350 a week for a one and a half- to two-bedroom unit'.

However, renting in Sydney was especially difficult. At the time of the interview in 2005, Judith was paying $250 a week for a small cottage in Sydney and was struggling to cope. She had been living in a caravan in a regional area but moved back to Sydney to help look after her grandchild. She constantly had to draw on her capital in order to cover her costs:

> I pay $500 a fortnight. But of course for my pension I get $517 [a fortnight], so I have $17 for 2 weeks [excluding Rent Assistance] … If I had somewhere with a reasonable rent that I could afford on the pension, because the pension is not a huge amount and one doesn't expect it to be a huge amount, but it's nearly impossible to rent in Sydney [on the Age Pension].

Judith's situation improved dramatically after she managed to secure community housing (see Chapter 7).

Barbara lived in a comfortable one-bedroom apartment in the city. In 2005, her rent was $295 a week and consumed all of her income. Fortunately, she had some family monies that she could draw on:

> I'm usually short. I've got to call on funds that I had put away; about $200 000 that isn't available if you know what I mean. It's sort of been helping the family in different matters, but it's sort of there in the background ... and that's what I've been using. So I would say I'm short of between $500 and $700 a month.

Nancy had been a homeowner but after her husband passed away and a business failure, she lost her home and became dependent on the private rental sector. She had moved into community housing shortly before the interview in 2006. In the extract in Box 3.1, she talks about the difficulties of being a private renter and how moving into community housing and lowering the cost of her accommodation changed her life.

'If you own your own house ... it is the cheapest way to live': Older homeowners' perceptions of the cost of their accommodation

Older outright homeowners are clearly in a different position to older private renters and social housing tenants. Their main expenses related to housing are maintenance, rates and insurance. Homeowners in apartments and villas also have to pay strata fees. Besides the rates and strata fees that have to be paid, homeowners can usually decide how much money to spend on their homes and whether they should take out home insurance. Almost all of the homeowners felt that they were able to cover their housing costs and lead a decent life. Joe lived by himself and was adamant that because he owned his home it was easy for him to cover his housing costs and live well on the Age Pension:

> If you own your own house and you own everything, it is the cheapest way to live as a pensioner and if you don't drink and don't smoke, which I don't and I do not gamble, never ever had, well I find it easy [to live on the Age Pension].

Most of the homeowners had some savings so that when maintenance was needed they were able to do it. In some cases, they drew from historical savings, but their low accommodation costs meant that many were usually able to save from the Age Pension:

Box 3.1. Nancy's story – renting in the private rental sector and in social housing

I think I was lucky because it was a friend's home, well a unit in a friend's home, and I did get it cheaper than most in Sydney. I got it for $250 and I think it was probably worth $350. I still had a lot of trouble paying $250 because it's virtually what you get from Centrelink. So in my case although under Centrelink you can't do it,[15] I had to go out and babysit and that was all I could do. My husband had kept me very well for many years and I was too old to really get in to the workforce so that was the best thing to do. So I looked after children as many days as I could and of a night and but as I'm now 66 it just got too much for me and I was too tired especially with the children, so I cut it down to a couple of days and just a few hours and I was coping with that, but other than that I wouldn't be making ends meet at all. I really had to earn that extra money to live and not very well at that. Luckily, I have a lot of things from my marriage and I didn't have to go out and buy anything so that was fine but just the day-to-day living and your bills took virtually everything.

It [the pension] is unrealistic. I mean I thank God for it because I'd never make ends meet otherwise. I really thank God for it, but it's unrealistic. You cannot live on that. I mean what would you live on. It's a joke. I was lucky that I had the income from working on the side … I couldn't have lived like that without working a bit and the system is ridiculous because they don't help you. They hinder you. You've got to tell lies [that she had no extra income].

… I'm now in a place that they let me in here [community housing] without a deposit, which was marvellous. I only pay $100 a week and that stress is gone. I feel a different person, I really do … I am so happy here and I've really only got myself so although it's cramped you know you manage. Much better than being out there in that private market, I was stressed when the people [landlord] told me I had to go because they were putting the rent up. I couldn't afford it. Very stressful. I didn't know where to turn but luckily through community housing I just got on to this and I've been very lucky. I look upon myself as very lucky …

The maintenance on this place, we've always kept up-to-date, 100%. (Edward)

As a homeowner you always have to have something in reserve for maintenance. (Linda)

There's always a concern if there's a major repair. If there's an emergency. But I've got my backup [savings] you know. Others may not. (Sylvia)

> I did draw some money out cos I'm getting a new back fence. The people at the back asked if I could go halves in a back fence... So I drew out $1000 for that. It turned out to be $600 so that was all right. (Helen)

An important feature of being a homeowner is the capacity to plan expenditure. Homeowners spoke of doing maintenance 'bit by bit' and by delaying expensive work until they had the necessary finances in place:

> We budget for that [maintenance] ... We do it bit by bit rather than the whole. (Walter)

> And there's another $100 a week going to my ... savings account for ... yeah that's for my courtyard for what I want to have done and that's how I'll save to have the townhouse painted .... As I get the money, I'll get the jobs done. (Jennifer)

Calling on family for assistance appeared to be common:

> I've just got my son-in-law to paint out the villa for me. Fix up some little bangs on the walls from the wheelchairs and everything. (Susan)

> I've got the maintenance of the house but I have a son who is a carpenter ... and the other one's an engineer so between the two of them I figure they owe me enough so ... (Thelma)

A couple of the interviewees viewed maintenance of their home as their primary activity and did everything themselves. Joe (80) was exceptionally handy and had built two garages on his property virtually single-handedly:

> I do all my own maintenance. I do the lawn mowing. All painting. All maintenance. I do it all myself. I don't rely on anybody for anything.

Not surprisingly, homeowners dependent on the single pension who lived in large, old homes by themselves, were more likely to find maintenance a concern:

> The house is well over 60 years old and being out here [the area concerned is lush] we have a great emphasis on retaining trees so you know the plumbing is the old clay pipe one, which now has got roots invading it sort of thing ... And now the roof has gone so I do have a roof leaking and I feel that has to be replaced ... I've got a back injury so I'm not able to look after the pool ... so I have someone come to maintain the pool for me now. But that means every month I'm up there for $135 ... I made enquiries about filling the pool in and the cheapest quote that I got was $21 000 so I'm caught between a rock and a hard place. (Shirley)

Not all of the homeowners were able to cope with the cost of maintenance. Doug and his wife had sold their large home because they were finding it impossible to maintain:

> We'd lived in the house nearly 50 years ... It was starting to show its age and with all the drainage and sewage and new regulations we just couldn't afford the upkeep and to keep it modernised. If we'd stayed there it would have been like a typical old age pensioner's house falling down around our ears because we didn't have enough money coming in for the upkeep of it ... We didn't have the money to do the necessary maintenance ...With the pool degrading, the sewage system degrading and we had to put a new roof on ... We would have been up for about $50 000 and that's $50 000 we didn't have.

They sold their house and moved into a smaller, more manageable home. Their situation was unusual in that they had to support their son who was unemployed and renting privately. Assisting him was a major drain on their resources.

A substantial expense for many homeowners was insurance. Most had home and content insurance, car insurance and private health insurance. A couple of the interviewees, especially those on the single Age Pension, found that the cost of insurance had a significant impact on their capacity to maintain their homes and quality of life:

> I have a Visa debit card which I try to pay off, but, yes, I just rely on the age pension. … I get the electricity [bill]. I get that taken out of my pension and the council rates and my insurance all taken out before I get the pension, so it's sort of not such a big thing when it [the pension] comes. It doesn't leave you much to do the things but we survive. But I find the maintenance is the problem. (Doreen)

Maureen's various insurance premiums meant that her disposal income for other items was minimal:

> My house insurance per annum is $2700. My medical insurance is $2100, I have a car and I don't know how much I pay for insurance for that. I haven't got it off the top of my head. I allow myself $200 a fortnight to live on for food and incidental expenses.

Thelma was also battling because of the cost of insurance:

> Another thing that's getting out of hand is insurances … The house and contents insurance is going through the roof. I mean mine was $1500 and what I did was increase one of the excesses because every year it goes up …

For Doug and his wife, the cost of their home insurance hastened their move:

> And also with the global warming they predicted that … it would flood there … And because they said that, the insurance went up by over $1000 a year and the rates just about doubled so we couldn't afford that either so we had to move out … [combined] with the upkeep of the place [it was impossible].

Although a major expense, almost all of the homeowners had home and contents insurance. Like maintenance, most said that they were able to plan for it and it was not too onerous:

> You ask if it's a financial burden. Yes, it would be a problem if it fell due in any other month. I'm fortunate renewal falls

> due in October, outside the quarterly power/water/rates billing times and sufficiently in advance of Christmas, so I am able to pay it in a lump sum instead of spreading the agony. (Tina)
>
> Always budgeted for it in all of my homes I've had. (Walter)
>
> No, it isn't [a burden] because it is something we know it has got to be paid and that's that. We have money left over at the end of the day ... (Paula)

Rates were another expense that homeowners had to bear. Again, most homeowners were able to budget for rates and they were not viewed as a major burden. After the rebate for pensioners, interviewees in Sydney were paying about $100 a month for rates in 2015. For those homeowners who were struggling with maintenance, insurance costs and other expenses, rates were an additional burden. This was especially so in regional areas where rates in some areas were a lot higher than rates in Sydney:

> I think the hardest part is the rates. My rates are $2000 a year. Orange has one of the highest rates in New South Wales. Higher than lots of Sydney places ... So that's sort of a $100 every fortnight that has to come out to pay the rates and if anything goes on, like people next to you need fences or your roof needs cleaning, all these things, it proves a bit hard. (Doreen)

Christine also lived in a regional town: 'Our biggest outgoing here would be our land rates, $2100 a year'.

The few interviewees who lived in a villa or an apartment and had to pay strata fees appeared to be managing. Their strata fees were relatively low:

> I only pay $600.87 a quarter, which isn't very much. I know a lot of people, well I have friends, who live in apartments more modern ones where there are lifts and swimming pools and things and they pay quite a lot of money. (Linda)

> I pay $110 a fortnight ... and I don't miss it because it comes [automatically] out of the pension. (Jennifer)

Henry paid $690 a quarter that he said was 'no problem'. Sylvia was paying just under $2000 a quarter, but was coping:

> Well actually I manage quite well cos I sold my car when I came here and that's another reason to be living where I am [her neighbourhood was well-served by public transport] and so I think that makes a difference. I haven't got that expense.

Conclusions

It is evident that there is a strong relationship between housing tenure and the cost of accommodation. Almost all of the social housing tenants felt that their rent was reasonable and manageable and that it left them enough disposable income to live a decent, albeit frugal, life. In contrast, many of the older private renters were in a dire situation due to the high cost of their accommodation. Many were having to use more than half of their income to pay for their accommodation. As is illustrated in Chapters 4 and 5, the high cost of their accommodation restricted their consumption and made it difficult for them to lead a decent life. The chapter gives credence to Kemeny's thesis that, in Australia, if you are dependent on the private rental sector and on the Age Pension it is likely that your circumstances will be grim. Home ownership or a heavily subsidised rent (social housing) are essential if a person dependent on the Age Pension is to have adequate financial resources. Most of the homeowners were able to maintain their homes and pay for home insurance and rates without too much effort. For some homeowners, home ownership was a burden. This was especially so in the case of homeowners living by themselves who had minimal savings or homeowners who had ongoing excessive expenses that impacted on their disposable income. However, in the main, homeowners were able to control their accommodation costs and had the resources required to lead a life they valued.

4
'You go past the shops and you look and you can't buy': the cost of accommodation and the ability to lead a decent life on the Age Pension

Introduction
This chapter discusses the impact the cost of accommodation has on the ability of people on the Age Pension to consume and live a decent life. The discussion is confined to shopping for basic items such as food and clothes, the capacity to purchase large items such as appliances and the ability to pay for utilities and run a car. The ways in which the cost of accommodation shapes leisure and social contacts are discussed in Chapter 6 and medical expenses are discussed in Chapter 7. The capacity for adequate consumption plays a key role in shaping older people's capabilities and quality of life. In regards to older people, Twigg and Majima (2014: 24) make the important argument that:

> consumption offers a possibility of counteracting the cultural exclusion traditionally associated with age, as they join younger cohorts in a common pursuit of consumption oriented lifestyles. Such integration, of course, rests on resources.

The capability approach is a useful way to understand consumption because it refers to how much agency an individual has to determine the way they live their life – 'an impoverished life is one without the freedom to undertake important activities that a person has reason to choose' (Sen 2000: 4). This chapter argues and illustrates that in Australia, for people dependent on the Age Pension for their income, the cost of their accommodation is a crucial shaper of their capabilities and capacity to avoid what Sen calls a 'deprivation of basic capabilities'.

It must be said that for many of the older interviewees their consumption patterns were moulded during the 1930s and 1940s, the great depression and war years, and modest consumption and living within their means were deeply internalised. An older private renter captured this orientation or to use Pierre Bourdieu's term, habitus:[16]

> My friend and I have said, 'We can live with poverty'. We cope with it ... We didn't grow up with all that brand thing. So we're very lucky that we grew up, coming out of a war, you know, and the 30s, the depression, our parents went without. So we probably wouldn't starve. Probably, if these children today were in our position as grown-ups, I think they might starve. (Marie)

Higgs *et al.* (2009: 105–6) talk about a 'generational habitus' – the notion that people that grow up in a particular context have similar dispositions and ways of perceiving and operating in the world.

In regards to the most basic consumption item, food, what an individual chooses to eat is a complex process and, by the time people reach retirement age, their food choices are usually set (Brownie and Coutts 2013; Furst *et al.* 1996). However, this presumes that individuals have the capacity to make choices. The financial resources households have fundamentally shape food shopping and, not surprisingly, research has found that households with higher disposable incomes are likely to have higher quality diets and a greater variety of food than low-income households (Brownie and Coutts 2013; Darmon and Drewnowski 2008; Worsley *et al.* 2003). An Australian study found a three-fold difference in the non-consumption of fruit the previous day between the top and bottom quintiles of income (Giskes *et al.* 2002). These differentials are significant because diet quality impacts on health status (Margetts *et al.* 2003). The interviews indicated that there were clear differences in the capacities of interviewees to eat healthily. Almost all of the older social housing tenants and homeowners appeared to have the capacity to shop for healthy food if they so desired, but many of the private renters did not have this capacity due to limited financial resources.

The chapter first examines the consumption capacities of older private renters. It then investigates the situation of social housing tenants and concludes with an analysis of the consumption capabilities of older homeowners.

'I have never felt this squeeze like this, so desperate': consumption and older private renters

The capacity to lead a decent life

Extreme frugality and self-deprivation were central features of many older private renters' lives. Many battled to purchase essential items. Beverley's total income at the time of the interview in 2006 was $290 a week. After paying her rent of $240 a week she had $50 a week for all other expenses. It was evident that she was battling financially and emotionally:

> Well, it just worries me. Sometimes I think, I just wish, not so much worry, but I just wish sometimes I had a little bit more you know to do what I would like to be able to do. You go past the shops and you look and you can't buy.

Gloria gave a meticulous account of her situation:

> My pension (in 2014) was $951 a fortnight, and that included rent assistance, which at that point I think was $121 a fortnight included in that figure. Now you take $640 off that $951, I think it left me $311. Now that $311 out of which I would have to pay for 2 weeks food, but I buy quality food, I don't buy junk ... So I had to stretch that $311 each fortnight to cover my mobile phone, PC equipment if I needed paper, possible bike maintenance maybe, put some

> aside for water and electricity and my food bills fortnightly were around about $130–$140 a fortnight. That leaves me virtually nothing.

She was intrepid and managed to get around on a bicycle. Gloria eventually managed to access community housing. She had been on the waiting list for just under 10 years. She was interviewed a few months after she moved in. The move had transformed her life.

> My current rental is $325 per fortnight 2015 … and I am very, very grateful for this reduction in my basic living cost from $640 per fortnight private rental … The rent reduction has made an enormous difference to my ability to save for a new fridge, new stick vacuum cleaner, replace my PC HD/Screen/Keyboard with an ex-rental model …and meet my electricity costs and food and general household expenses.

Private renters told of how hard it was to look after themselves. A haircut was unaffordable for Marie: 'Things have got harder lately. They have got harder. Food and you know I couldn't afford to get my hair cut regularly. I trim it myself'. The inability to groom oneself adequately can be debilitating. As Twigg and Majima (2014: 24) argue: 'Controlled, clearly managed, hair is particularly significant for older women in avoiding the status of dereliction or derangement, signalled by wild or neglected locks'.

Most of the older renters could not afford to buy new clothes and relied on charity shops. Valerie, interviewed in 2006, was paying $200 a week for her cottage:

> You can't go and splurge on anything and you definitely can't drink alcohol or smoke cigarettes, use drugs, gamble, or use cosmetics or get your hair done, or buy clothes. I don't buy clothes. I get all my clothes … from the skin cancer shop.

Judith[17] commented, 'Apart from the shoes that I have to buy to get around, I don't buy new clothes. I never buy new clothes'.

Even private renters on the couple pension battled:

4 – 'You go past the shops and you look and you can't buy'

> We cope. Don't get into debt or anything but there's certainly nothing left over for luxuries or living a quality of life that other people might see to be necessary. You cut down on everything that's not absolutely necessary like insurance and things like that. You don't pay anything you don't have to pay. (Greg)

Running out of money before their next Age Pension payment was not uncommon and was a persistent anxiety. Any expense beyond rent, telephone, utilities and food was difficult to accommodate. After her washing machine broke down, Arieta had taken her winter blanket to the dry-cleaner:

> Laundry charge $20 for it, but if I go and get it [the blanket] today, then I haven't got the money when I go. I'll find the money somewhere and go and get it tomorrow … Very hard, very hard. I can show you maybe $3 something in my bank left over. No savings. Can't put away any money. This week I pay the bills, all of them. Then next week my money is gone. I pay $300 [per fortnight] my rent, then every month my telephone bill. And then I buy my food. This time only $20 for the fortnight.

Marie was battling to come out on the Age Pension and rent assistance despite having found relatively cheap accommodation:

> I mean [after paying the rent] I have $270 a fortnight to myself, but that's to pay everything and I always try to keep at least $20. If I've got $20 by the next Monday I'm doing it good … It is depressing. It is.

Some interviewees could not afford what are generally considered essential items (see Saunders 2011 for an analysis of what low-income households consider necessities). For example, Malcolm had a mobile phone but he only used it to receive calls:

> I haven't recharged it for 18 months. I give people the phone number and they can ring me, but I can't ring them. I've got

> to go to the local phone box ... And one thing with mobiles, I mean the minimum recharge you can get is $30. That's a whack out of somebody's pension.

Everyday life was constituted by a constant balancing act as decisions were made about what they could and could not spend money on:

> Because, as I say, I don't like to act poor ... [but] you have to go without. I'd love to go, I mean I'd love to go to the Opera. I'd love to go, not every day, not every week, once a year. ... We do go to the movies. I think you have to treat yourself. I think it would be more depressing if you didn't make that effort, but you do have to balance it, your budget. I've got two birthdays this month, grandchildren. Now you could say why don't you give them $10. I want to give them $20 each and I'm going to, but I've had to balance, you know, and I've had a phone bill. So some people would say let them go without, but not me. (Marie)

Chris, after paying his rent ($220 a week in 2006), had $70 a week for all other expenses. He had worked until the age of 64 but had then had an operation that depleted his savings. His ill-health also contributed towards him losing his job and eventually he had to declare bankruptcy (Box 4.1).

The extract illustrates how limited Chris's agency is. His options or to use Sen's term, capabilities, are negligible. His days and his thoughts are consumed by his endeavour to meet basic expenses. Even daydreaming is a luxury.

Food shopping and diet

There is little doubt that many of the older private renters were struggling to maintain a nutritious diet and it is likely that their ability to lead an active and healthy life was being compromised as a result. Many suffered from 'food insecurity'. An expert working group of the American Institute of Nutrition defined food insecurity as the 'limited

> **Box 4.1. Chris, on being an older private renter and consumption**
>
> My only income is through the aged pension but my main outgoing is $220 a week for rent and so it means that there's a very skinny situation as far as surplus, and the things that I actually couldn't maintain, accounts and things. I had to seek advice through the Lifeline people and I was forced into voluntary bankruptcy to pay outstanding amounts ... I don't have a credit card; I don't have anything except the pension that comes in and I literally have to budget to the last dollar, even less than the last dollar.
>
> And quite often it's even little things. Like now with the train travel going from $1.10 to $2.50. It's a pretty small amount, but it's substantial in my sphere ...
>
> Well the last 2 years have been very difficult ... thinking virtually daily and nightly how I'm going to do something with the money and plan what I'm going to do, and of course it's almost as difficult as maintaining a full-time job ...
>
> That's what is happening. What can I do about this and what can I not do about that? And then it is, mindful of all those things, and you know I don't buy newspapers any more. I just miss that ... Yes, I really need to move [house] now because there are lots of things that I'm cutting corners on, that I can't. I'm just hoping that nothing breaks down. If the fridge goes, what do I do? If the washing machine goes? I can't buy clothes.
>
> Well I can't sort of plan anything. That's the thing. The lack of looking forward to something, [is something] I miss. I love spontaneity. I love to look forward to something. You can say, 'Things are not so good at the moment, but, I'm going on a holiday' ... Or if you're working you can say, 'Things are pretty tough. I'm working 7 days a week, but, at the end of next month I'm going on holiday' ... That option is not there for me.

or uncertain availability of nutritionally adequate and safe foods or limited or uncertain ability to acquire acceptable foods in socially acceptable ways' (in Cook and Frank 2008).

The interviews indicated that many of the private renters were not able to buy fruit, fish and meat regularly and that running out of money a couple of days before the pension pay day was not uncommon. They spoke about having to depend on unhealthy processed food and, at times, of not being able to obtain food in 'socially acceptable ways' and of having to depend on charity. Shopping for food was a stressful and methodical process and a central part of their day. Every cent was accounted for, advertising booklets were studied, specials taken note of and much time spent:

> It's a very careful exercise. Every day of my life I write down and I've now found that at 7 o'clock at night at the shopping centre across the road, I can sometimes get bread for $1. They put it on special, so I go and I'll put some in the freezer ... I don't buy what I want, I buy whatever is on special. So whatever is on special, I'll eat that. ... I can get pizza for $4. I got that last night ... I never, never buy things at full price, ever, unless it's dishwashing liquid or something like that and then I'll go to the cheap ones ... I shop around ... I can keep my costs down by doing that, and again, I don't smoke or drink alcohol, so I don't know how much those things are these days and I don't go to the clubs and play the pokies or anything like that ... But then again I have the little dogs to feed ... (Judith)

Judith was one of the few private renters interviewed who had a pet. Although her dogs gave her a great deal of pleasure, they certainly added to her financial stress.[18] Like Judith, Eileen carefully considered each potential purchase: 'I have to be very careful and I have to you know get an item and turn it three or four times in my hand to see if I need it or if I don't need it'.

After paying her rent, phone and power bills, Beverley had $30 a week for food a week. Not surprisingly maintaining a healthy diet was difficult:

> I mean, you don't have any luxuries. You can't afford luxuries, no ... What I've been sort of trying to do is get what I can for the 2 weeks and that sort of gives you $60, which gives you a bit better [choice] than going with $30 ... If I run out of bread or milk or margarine ... towards the end of the next pension, I've got $10 or something that I can use, but I certainly don't have porterhouse steak or rump steak or anything like that ... You know, well fruit is a luxury. You

> don't get much opportunity to buy fruit and you know a lot of vegetables … I like tuna, tinned tuna. I sort of get that. And then there's noodles and mince and sausages and bread. Perhaps the odd biscuits if they're on special … I might have fruit maybe once a month or once every couple of months, because you can't … afford to go out and pay 80¢ or 90¢ for an apple. You just can't because … it's not only your food you've got to buy. It's your toiletries, your washing up powder and soap and toothpaste and all those things that you have to buy as well.

She felt that she was not eating as well as she should:

> I mean if I had the money I would [eat far more healthily]. I'd buy, I quite like fruit and I really love vegetables and a nice piece of steak and perhaps a chicken and all that sort of thing. Most definitely.

Private renters told of how at times they had had to restrict their food intake:

> Things have, lately things have, they're squeezing us. They're[19] absolutely squeezing us. I have never felt this squeeze like this, so desperate. Yes, there have been times where, a couple of weeks ago I had eggs for 3 days and I bought a-cup-of-soups. Yes, there's been times. (Marie)

Towards the end of the fortnight (the Age Pension is paid every fortnight) some of the private renters told of how they had to limit their food purchases dramatically:

> It costs me at least $50 a week for food. If things get really tight I can get by on about $2, $3 a day for food. Basically a loaf of bread and half a kilo of Devon (processed meat). Something like that … I mean that would keep me going for a couple of days. (Malcolm)

Arieta, despite having very reasonably priced accommodation, on occasion found that once she had paid her essential bills she had no money for food and had to resort to charity. Charities were an important resource for many of the older private renters:

> Yesterday I got money [the Age Pension]. I pay off everything, then I buy two things for myself and then I got no money to buy the grocery. Then I go and talk with Salvation Army. They give me the voucher for $20 to buy the food.

Chris had had a heart attack a few years before being interviewed and was health conscious, but his lack of financial resources meant that he found it difficult to maintain a healthy diet. On average, Chris spent $30 a week on food:

> I don't eat all the right food because I can't afford to buy all the right things ... I'm the best shopper in the world. I buy according to price and not according to quality ...
>
> What I try to do is have a big shop as I call it when the pension comes in, which is every fortnight on a Friday. And then I have a great list of things. I only buy what's on the list now.

Lists were a crucial accompaniment to shopping. The limited research that has been done has found that shoppers who shop with lists tend to spend less as it lessens impulsive purchases (Thomas and Garland 1993). Betty was determined to maintain a healthy diet and by strictly adhering to her list she more or less managed to buy what she needed:

> I go around with my list and I don't waiver from it ... It's really important. If people don't do that [have a list] when they're on a very limited budget then they are going to be in trouble because the temptation in those supermarkets is just unreal.

Her well-developed cultural capital helped her accomplish her goals of eating well and sticking to her budget. She was able to calculate exactly what was required and her cooking skills meant that she was able to eat healthily on a small budget.

Beverley never deviated from her list: 'You see you have to budget for what you get and things like that … You go with what you have to get and that's it'.

Some interviewees were skilled at finding cheap food. For example, Valerie bought most of her fruit and vegetables at her local street market late on Sunday afternoon when they were marked down significantly:

> I go to Paddy's Market every Sunday at 5 o'clock and you can get a huge tray of apples for $1 and you can get really cheap everything else. It's all cheap at that time of the day and so I just buy all my fruit and vegies there at Paddy's on a Sunday afternoon.

Their limited resources increased the possibility of inadvertent malnutrition (Sampson 2009). Valerie said that generally she was able to manage, but it appeared that she did this by buying the bare minimum:

> I don't really kind of make a budget for spending. I just hardly ever spend anything. I see if I can get away with it and I'll just draw out of the bank what I need for everything and then just pay the bills and with what's left I buy food and occasionally … I'll go to Exodus [charity that provides food] and I'll get free food.

Coping with utilities

Research has indicated that energy costs are a major issue for people on the Age Pension (Chester and Morris 2011). Between 2007–08 and 2013–14, electricity prices in NSW increased by 115% (Chester 2015). Almost all the older private renters suffered from what has been called 'fuel poverty' or 'energy poverty'. Energy poverty is generally defined as low-income households having to use more than 10% of their income to pay for power combined with an inability to heat or cool their homes adequately (Chester and Morris 2011). For older people, the implications are potentially severe (Wilkinson *et al.* 2001; Wright 2004). One implication of energy poverty is that in order to ensure that they are able to pay for electricity and gas, households tend to cut their energy consumption. This is potentially deleterious – indoor cold, dampness and mould can have serious health consequences, as can excessive indoor heat (de Vries and Blane 2013).

In winter, Gloria never used her heater:

> I'm warm-blooded. I'm lucky … In the winter I wear three dressing gowns, woolly socks, woolly boots, gloves without the fingers in you know … a hat and I wear a giant shawl around my shoulders and then I get in [to bed]. The only warmth I have is an electric blanket and it's on for about 2 hours till the bed's nice and warm and then I turn it off, pull the plug out and … listen to the ABC.

Like Gloria, Carmel hardly used a heater:

> I never had a heater on for the last 2 years in the house. I bought a little, they're like an electric throw. If you put it over you it is like an electric blanket … If you put it over you right up to your neck and turn it on and then as soon as it gets warm turn it off it is like a little tent … So I do think people find all the tricks that they can.

Beverley did not have a heater and said that even if she did she would not use it:

> No. I couldn't afford the electricity. You see my electricity, even though I just use it for cooking, and washing, and showers, and my electricity bill runs out to about $180 every 3 months, just for that … Ah, it gets cold in the winter time, yes. It's cold. I usually go to bed about 8.30, something like that and I listen to my radio …

Several of the older private renters said they went to bed early to save on electricity:

> Well you've got your utilities which are a pain. Last 3 months power bill was $265 and that's [only] me … I live in the dark

> more or less cos I go to bed at 8 and I get up at 4 so there are no lights on. (Robert)

Another health implication is that expenditure on utilities can mean less money is spent on food (Beatty *et al.* 2009):

> I don't like to say it is a hand to mouth existence because I mean to say there is a bit of money there, but it is going off on electricity. (Bruce)

After the rent, electricity was usually their biggest ongoing expense:

> You don't pay water when you're renting but your telephone and your electricity and your gas, yeah, that keeps you poor. (Nancy)

Energy poverty can evoke much stress (Walker *et al.* 2009) and certainly many of the older private renters were highly stressed by the cost of electricity and gas:

> Occasionally I would wake up in the middle of the night and switch the BBC world news on and listen to that because it seemed preferable to me lying there and thinking, 'Gosh the electricity bill'. (Gloria)

Major expenses and running a car

Most of the older private renters had minimal or no savings so any unexpected expense was usually a serious blow and had the potential to cause significant distress. When Arieta's washing machine broke down she was unable to replace it:

> The machine is break down ... Then I call the man to come and look and repair, but he can't repair. Lot of money to do repairing, but I can't get another one. What am I [to] do? Then I go and talk with Salvation Army. 'Can you help me for the washing machine?' Nearly 2 months I haven't got a machine. Sometime I wash by hand. And now the day is come, I can't wash by hand ... My heart is not working

properly. When it is cold then my hand is all blue. Then I can't touch anything ... Very bad.

Faye had been unable to replace her fridge. She had just moved to cheaper accommodation so was hoping that with the lower rent she may have the means:

> My fridge was broken so everything I had in there went off ... I can't afford a new fridge so I haven't got one at the moment.

Even small appliances were difficult to replace:

> Well I've had a few things break down since I've been here that I can't replace. I mean I haven't got a microwave oven. That's sitting out on the back out there ... I'll eventually get that out on the street for the [council] pick up. And I don't own a vacuum cleaner and I haven't got a heater. (Beverley)

When they did replace an item, they usually could only afford a cheap model:

> And then something breaks down. The vacuum cleaner blows up ... and then you buy one which is $40. You get what you pay for. It blows up ... So you get the broom and you start sweeping. (Gloria)

Surprisingly 21 of the 40 private renters interviewed had a car. Usually the car they had was purchased when they were still employed. It was a major part of their budget but viewed as a necessity rather than a luxury. Renting in convenient locations is usually expensive, so many of the private renters found themselves in locations that were not close to amenities and where public transport was poor. In these situations, a car was usually essential. It enabled them to shop and maintain social contacts. Rhonda's situation was not unusual:

> Well where I live I've got to run a car because it's, well the name of the Road is Hill Road so it's up high and there's no way in the world I can walk into town ... I really don't know

what the future holds but as I told you the other day I'm 78. I'm going to be 79 in January and, you know, like you're getting older and you don't know how long you're going to be able to drive and if I can't drive I will never be able to get out the door.

Robert lived on the outskirts of a regional town and his neighbourhood had poor public transport. Having a car greatly increased his quality of life: 'Well where I am here, I'm 4 kilometres from town. I mean in a pinch I can walk there but I couldn't bring anything back that's of any size …' He also emphasised how important it was to have a car when looking for accommodation. Asked whether he would have been able to find a place if he did not have a car, he responded:

> Well I wouldn't. My daughter would have had to take time off work and drive me around the place. So yeah, that part is very difficult to negotiate for anybody being a pensioner or otherwise. If … you're told to leave … then you're placed in great difficulty.

Keeping their car on the road was a major challenge for most of the private renters. Bruce was struggling:

> I have not been able to afford to get the car serviced … Fortunately, it is in reasonably good condition. And you were talking about, 'What would I do if the rent went up anymore'? I'd have to consider getting rid of the car. As I've told you, you cannot go about with a car uninsured.

Although his car was a major financial burden, Bruce was reluctant to relinquish it. He was concerned about the impact of not having a car:

> Put it this way. Yesterday I was able to take a rod and go down to the river and have a fish and sometimes I have to flog myself to get out … As for the car, other people say I'd probably be very depressed without it … Yeah, well. I would think things would be a bit grim without the car.

Most used their car sparingly and had minimal insurance:

> You've got to have a car that runs on low amounts of petrol ... We don't go very far because you know you can't afford long trips or anything like that, so it's just like the shopping. You trim off the fat and you get the basics ... Again, no insurance or anything like that. Nothing superfluous. (Greg)

Several of the private renters depended on their children to keep their car on the road:

> Like last month I had, well the rego's free but the third party's not free. The pink slip's not free, so that's $300. The insurance was $400 and the power bill that was a thousand bucks in one hit. Unless you save, you can't [keep the car on the road]. So what do you do? So your daughter helps. If I didn't have her, I wouldn't have a car cos there's no one to borrow anything off. (Robert)

'I do all the things I want to do': social housing tenants and consumption

The capacity to lead a decent life

None of the interviewees in social housing felt that they suffered from significant capability deprivation in regards to consumption. Almost all were firm that because of their reasonable and predictable rent they were able to manage on the income from the Age Pension and live a decent life. An 85-year-old public housing tenant who was a capable artist, succinctly captured her capacity to live a life she valued mainly because she had the necessary resources due to her low rent:

> I have no interest in a lot of money because I've been there, done all of that. I've had everything and I still have got everything because I'm living the way I want to live. As you can see, I can paint, I can crochet. I do all the things I want to do. (Norma)

Unlike their counterparts in the private rental sector, the social housing interviewees were generally not anxious about getting by:

> I've got enough to be able to look after myself and I find that the money that I get from the pension, people complain about it, but I wouldn't complain about it cos I find it quite adequate … I hear one of the girls who … live down here in private rent and they're paying over $300 and they've got no money … They've got no extra money. They've got nothing. She goes to the shop where people take clothes to get rid of and she buys clothes from there but I buy clothes from a proper shop. (Jeanette)

A key requirement for adequate consumption was not to smoke or drink in excess:

> I think that anyone [in social housing] that doesn't smoke, doesn't drink, I think you can live quite comfortably on the pension. It [the pension] has just gone up. There was a time when it was a bit iffy, but umm, I think that now anyone that can't live on it, they're doing something [wrong]. (Daisy)

However, being dependent on the Age Pension certainly meant that frugal living and careful budgeting were necessary:

> You can manage. If you budget, you can manage on it. There's no problem with it. It's a tight squeeze, but I manage … I just can't run out and say, 'I'll buy this and I'll buy that'. I just, like I buy what I need and make sure that I've got enough for the medication and everything, you know, and anything that I have to have and if there's anything left I can save it and there's usually never that much … I'm having a good fortnight this fortnight. I've got about $100 and something left, but next fortnight, I won't have that much because I have to pay a couple of bills. So I always try to keep a little bit in there if I can so I've got a little extra. (Patricia)

There was an acute awareness of the relationship between their low accommodation costs and their ability to consume adequately:

> If I weren't in public housing, in the Housing Commission, I wouldn't be able to live like I live. I'm not living like a Queen, but I'm not a pauper either. (Doris)
>
> But I find that, yes, I'm quite comfortable. I don't really want for anything … If I want anything I can just save up for it. (Dan)
>
> You came here to see how I manage with my money. I don't know how I would manage if I were not in here [social housing]. (Edna)

When asked whether she had to be careful about her spending, Rita responded, 'That's for sure, but it comes easily to me because I've never had much'. She was very pleased with her present situation: 'Actually I'm better dressed and I have a better home than I ever had'.

Jeannette spoke about how she could buy new clothes but had to shop at a particular shop that catered for low-income households:

> I can buy clothes. I mean I go to Millers … and they cater for people that haven't got much money. You can buy something. It doesn't have to be expensive clothes.

Norma prided herself on her wardrobe. She waited for the sales:

> Now if I want a dress or a skirt or slacks and I need it and there's a sale that's where I buy it … and if people like to dress nicely like I do, now I don't want to go out and pay $200 for dresses that I would like to wear. I wait for the end of the season sale then I buy it. I've got a beautiful wardrobe.

Another mechanism used was credit. Interviewees told of how they paid off purchases over time:

> You have to plan for that. I have an account with Lowes [a clothing outlet] so if I want new clothes I usually go to them, get them and pay it off on a monthly basis because the price of clothing, and some shoes in particular, would make a big hole in the pension if you had to do it in one hit. (Graham)

Choices had to be made, but the essentials were almost always covered:

> I was with an exercise class, a diabetic exercise class for 9 years and then of course when we didn't have any of Stan's income [her husband passed away] I couldn't go to it any more so I just have to do the exercises that I remember [at home]. I miss it, but it simply cannot be … You have to be sensible about these things … But I don't go without. Not the essentials. (Rita)

Anne had decided that she could not afford to subscribe to the internet or have a mobile phone and would rather use the money saved for socialising:

> So the phone and the internet, they're two of the things that I sacrifice for a life where I can go out and have coffee with someone. You've got to make choices. You can have this or that, but you can't have it all …

Doris was asked if there was anything she regarded as essential but could not afford: 'Apart from a house, I don't know. I think I'm happy the way I am'. She did feel constrained and felt the pension could be more generous:

> I don't think they (the government) give them [age pensioners] enough money. I think it's sort of, it's not the poverty line, but it's not far from it … Even if it was say another $50 a fortnight, it would be lovely … I just think that you could buy a little bit more. Live a little bit … nicer.[20]

Dorothy was certainly restrained in her consumption, but interestingly was saving for a holiday:

> I don't go to the theatre. I don't go to the pictures very often. I don't drink, smoke or gamble so I'm lucky in that respect … I have to save up for things … I've got special shoes. I have to pay $100 for those and everything comes in one go

> ... but on the whole [I'm fine]. I'm even saving up to try and go on a holiday with my friend next year.

Not surprisingly, couples seemed to cope better than social housing tenants living by themselves. I asked an elderly Russian couple whether moving into public housing had changed their life. The husband responded, 'Of course. It has made life much easier now' (Boris). His wife added, 'Since we now have money left over after paying the rent, we have enough money to organise our life' (Alina) A tenant in the same public housing complex who had been a private renter, commented, 'Since we moved here it has become a lot easier for us to live. Just to live normally' (Raisa). Implicit in Raisa's emphasis on living 'normally' is that after moving into public housing, the anxiety and stress about spending money on essentials eased considerably.

They were highly appreciative of any extra government support. It gave them the ability to purchase larger items:

> We don't really buy anything. If something is on sale we might buy a few pairs of shoes. I recently bought my husband two pairs. I buy shoes for myself once a year for maybe $100. But like I said, we have enough. Recently, they gave the elderly $2100.[21] And then they also gave me another $1000 for being a carer to my husband – $3000 altogether they gave us. That's big money. Last time, they gave us $1600, so I bought a flat screen television. I'm not going to buy another one. This will be here for as long as it lasts. So I think we have enough to live off. (Lada)

Food shopping and diet

The low cost of their accommodation meant most social housing tenants were able to purchase the food they wanted and eat healthily if they so desired. They were careful and moderate. 'Yeah. I eat all right. Like you know I can't get lobster or anything like that, but vegies and fruit, yeah' (Valma). Lada's comment captures the situation of having few luxuries but having enough for an adequate diet:

> We have enough. Of course, we're not eating bread with caviar each day. Of course now there is the financial crisis but we don't feel it because we cook at home and we don't go out for coffee. We won't pay $3.50 for coffee. We'll buy a jar and we can drink it at home all we like. I wouldn't pay for health food, but we try to buy cheap groceries …

Patricia commented:

> I love fruit and vegetables. I think you've got to eat vegetables and I have a bit of meat, you know. Chicken and that. But I don't' eat a lot of it … I buy what I need, definitely … And sometimes I might make myself a fruit cake, you know. But as far as just splurging out on like take-away or a lot of sweets and stuff like that, that you don't necessarily need, I don't buy them.

Asked whether she was able to have a healthy diet, Alice responded emphatically:

> Yes, yes. For dinner I'll have potatoes and vegies. Then I'll cook my meat. I'll have that for the night, and then sweets, and then I might have a sip of my little red wine, but not a lot, but no, it's good living.

An interviewee who had moved from private renting where she had been struggling to maintain a healthy diet commented on the positive impact moving into social housing had had on her diet:

> The thing I've been able to readjust since I've been here is the management of my food. I've learned skills of how to prepare enough for a few meals you know to save on costs with electricity and that sort of thing and [I'm] busy going in and out having a social life, not having to come home and then to start cooking. I've already got prepared meals, but they're nutritious meals. (Anne)

Norma was very concerned about eating well and was able to do so:

> I will have a salad [and] every day I will have three different types of vegetables. I have meat maybe twice a week, and fish other times or tofu …I go down to the market, [and] … for $7 or $8 I buy all the vegetables that I need.

Graham commented, 'I'm a diabetic so I have to shop according to my requirements, so I don't miss out on things I need to have'.

Most of the social housing interviewees were extremely careful shoppers: 'I shop furiously – check prices, check comparisons. I have gone gluten free and that is much more expensive than ordinary stuff' (George). Evelyn commented, 'I buy the fruit and vegetables only when I really need it, which is not now. They're too expensive nowadays'. She did say that she liked fish for her dinner. Some tenants did not feel the need to be so careful: 'I personally don't look for cheaper. I have enough to buy the best of what I want' (Marina). 'We don't limit ourselves with anything' (Olga). . 'In terms of food, we can buy whatever we want' (Abram). Perhaps Marina, Olga and Abram's greater capacity was due to them being in receipt of the couple Age Pension.

A few of the social housing tenants frequented community centres that provided food. This allowed them to eat healthily for very little: '$4.50 and you get a lovely hot meal or a lovely salad. What more could you want. I'm quite happy' (Doris). In some of the larger public housing complexes, charities distributed food from restaurants and bakeries that would otherwise be discarded. A few interviewees occasionally used this service.

The capacity of social housing tenants to eat well was also dependent on what other expenses they had besides accommodation. Edna had a serious chronic health condition and spent a good deal on prescribed and alternative medications. This restricted her capacity to purchase good quality food: 'I've been living on spaghetti and rice and things like that, so that I could fulfil all my obligations'. Smokers found it difficult to maintain a healthy diet:

> I've given up smoking now for 12 months so I have a bit more money. I [have] saved so much money by not smoking.

> I have … more, more [money] for proper food. I'm eating better. I eat really good stuff now - fruit and vegies, yoghurts, mangoes and all that kinda stuff. (Hazel)

Coping with utility bills[22]

Certainly, the cost of electricity was a concern for older social housing tenants. 'If there's one thing that's a worry, and I don't think it's just me but all pensioners, it's the cost of electricity. It went up enormously' (Ben). Most social housing tenants said that they could afford to heat or cool their dwelling adequately and pay the bill:

> Yes, yes, we heat it [the apartment]. We have air conditioning and when it is cold we heat and when it is hot we also turn it on. Of course we don't let it run all day. Electricity takes up a lot of money, but personally we have enough for what we need. (Raisa)

There had been times when Olga and her husband had had to approach a charity for assistance with their energy bill: 'And if we have a large light bill then there are organisations that can help … If we have large bills, they try to help us'.

Some interviewees severely limited their energy consumption: 'I don't have the radiator on during winter and I only have a fan in summer' (George). A husband and wife commented:

> Boris: To heat the apartment. We can but… we don't always allow ourselves to do this because electricity is…
>
> Alina: Very expensive.
>
> Boris: Very expensive, and the price of electricity is always increasing. It increased recently. And when it is very cold outside we allow ourselves to turn on the heating periodically to feel more comfortable.

Dressing very warmly and limiting heater use, was a common response: 'I've got a little fan heater and my bedsocks and I put more clothes on. That's all you do. Put more clothes on' (Patricia). She always managed to pay the electricity bill: 'I pay maybe a day late, but, well it all depends on when the pension falls, see'.

Several of the social housing interviewees had money for electricity taken out of their pension. This helped alleviate anxiety:

> You know that your rent is paid which is your number one ... and I get my electricity something taken out every 2 weeks for my electricity. So at least I know that I've got a roof over my head and I can put the TV on if I want to and I'm covered. So yes, it is a great relief to have that. (Judith)

Major expenses and running a car

For many of the social housing tenants, major and unexpected expenses were a concern:

> I wouldn't mind an air-conditioner. I can't really afford that ... If the washing machine broke. Things like that, I'd be stuck. (Valma)

Few had the ready cash at hand. An analysis of the HILDA data found that ~42% of older (65 or over) public housing tenants living by themselves and ~30% of couples in public housing would have difficulty raising $2000 in an emergency (Naidoo and Morris 2014).[23] Many of the interviewees found saving a significant amount difficult:

> I manage well and I have a good life but even with that managing well there's not enough to put away for a rainy day to any large extent. (Anne)

Judith was able to run a car and had a dog, but had minimal savings:

> But the pension does just see you through. You can just get through on the pension if there are no unexpected extras, you know.

Interestingly, the intense anxiety that plagued the private renters around unexpected expenses was rare. Most of the social housing tenants said that if they had a large expense they could cover it. However, it may take time and planning was important:

> At the moment my fridge is playing up … so I'm considering putting some money aside to buy a small fridge, which should be around $400. So at the moment I'm just waiting for the sales. It's close to Xmas so I might pick up something soon. (Roy)

> You've got to put some money aside. You've always got other things that pop up, like you know, my little dog. Like she costs me a fortune. Like you know, I get her clipped, then have to pay for the Vet … You just gotta put away for it all you know, but you work it out. (Marion)

Some of the interviewees who did not have savings were confident that if in need they would be able to borrow money from Centrelink or if they were in community housing, their housing provider:

> I don't have the ready cash to do it but fortunately again St George (the community housing provider) have a loan scheme up to $1000 that [you can use] if you have an emergency and then pay them back. I think it's about 2% interest. (George)

There was the odd innovative response to a lack of funds. Ben had resorted to renting his fridge:

> I had to rent a fridge, I had about five fridges in about 18 months and they all broke down. Well four of them broke down. This one is still working. It's about $17 a fortnight, $17.60, just under $40 a month. (Ben)

Several of the social housing interviewees said that they could rely on family support if absolutely necessary: 'I needed a new fridge and my daughter bought it and I paid her back' (Doris). Betty has three sons: 'I can rely on them for a loan … It does make a difference. Peace of mind … Yeah. I can always ask the kids'. However, asking children for assistance was generally avoided. The prevalent view was that they had their own financial concerns:

> No, because they've got their problems. He's got two kids … I never ask anything from them. I try my best. I try to manage myself … No, because it's very hard to survive in these days with two young kids and they're both working. They have expenses. I never ask anything. (Gwenda)

About 30 of the 55 social housing tenants interviewed had a car. Not having the expense of running a car certainly helped social housing tenants cope on the Age Pension. Many of the interviewees, especially those in inner Sydney, lived in well-serviced areas and they could generally rely on public transport. Also, the community transport service was viewed as a major benefit. A couple commented:

> Abram: This building is also well situated. Close to the city.
>
> Nina: Close to shopping
>
> Abram: … We have no driver and we have no car. It's very important for us [to be well-situated]. Very close to shopping. Shopping is very important.
>
> Nina: And service is very good. Now, every Thursday comes a bus and takes us to do shopping for free. They take us there and back and help us take the [bags]. And once a week they take us to market for free. Community transport. We have a very good life. For pensioners it's the best.

For the social housing tenants who had a car, the running expenses were a burden. George was thinking of selling his:

> One thing that I am thinking, my car is due for re-registration [in] December. Do I keep [it]? Cos that in itself probably costs $50 a week by the time you pay petrol. By the time you have repairs and maintenance. Now I'm seriously thinking $50 a week [do I keep it]. If it is an emergency I can catch a cab.

Financial support from children was often essential to keep the car on the road:

> I've got kids and I've got a car. That's the only reason I've got one. I wouldn't be running it without help from my children … I usually pay for the insurance. They help me with the servicing and all that sort of stuff. New tyres and all those things that have to be done … (Betty)

Judith bought her car when she was still working. Like Betty, without the support of her children she would not have been able to keep her car running:

> I've got a car but my family put it through [the registration] this year for me. It was due for rego (registration) and… my son and my daughter put it through for me … They paid the comprehensive insurance. They did all that. Next year, well really this year, I would have got rid of it because I can't afford it.

Lois had had a car, but she found the running costs too burdensome and had sold it:

> I found the expenses of the car were considerable. It meant that I didn't have any spare money left over at the end of the fortnight so I just lived from one fortnight to the next.

Mavis had no support from her children and had decided that she could not afford a car:

> For me to buy a car, I just couldn't afford it. Not on the pension, single pension, but if I did go and try I would have to go without a lot more than I am now … I thought more than once, 'Gee. I'd like to get a car'. I really can't afford to get a car so I've got to settle for charging the battery up and going on the bike (motorised scooter).

For Kevin a car was necessity. He had a serious bladder problem and could not use public transport. The car greatly increased his capabilities:

> The trouble is I can't go anywhere unless I'm sure that there are toilets available … That affects me everywhere I go. That's why I had to get a car and that's why I don't go on bus

trips. That's why I have to have my own car ... I'd be completely lost without the car.

'I can't see anywhere we've cut back to what we used to do': older homeowners and consumption

Capacity to lead a decent life

Whether homeowners felt that the Age Pension was adequate and they had the capacity to lead a decent life was, to a degree, dependent on their lifestyle, whether they received the couple or single pension, had constant ongoing health or other expenses, their capacity to budget and their level of savings when they first went onto the Age Pension. Henry and his wife are a good example of a couple that were able to live a decent life on the Age Pension. They lived in a home that required little maintenance, they had minimal extraneous expenses and had about $100 000 in superannuation (savings), which they rarely drew on. Although Henry had serious health problems, maintaining his health was not a major expense:

> Well, if you don't have a mortgage, I think the pension is quite adequate for our lifestyle anyway. Yeah, well you get other benefits. We get 25% rate reduction, $2.50 transport, [cheap] prescriptions ... I can't see anywhere we've cut back to what we used to do [when working].

Henry and his wife had done a fair amount of travelling since retiring:

> Since we've both been on the pension, we've been to Perth, Indian Pacific [train], both ways for me. My wife flew back. We've been on two small cruises to Darwin, 11 nights, and Brisbane, four nights. Canberra, a couple of times. A driving trip around Byron Bay ...

Paula and her husband lived in a regional town and were very active:

> We holiday a lot and it just amazes me when I hear people [say] you can't manage on the pension cos we do a lot. We're

> off cruising for a month next week ... We bought a new car this year ... We have a small nest egg and by saying a nest egg I'd say we've probably got about $55 000, which is all the money we have but that sort of went down a bit. As I said, we bought a new car but we can manage to live with our pension and save money to go overseas.

The capacity to budget and spend sensibly was viewed as critical. Edward was married and budgeted carefully:

> The pension is adequate provided you live wisely. Now, I don't think you can go for a world trip every second day of the week, cos you'd soon run out of money but if you... wanted to go overseas say to see family you have to save up wisely and after 12 or 18 months book for 3 weeks.

Another recipient of the couple Age Pension felt that he and his wife lived well and, if need be, they could call on their children for any major expense:

> We live fairly well because we've got nothing else [but ourselves]. I haven't got children other than grandchildren to be a financial burden and so therefore we budget fairly thoroughly to almost spend everything you know. If anything major was needed, I'd call on my son and my daughter. I don't want to but I will if I've got to ... I mean I use every convenience. I use the seniors card, and I use the $2.50 card [public transport concession] ... I really can't complain and there are times when you need to rationalise and say, 'Gee, I'd like that', but you know you can't do it, or if you do, something has to suffer and you don't do it. (Walter)

As mentioned, a key factor determining whether older homeowners are able to manage on the Age Pension is for them not to have any major ongoing expenses. A couple, who every month had to spend a good deal of money on supporting their unemployed son, were struggling to cope. Their son was a private renter and the parents were paying his rent. When Doug was asked if they were able to save he responded:

> Very little you know with the position we're in with our son. We've got enough to get by but not enough to put aside each week for other things ... We put so much aside for rates, another lot aside for house insurance, car insurance, electricity and phone so you know we're budgeting all the time. My wife's at the table 3 or 4 hours a day budgeting ... We've got to know where every cent goes and where it's coming from and if we want something how long it is going to take for saving for it.

Homeowners on the single pension were generally less sanguine than those on the couple pension but generally appeared to cope well. Thelma felt that single pensioners were certainly in a more vulnerable position than their partnered counterparts:

> I guess I'm at a disadvantage on a single pension. I've got friends living in a similar situation on a married pension. I virtually have nearly the same bills, electricity services, rates, etcetera as they have, but I have got half the money.

There were activities that Thelma could not afford that her friends on the couple Age Pension could:

> And you know some of them understand it when I say, 'No. I can't do that. Can't afford that this week', but others don't understand.

Doreen was struggling with her expenses. This was partially a result of the excessive rates she had to pay in the regional town she lived in. She also had a pharmaceutical bill of ~$60 a month:

> I think the security of having your own home is great. I mean I wouldn't like to have to pay rent but then when you look at the $2000 a year for rates and $80 for water four times a year, things like that ... and you still have to pay electricity and phone and all that, it restricts you. I mean I am on the internet but it's only wireless. It's not very good ... I need a new computer so you just think about it but you don't ever buy it. All those little things.

Although Joy was financially stretched and felt restricted, she was connected to the internet, she had a car and private medical insurance and led an active life:

> If you live in a house all it [the pension] does is cover the basics. It doesn't sort of allow you, particularly with all the utilities that you have to pay, [to live well]… and if you own your home of course you've got to think of the rates and insurance.

Maureen was battling as a single person on the Age Pension. Insurance and running a car were major expenses, but she felt that these were essentials that she could not forego:

> I don't eat out at all. I don't buy a cup of coffee when I'm out. That would be way above my ability to pay for that … I buy food to cook at home … I occasionally go to the movies which only costs me about $8.

Helen said that she was able to purchase what she required, but she felt that if the pension was a bit more generous it would certainly make a difference: 'I probably wouldn't go out and spend it on things but I would just feel more secure and maybe just have a treat here and there maybe'.

Most homeowners on the single pension felt that they were able to lead a decent life but had to be careful:

> So I can't say that I'm rich but I can't say I'm poor either. I don't have to think I can only go and buy a bit of butter and I don't have to think like that you know … I absolutely feel that the pension is really adequate if, as I said before, you don't gamble, you don't smoke or drink. (Denise)

Francesca brought up four children by herself. She was content and had all she needed, but lived frugally:

> I'm thankful that it's [the pension is] there and I can make do. Of course I don't go to the Opera House every weekend but … I mean I'm happy … I should say I'm content with the

life I lead. I've never been one for strings of pearls or diamonds. I've never been like that.

Some of the homeowners were able to keep expenditure to a minimum. As mentioned, Joe was a superb handyman and able to maintain his home himself. He rarely engaged in leisure activities and had no energy bills:

> I live on the Age Pension quite well I'd say as I own everything. I own a vehicle and a scooter and I have to pay rates of course, insurances and then that leaves me roughly say $600 a fortnight, which I never ever spend because I don't go anywhere. I just live here. I go to Sydney every month or so. I go to Bathurst every week and that's about my life ... I haven't got any [major] expenses. As I say, I own everything. I've got solar on the roof and I've had that for the last couple of years and they [the electricity company] now owe me $70.

Jennifer also coped well on the Age Pension. She had learnt to budget from a young age and lived modestly but did not feel at all deprived:

> I find it amazing that people complain about the amount of money in the Age Pension. I find that I'm very well off with the Age Pension. Mind you, I don't have a lot of illnesses so I'm not on a lot of medication, no medication costs. I don't go to clubs except on occasions to have a meal ... I don't play the pokies and I don't go to the shows ... I don't go to the theatre any more ... and I got all these habits when I first bought my unit and I was living on $6 a week and paying a mortgage ... I don't deny myself anything [but] I don't spend money frivolously.

Food shopping

Everyday food shopping was not a problem for homeowners. They were vigilant, but all of the homeowners said that they were able to purchase what food they wanted and were able to eat healthily. Francesca was typical:

> I have never once bought something without knowing its price … Like say fruit … I'm buying less now and you know like I like lychees. It was $17 at one shop and I found them at $9.50 at Woollies [Woolworths]… I didn't buy a kilo. I bought some but I still satisfy my taste buds but I don't have to buy that many you know. I really think that because I don't gamble and I don't smoke, I'm able to do those things.

Henry emphasised that when it came to food he and his wife did not eat a great deal but purchased whatever they felt like:

> Like I said, in the food [line] we buy what we like. We don't skimp but we don't buy excess either. I mean half a kilo of prawns will feed us adequately whereas for other people it would just be a starter … So yes, we have prawns, we have oysters, we don't have caviar … and we have smoked salmon.

When asked if there was anything that she would like to buy but cannot, Shirley responded:

> Not really. I have all my wants here. I can't think of anything. I think to myself I'm definitely not going without, and … I don't skimp on food. I'm not eating cereal for dinner at night or anything like that.

Coping with utility bills
In the case of utility bills, the homeowners were able to cope but generally kept their usage to a minimum and were watchful:

> I make sure like my electricity everything's turned off. I don't even have the microwave on except when I need it, so the only thing that runs is the fridge and the hot water service. So I don't turn the heater on and I don't have the air conditioning on, only if I really need it … I think most people learn to cope but I do think that these $600/$700

> bills for people unless they like me get it taken out [of the pension monthly], that's a shock. (Doreen)

Doug, the one homeowner interviewed who had a major ongoing expense, found the electricity and gas bills difficult to deal with and he and his wife restricted their usage as much as possible:

> There's days and nights you'd like the air conditioning on but you know it is going to catch up with you when the electricity bill comes … We haven't got a gas heater but … if you put one of them on and you put it on in the winter and left it on through most of the day you probably wouldn't be able to pay the bill.

Tina was an exception. She did not feel constrained in her consumption of energy:

> I try not to put the heater on till 6 o'clock at night just now because it is getting colder but if I want to put the heater on all day, I put it on all day. I am very aware that I'm going to get a big bill but really I'm fine … I do sound really stupid I know but I just don't want to have my whole life crippled by watching whether I've got the lights on, my washing machine or the television. I just won't go down that route, so we use as much energy as we like. We do use too much.

Running a car and other major expenses

Running a car and replacing large items did not appear to be a major burden for most of the homeowners. Only five of the homeowners interviewed did not have a car. In many instances, a car was viewed as a necessity because many of the homeowners lived in areas that have inadequate public transport and are not in walking distance of facilities. A car significantly increased their capabilities and allowed interviewees to age in place. Joy had a beautiful view of the ocean but staying in her home was dependent on her having a car and being able to drive:

> It's a good position if you can drive. If you can't drive, you become dependent on neighbours or other people.

For Helen, having a car allowed her to walk her dog at the beach. This was a critical activity for her:

> I'd be pretty stuck I think, yeah. I could get a bus but I can't take the dog. I could take the dog for a walk around here but it's not [the same]. You miss out on seeing all the people on the dog walk.

Francesca lived a fair distance from the shops:

> And it [the car] helps me. Imagine if I had to walk all the way. I'd collapse in the heat. Instead with the car I can take it (the shopping). It's a luxury for me [but] at the same time it is a necessity. I mean a necessity is not a luxury.

Most homeowners appeared to be able to keep their car on the road with little problem:

> I have a car that's 1997. I feel I'm too old to change it. That's the only reason [I don't change it]. I have it serviced whenever it needs to be serviced and it goes from point A to point B. (Ian)

When she was asked if 'running the car is an issue', Denise responded:

> No. I bought a brand new car ... This I bought in 2010 so this should last me out cos I'm going to be 75 this year and I think this should do me.

Linda was 87 at the time of the interview and was of the few homeowners who did not drive. She lived close to services:

> Living where I live, I'm very close to the shops. It's level walking and not far to go and at times I think it'd be great if I could hop into a car and go somewhere but it's not [to be]. I've managed very well without it.

Most homeowners said that if a large appliance needed replacing they would manage. Many had savings that they could draw on:

> Yeah. I think there'd be $10 000 or $11 000 that's a working account ... This $10 000 or $11 000 is just for the things that might go, like you say, a fridge or washing machine. (Henry)

Those without significant savings would save over a period of time:

> When the washing machine busted, I didn't go straight down and get it. I think I waited awhile and put a bit away each month until they had a special on and then I went and got it. (Ben)

Alternatively, they would use their credit card:

> And we just recently our cooktop died, so there was $600 or $699. So that's where I'm so lucky that the credit card system is available but then it's spread over 6 weeks. You have to find it. (Tina)

Conclusions

Nussbaum (2003: 35) argues that equality of resources is not enough to ensure equality 'because it fails to take account of the fact that individuals need differing levels of resources if they are to come up to the same level of capability to function'. In the case of older Australians dependent on the Age Pension, this is certainly apparent – the housing tenure occupied plays a fundamental role in shaping capabilities.

The chapter has illustrated the tremendous and pervasive impact that the cost of accommodation has on the ability of older private renters, social housing tenants and homeowners to consume and lead a decent life. The predictable and fixed rent of the older social housing tenants interviewed meant that their rent was usually not a major burden or concern and they generally had enough disposable income to lead a decent, albeit modest, life and avoid social exclusion. They were generally able to purchase what they required and engage in the world (see Chapter 6 for a detailed examination of social contacts and leisure activity). However, their dependence on the Age Pension for their income did mean that they had to be frugal and there was consensus that social housing tenants who smoked and/or consumed large quantities of alcohol, faced major consumption challenges.

In contrast to the social housing tenants and homeowners, the consumption possibilities of older private renters were restricted and many struggled with basic items such as the ability to maintain a healthy diet. Any unexpected expense was a major blow and precipitator of anxiety. Not surprisingly, the older private renters who lived by themselves and had not had the good fortune of finding reasonably priced accommodation and who had minimal or no family support and were totally dependent on the Age Pension for their income, were in the worst position. Their capacity to consume was fundamentally determined by the cost of their accommodation.

Older homeowners were generally able to purchase what they required, providing they did not have any major recurring expenses. Most of the homeowners interviewed were able to save (the amounts varied considerably), run a car and engage in costly activities such as going on holiday. Not surprisingly, the ability to save was most pronounced in the case of interviewees receiving the couple pension. Some of the homeowners on the single pension were struggling financially but nevertheless they generally had enough resources to lead a decent life.

5
'Exceedingly miserable and bloody cold': accommodation and housing tenure

Introduction

This chapter reviews the accommodation of older private renters, social housing tenants and homeowners. There is consensus that an older person's accommodation can play a major role in shaping their wellbeing and capacity to live a decent life (Allen 2008; Lawton 1985; Oswald *et al.* 2007). Research has shown that poor quality accommodation can contribute to poor mental health, respiratory disease and injuries (Bentley *et al.* 2012; Howden-Chapman *et al.* 2011; Krieger and Higgins 2002; Phibbs and Thompson 2011). Older people, especially if they are on a low income, spend a good deal of time at home, so the quality of the accommodation is especially significant. As Easterbrook (2002: 9) notes:

> If you have any mobility problems, or you're a carer, or you're old, or on a low income or depressed, your home becomes more important, not less, because you're spending more of your time at home. When you're working, you're out all day ... home is much more the place where you sleep, not where you spend most of your life.

The ability to age in place is viewed as beneficial in most instances (WHO 2007; Wiles *et al.* 2012) and an individual's housing tenure can be a crucial factor influencing this capacity.[24] The interviews indicated that older homeowners and social housing tenants are usually able to age in place. Older homeowners are often in a position to choose the type of housing they want to live in and where they want to live and are usually able to move to more appropriate accommodation or modify their existing accommodation if they so desire (Phillipson 2007). Older social housing tenants are generally in situations where they have virtually guaranteed *de jure* security of tenure in perpetuity and most are in age-friendly accommodation. However, as discussed in Chapter 9, the increasing residualisation of public housing is impacting on the age-friendliness of some public housing complexes. The capacity of older private renters to age in place is often negligible (see Chapter 8). They usually have minimal *de jure* or *de facto* security of occupancy and if their accommodation is inappropriate for ageing in place, their capacity to request appropriate modifications from the landlord is often limited.

Although there are always intervening variables that may increase or diminish the impact of inadequate and insecure housing on older people – for example a frail and unwell older person is more likely to be affected by inadequate housing than is a healthy older person – the research does illustrate that housing quality, security of occupancy and affordability (see Bentley *et al.* 2011) all play an important role in contributing towards physical and mental health (Danermark *et al.* 1996; Evans 2003; Howden-Chapman *et al.* 2011; Oswald *et al.* 2007). The health implications of the different housing tenures are discussed in Chapter 7.

The chapter first discusses the accommodation of older private renters and their capacity to move out of poor situations. The accommodation of older social housing tenants is then examined as are their thoughts around moving. The chapter concludes with a discussion of older homeowners' perceptions of their accommodation.

The accommodation of older private renters

There was much variation in the accommodation of the older private renters. Many lived in reasonable accommodation, despite their minimal income. A common feature was a determination to live in decent accommodation even if it meant using a substantial proportion of their income to pay for it. Beverley's comment captures this:

> And as I said, I really couldn't go, couldn't just move anywhere. I couldn't. All my life I've never lived like that.

Historically, she had been middle class (as had many of the other older private renters interviewed) and had lived in comfortable circumstances before falling out of homeownership. At the time of the interview, she was living in a comfortable two-bedroom apartment in a pleasant neighbourhood. One of her three sons had been living with her, but had moved out a few months before the interview:

> It's a two-bedroom unit, yes and it's, what I like about it is that it's in a security block, and yes, it's quiet. But I really would like to have a house of my own, but I know that's not possible. But it's quite a nice flat really. It's got everything that I want.

Although she only had $50 left after paying her rent she was adamant that she wanted to live in 'respectable' accommodation.

Maria was using ~60% of her income to pay for accommodation but was determined to live in adequate accommodation: 'You see I don't like to live poor. I don't like to live as if I'm poor, which I am'. She was pleased with her current accommodation:

> At present I'm in a little granny flat, which is like a bit of a ski lodge. I pay $300 a fortnight rent [interviewed in 2006]. It's like a big room. It's like a bedsit. It's quite long. It's really pretty … Everyone loves it. It's really very comfortable and I like it because it's … surrounded by trees.

Having a car had allowed Paul to canvass several real estate agents and areas and he had managed to find adequate accommodation for a reasonable rent:

> It's quite a nice place. It's a two-bedroom unit. It was originally a two-storey single house, but the owner has converted it into two units, downstairs and upstairs. Now I've got the downstairs section and it's fully self-contained … The rent is reasonable … It's very ideal for me. It's very secure.

Chris lived in a converted house and was happy with his accommodation and relieved that he did not have to share:

> It's good. I've got a garden and there's trees, and it's a bit of a rambling sort of a place and I can do a little bit of gardening and I can take a bit of pride in that. But it's an ageing place, and it does need something. I'd be happy to sort of stay there because it suits me, rather than living in a place with a multitude of people.

The interviewees quoted had been fortunate. They had managed to find adequate accommodation for a reasonable rent. The Sydney private rental market meant that it was not always possible for interviewees to find decent housing. James (interviewed in 2015) lived in squalid accommodation (Box 5.1).

The house Valerie rented in Sydney was clearly unacceptable, more especially for an older person:

> I've been there a year and a couple of months I suppose and when I moved in there it was rat infested and cockroach infested and it smelt so badly that I couldn't sleep there at night. I had to go over and start cleaning during the daytime and go somewhere else to sleep. I asked a friend if I could stay there at night at her place because I couldn't bear it … Previously there had been about five young people there and they only stayed for a couple of months. I think because they found it was rats and everything else and also the area of course didn't agree with them as far as the drug dealing and alcohol and the criminality that's around … but it suited me because I find this is a most desirable area to live, near the city, and I like being close to markets and the city as well.

A lack of capacity to choose meant that there was always the possibility of landing up in a bad location. When Norma first started renting she found herself in a confronting situation:

> I went into a unit and I had drug addicts upstairs and … we had the fire brigade and it was so foreign to me … That

5 – 'Exceedingly miserable and bloody cold': accommodation and housing tenure

> **Box 5.1. James – living in a 'serviced' room in inner Sydney**
>
> The place I live in, I've been there for 14 years. The reason I want to get out of there is because it has become untenable insofar as the condition of the place. It has never been maintained. It is a dangerous environment and it is unhealthy. I do have a health problem, which is exacerbated by the place that I live in and the immediate surrounds. So I pay $195 a week to live in this place and if most people saw the place they wouldn't believe it … It is an old building … There's 100 rooms in the place. Single rooms, shared bathroom, four floors. I would say 50% is transient, the other 50% of people are in the same situation such as myself … The room comes supplied with a microwave, a bar fridge, a television, which in my particular case doesn't work. It hasn't worked for 3 months and they refuse to fix it. It [the room] is supposed to be cleaned but the place has become so covered in mould and whatever that they now refuse to clean it and they just give me clean linen every week. I've asked for another room and despite the fact that there's been vacant rooms [that have] become available [and] that have been renovated they keep putting me off and I'm still in the same place … Yes, there has been one murder on the premises that I know of in the last 14 years and numerous bashings and affrays. The police and ambulance attend there usually every 1 to 3 weeks. The common bathroom is full of syringes from time to time and other times there is just shit thrown up the walls. It's a hell-hole. … You try and go to the bathroom before you go to sleep and don't go again before the morning … I have a daughter. She's now 18. No way can she visit me. There's no way she can visit me where I live. Not possible to bring her there … It's like being in jail … I'm convinced that the environment I live in has helped to make me sick … It is very busy at the moment with transients because of holidays so you get people from interstate plus overseas and they couldn't care less about the place … They're on holidays so you can imagine most of them are pissed every night or out of their minds and they come and go and it is a pretty noisy environment. Noise is a big factor, but also violence is a factor. You can hear everything in the place. I can hear arguments four floors away and quite often rooms get wrecked and thrashed. I had a television got thrown out of a floor directly above me two floors up that landed outside my front window. 'Smash', looked out and there was a television just smashed to pieces. People throw bottles out the window cos they forget to open the window…

[private] rental market is horrible unless you can find somewhere decent … You're living on your nerves. I mean anything could have happened.

Too little space, poor security and challenging neighbours were not the only problems. Rhonda had been forced to leave her previous accommodation because of a major damp problem that she said made her ill:

> It was ... very damp and my clothes were getting mildewed and I was throwing my clothes out all the time ... I kept on complaining and they wouldn't cut the tress back, all that sort of thing, so I was constantly sick because of the dampness in the place.

She was also very unhappy in her present accommodation that she said was overrun with spiders and flies:

> Well, when I first came here I was sort of very attracted to it because of the sunshine and everything but you've got to live in a place to sort of really know what it's like and I'm having terrible trouble with spiders and blow flies, etcetera. I had the house sprayed on Monday [she had to pay] because the spiders are so bad.

Phyllis had recently left her partner and had managed to find a tiny granny flat:

> Last May I started back into the rental on my own and I have found it very difficult cos it is very expensive ... All I could fit in was my bed and a lounge, you know. I've got boxes and the washing machine and dryer and everything sitting around the lounge room and the bedroom. So, yeah, there's not much room ...

A few of the interviewees had been forced to live in boarding houses or shared accommodation. For a period the only accommodation Anne could afford was bedsitters or rooms in shared accommodation. She found it extremely stressful:

> You are cohabitating with the most desperate people in our community ... apart from people living in the street. Safety is an issue. Learning to share with people that have no concern over sharing and they have their own agendas that they're concerned about and they're not concerned about others is a

very difficult thing with sharing bathrooms and toilets and all that sort of thing and kitchen areas. So it is very confronting and you feel very isolated and alone and helpless because there doesn't seem to be anyone you can go to.

Anne was paying ~$200 for this accommodation. Her situation totally overwhelmed her:

> I was so entrapped in my own despair that I couldn't, I didn't know how to reach out to services that probably were available and no one was offering anything and everywhere I went the doors were closed so I sort of gave up.

At the time of the interview she was living in social housing and, as a result, her life had been completely transformed: 'If you've got a roof over your head you've got everything'.

For a period Leonie had been forced to live in a pub in a country town:

> They gave me a room, the manager of the bar, a female. I got on very well with her … and she sort of looked out for me and she said, 'You can live there for as long as you want.' … Initially I started to settle in there and thought this is all right … but it was the nature of the guests coming into the pub, not so much the four or five of us permanents … It was the people who came into the pub [accommodation] for one or two nights … Some of them were pretty dodgy characters and they were unknown … I realised I had to move.

Older private renters who were heavy smokers found it especially difficult to access reasonable accommodation. Malcolm spent $70 a week on cigarettes and could not afford an apartment. Also, he had no furniture and was thus dependent on rooms in boarding houses or pubs. The boarding house he was staying in at the time of the interview (2005) was grim:

> Well it's an old house that's been converted. Downstairs what would have been four rooms is eight bedrooms. Upstairs, I'm not really sure of, but I'd say that that's probably 10 rooms,

> maybe more and it's only partitioned. It's cold, ... the furniture is substandard. There's gaps in the floorboards. There's gaps in the walls ... exceedingly miserable and bloody cold, especially now that winter is coming on. But that seems to be the standard.

All of the places he had rented since losing his home after a divorce had been dismal:

> I mean I've been renting for 7 years, 8 years, ever since my wife threw me out, and most of them basically are substandard accommodation ... They tend to charge as much as possible for as little as possible. That's what I've found. Finding good accommodation is very difficult.

He often had to live in close proximity to challenging people:

> Psychiatric patients, ... living with them is exceedingly difficult, and living with alcoholics and I mean, yes, it is difficult, without belittling them and their problems and things like that.

He felt that there was no possibility of him ever being in a situation where he could contemplate renting conventional accommodation:

> Well, I look around the real estate agents, there's a real estate agent in Campsie [an area in Sydney] that's advertising a one-bedroom flat for $150 a week, but it's got no kitchen ... I mean I've got no furniture, so I've got to get furnished accommodation. You're looking at minimum 4 weeks bond, plus 2 weeks in advance, and you're looking at something that's going to cost you $200 plus a week. So you're looking for a minimum of $1200. Where do you find it on a limited income?

The option of sharing rented accommodation so as to broaden possibilities was not viewed favourably. None of the interviewees were keen to share. Faye told of what happened to a friend of hers:

> I had another friend ... She got a good house and then asked people to share, but it just doesn't work. She ended up virtually hiding in the bedroom from a more domineering personality and she ended up going away to Tasmania because the public housing is better.

Private renters and moving house

Unlike older homeowners who usually voluntarily decide to move and are often able to choose alternative accommodation in accord with a preferred lifestyle (Phillipson 2007), older private renters usually have little or no choice and when they do move it is usually not a voluntary move (Morris et al. 2005). They have to move because they can no longer afford the rent, the accommodation is untenable or the landlord has given them notice (Morris 2007). The thought of moving is viewed with much trepidation. Interviewees were acutely aware of the financial costs of moving:

> Moving is costly ... Four weeks rental upfront and 4 weeks bond and moving costs, finalisation of utilities on leaving, reconnections at the new space and removalists. (Gloria)

Beverley was using most of her Age Pension for accommodation, but could not contemplate moving. She argued it was not financially possible:

> Well I couldn't afford it [to move]. I just couldn't come up with say for example $1500 for the rent or $1600[25] or whatever it might be, and then on top of that wherever you went ... you'd probably be looking at $600, $700, $800, $900 for the movers. You'd be looking at around $3000 and now that's an impossibility for me.

Besides the financial cost, there was the emotional and physical strain. Studies have found that the health of older people who have to move involuntarily is often negatively affected (Choi 1996; Danermark et al. 1996; Mowbray 2015a; Wiles et al. 2009).

> So they've got all the costs of moving again. All the worry; the trauma of moving house; packing up all the stuff and then getting a removalist to remove it, or getting somebody to do it for you and then moving into a new house. Yes. It's a lot of trouble for us older blokes. Younger people mightn't worry that much about it. (Paul)

Moving from a familiar neighbourhood was also viewed as stressful. Similar to the findings of Walker and Hillier (2007), the services and the relationships interviewees had in the immediate vicinity were often perceived as extremely important:

> Well, I'm settled there in lots of ways ... I can ring up my pharmacist and say, 'Can I put this on the account?' And she's very understanding ... It's like that I know a lot of the identities in the area and people know me ... and that was one of the things with the Community Housing that I stressed that I wanted to stay in the area because of the infrastructure of the church and my GP bulk bills and he's a fantastic guy and we can talk about all sorts of things and it's important that I have that. (Chris)

Beverley was also reluctant to leave her neighbourhood: 'Ah yes, well I know where everything is and when I go up the street I know where to go and how to get there and I sort of know the area reasonably well'.

Besides not wanting to move out of a familiar neighbourhood, there was a strong awareness that finding alternative accommodation can be enormously challenging. This was especially so for those interviewees who did not have a car and had nobody they could turn to for assistance. Often cheaper accommodation was only available in more remote areas. These neighbourhoods were usually poorly serviced and having a car was essential:

> But if you want to go right out to Glossodia or Freeman's Reach[26] you can occasionally get granny flats out there for $250 but if you don't drive and you're a woman on your own don't even think about it ... (Gloria)

Looking for alternative accommodation was an extremely draining experience for Faye. She had been staying in a two-bedroom apartment but decided she needed to move after her partner died, as she could no longer afford the rent of $250 a week. At the time of the interview (December 2014) Faye had just found a 'one-bedroom shack' in a regional area for $150 a week. The cheap rent was conditional on her being responsible for any repairs and maintenance. Despite her having a car, it had taken her 6 months to find:

> The process of getting there [finding the new accommodation] has been terrible. A few different factors and one of the major ones was trying to find something that didn't take all my pension.

Many of the older private renters were desperate to move into social housing and had put their names on the waiting list. Their attempts to access social housing were often intensely frustrating and there was much demoralisation. They usually had little idea as to how their application would proceed:

> And I have put my name down for public housing. I've been accepted [for eligibility] for public housing, but of course the waiting list is huge, huge. I reckon it will be 10 years, 12 years. The time between then and now concerns me … You know, how am I going to be able to cope … I think we need to find out how many older people are in this situation where they have no choices. There is no choice because you have the choice of going to have your name on the list for public housing, but it's not a choice because it's a 12-year waiting list.[27] (Judith)

Other interviewees had similar experiences: 'I've waited 10 years for a Housing Commission [public housing]. It's a joke' (Nancy). She described what happened when she went to the housing authority:

> What was happening with me with the Housing when I'd get desperate I'd go down there and I'd approach them and I'd get, 'Sorry'. I've just got to say it, a little upstart on the

other side of the counter that couldn't have given a damn and their attitude was just so bad cos they don't understand and couldn't care less ... and it really hurts when you've been waiting 10 years.

Paul recounted his experience with the housing authority:

> Well, the last time I was out there they were telling me about 10 years. I said, 'Thank you very much'. I tried to put my name down before I retired and I had to take them [NSW Housing] a statement about how much money I was earning, and they said, 'No, you cannot get on the Department of Housing list because you're earning too much money.' I said, 'But I want to put my name down now so that I can have a house when I retire because when I retire I won't be able to [rent privately]. I'll be dropping down from about $450 a week down to about $250 a week and that's a big drop.' And they said, 'No. There's nothing we can do about that. That's a government rule'.

Chris had been told that he was not eligible for the priority list and that he would have to wait for many years:

> But it's you know, paramount that I find cheaper accommodation ... I have been to Public Housing and Community Housing and the waiting list is enormous. Housing wrote back to me after I applied for [housing], after I went into bankruptcy, and I looked to be put on a priority list, and they declined that [his application] and said that I could find my own rental.[28]

At the time of the interview, Gloria had been living in the same house on the central coast[29] for 15 years and the house was now on the market. She was worried that she could find herself homeless due to a lack of social housing in the area:

> If and when that place sells ... I could become homeless because there is no affordable housing in this district that's

> available. And when I went to Community Housing to check on what level I was at, I am on their priority list, 'I have got about 2 years', she said to me before I might get an offer but the other problem she said, 'There's very little turnaround'. You see my generation are living longer and the second thing is there's been no affordable housing built here in this area as far as we are all aware since about 2000.[30]

Interviewees found the bureaucratic processes required by the state housing authority onerous. James was desperate to move into public housing:

> I gave them all my medical history. I filled out the housing application, then they wanted additional information. Bank statements, stuff about how could I prove that the house was no good. They wanted an independent living assessment done to show that I'm not wheelchair bound and whatever so that's got to be filled out …

The difficulty of finding affordable accommodation in the private rental sector and accessing social housing in Sydney is poignantly illustrated in the case of Peter who was interviewed in 2008 (Box 5.2).

Rejection of social housing offered

Some of the private renters had been offered social housing but had rejected what they had been offered. The size of the dwelling was often an issue. Research has indicated that the notion that older people require or desire less space is not necessarily correct (Gilroy 2005; Judd *et al.* 2010). Although she was struggling financially, June would not contemplate moving from her comfortable two-bedroom apartment into a one-bedroom apartment in public housing:

> Housing, well they've offered me two units actually since I've been on the list but they're both one-bedroom units which are just not big enough for me because I have one room that's full of sewing gear at the moment and I have other furniture that I would just have to sell it or give it away and I don't

> **Box 5.2.** Peter's story – forced to leave Sydney and move to a remote village
>
> At the time of the interview, Peter was living in social housing in a small town 3 hours from Sydney. He had been in this village for a year. Previously, he had lived in an inner-city neighbourhood in Sydney for ~40 years with his *de facto* partner. After she passed away, he was forced to vacate the house because his partner's daughter wanted to charge him a market rent.
>
> At the present I'm renting a one-bedroom flat [community housing] in R.... 3 hours south of Sydney and I pay $100 per week rent to Mid-South Council ... In Sydney I was on a [private] rent down there and the rent was going to be put up from $110 to $500 and that was the decision I had to make was to move from Sydney to the Central Tablelands because there was no possible way I could have stayed in Sydney and paid the rent down there.
>
> The lady that owned the house decided she can get more rent [and requested I] ... look around for something else and I looked around and I even went to places, rooms to rent in Petersham (a suburb in Sydney). They started from $165. You wouldn't have stayed there one night they were that bad and that was from $165 per room, ... absolutely terrible. There was nothing in it. There was one old wardrobe, would have been 50 years old, and that was it. There was no way that you could put all your furniture into that room. Shared sort of kitchenette and the rest of it was shared too ... and so depressing I just had to get out immediately. I looked at other places advertised privately in the *Trading Post*. I had some answers off them but they were out in semi-rural areas and they wanted just a shared room from $120. In Sydney, even studio flats in Glebe [a suburb] there would have been from $350 per week ...
>
> It was so depressing and then on me walks I'd see these poor chaps in the park ... I thought no wonder they're laying in the parks. Even on pensions or whatever they got off the government they could not have even got a room ...
>
> I went to the Department of Housing and I was sitting in there and they said, 'Where would you like to go?' 'Well', I said, 'You're not offering me anything in Sydney'. I said, 'I can understand that because of the accommodation. How hard it is' and they said, 'Where would you like to go?' I didn't really know. I said, 'Wagga [a regional town 460 km from Sydney] or anything you know'. They could not offer me anything and they knew that I had to get out ... I can understand now how people end up on the streets.

want to do that and I'm very comfortable where I am. I've been here for 4 years almost and I have a courtyard out the back. I have a garden and I have air-conditioning.

Arieta rejected the studio apartment she was offered. Besides the lack of space, she was also concerned about the stairs and location:

> They said they give me only the [studio apartment] … Bed here, lounge, everything in one space. No. I don't like that. When some people [visitors] come, then I want to get ready to go somewhere, I got no place to change. No privacy … [Also] I can't go up and down steps, very hard for me. And very small place. My things don't fit in there. Where I put the TV and my wardrobe? No place. And no transport. Shopping centre, railway station is very far away.

Carol would not consider public housing mainly because she needed a two-bedroom apartment for when her children and granddaughter visit:

> There are lots of problems with the Housing Commission here … In regional New South Wales if you are a single person on your own you will never be given any more than a one-bedroom flat, unit. You will probably end up in a bedsitter and I couldn't do that … They [her children] are half-an-hour out of town and they come into different functions in town and they may stay the night, so I need a second bedroom.

A perception that the public housing they had been offered was not safe was another reason for not accepting the accommodation offered:

> They offered me Waterloo [an inner-city neighbourhood in Sydney] and just right on the very top floor. And like when I went out to look at it, you had to step over drunks. So I went back there and said, 'There's no way'. I said, 'You put me right on the top floor and the lift, you have drunks outside, drunks inside.' I said, 'I wouldn't even consider it'. (Ellen)

She was offered public housing in another area but rejected it for similar reasons:

> I went there and took a look at that and said, 'No. There'd be no way'. I wouldn't even like going home in the light to where it was and see all the graffiti and stuff.

Peter was offered a place in a large regional centre 4 hours from Sydney. He describes his experience:

> I got out there and it was a battle zone. Graffitied [sic] everything and I said, 'This place comes up on TV regularly, disturbances and that'. And when I got there, there's a poor lady came out on a walking stick and she knew the lady that I was with was from the Department of Housing. She said, 'And what are you going to do with the chap on top of me? He's threatened to kill me again'. And she went on for about 10 minutes and she was shaking and I was taking all this in and I was thinking this is exactly what I thought it was going to be like, so I declined their offer. They had a bus shelter outside the complex that was smashed to smithereens and graffitied and all the brickwork over the units was graffitied. Just a depressing scene.

A couple of the interviewees would not contemplate a high-rise apartment:

> I did get the offer of a Housing Commission flat ... When I went into it, it was in high rise over at Surry Hills and it was on about the 17th floor or something and there's no way that I could actually live in that situation. I just like to be down on the ground. (Valerie)

A couple of the older private renters were fundamentally prejudiced against public housing and refused to consider it under any circumstances:

> Depending on where it is and what the people are like because I've found with a lot of public housing that they've got a lot of young members of society who are drug addicts and I don't want to get into that ... My son-in-law took me out to Green Square or somewhere and he said, 'What do you think of them?' and I said, 'I think they're depressing.' ... I think you need to be with people who've got the same sort of attitude as you. (Elsie)

> And to be honest I don't want to ever move out of private rental accommodation and go into Housing Commission. I couldn't. (Beverley)

The accommodation of older social housing tenants

Most of the older social housing tenants interviewed were adamant that their accommodation was adequate and created the foundation for a decent life. They felt fortunate and were highly appreciative:

> The day I come to have a look at this place … I thought, 'Gee I like this place'. And I went back to the Housing Commission and I said, 'That's my house. Don't give it away'. I said, 'I love it'. (Mavis)

> If I had to pay another $10 or $15 a week for what I've got, fantastic. I'm safe. I'm secure. I've got everything I need. Wonderful bath, shower, toilet everything. There's not a problem. (Gloria)

> I am happy. I am very happy. My place is clean. Nobody bothers me … I have everything. I don't know. Maybe some people complain, but I don't complain. (Lada)

> I can't say what I like best. I love my apartment. I have furnished it how I could. We are happy here with my husband. (Liliya)

> I'm damned lucky to have such a nice flat I think. I appreciate it and am very grateful for it. (Manuel)

> I'm grateful to be able to talk about this you know. I want people to know that I am grateful for my place, so grateful … (Joanne)

Joanne loved her apartment in Sydney where she had lived for 42 years:

> I have a three-bedroom place. It is absolutely beautiful. Anyone can come in at any time. When they done my kitchen up I went and bought some special tiles cos I wanted to have different colours instead of all white … When they done the kitchen, they done a new carpet. It's good. I'm happy with it.

Mildred had been in her three-bedroom terrace for 16 years. Her mother had lived in the same house for 30 years:

> It's just a lovely house. I love it. I wouldn't want to live anywhere else. My cousin wanted me to move up the coast to live with her and I was all for it, you know, and then I came home and wandered around and I said, 'What do I want to leave here for?'

When asked if she was satisfied with her accommodation, Joyce responded, 'Yes, I love it. They've just done the place up. Got a new kitchen. Got a lovely bathroom'. Joyce was the first resident in her inner city housing complex and had been in the same apartment for 46 years.

At the time of the interview, John had been in his apartment in Sydney's inner city for 21 years:

> When I first came here I thought it was a little bit of heaven and that's probably an over-exaggeration, but I still don't have any complaints except the type of people they put in here [in the housing complex] and maintenance.

For immigrants from the old Soviet Union, public housing accommodation was seen as an enormous step-up:

> This apartment is very comfortable, conveniently located in the city ... We have everything. We have a great bathroom, shower. We have a great balcony. We have two bedrooms and a lounge room. We have a separate laundry. All of this makes life better. (Alina)

In apartment blocks where residualisation and anti-social behaviour were significant interviewees, not surprisingly, tended to be far less satisfied. The chaos of the common areas spilt over into their perceptions of their accommodation. Doris was living in an apartment block that had several difficult tenants. When asked if she was pleased to be in public housing, she responded, 'No. I hate it'. She was then asked whether she felt at home in her accommodation:

> No. No, I couldn't say that ... You've got to share the laundry. You've got to go past the neighbours to get to the

chute room to put the rubbish. They fill up the chute room with stuff. You can't get in and then you have to get in touch with the Housing Commission and they take so long and things smell.

Doris's perception of her accommodation was also influenced by her housing history. She had been a homeowner before her divorce. Despite her dissatisfaction she would not contemplate moving into private rental.

Ellen was one of the few public housing tenants interviewed who was dissatisfied with her accommodation. However, she was not in actual public housing but in a private dwelling for which the Department of Housing had taken out a 'head lease'. The interviewee needed to be near her children because she needed assistance in caring for her husband. However, there was no public housing in the area and the state housing authority had placed her and her husband in a granny flat that was far too small for their needs. Due to her husband's ill-health she needed two bedrooms:

> My husband's actually now going in a nursing home because, one of the reasons is because of the [public housing] accommodation … It's very tiny and we're sleeping in a single bedroom … and I've got two beds in that bedroom and you can't move so you know basically I'm on the waiting list but there's no properties in the area.

Social housing tenants and moving

Almost all of the social housing interviewees had no desire to move and most said that they would like to be in their present accommodation until they died:

> I'm settled here till they take me out feet first. I have no intention [of moving]. If I die here, I'll go out in a box. (Norma)

> It could be one day [that I move] but when I'm in a box. (Mildred)

> The only way they'll take me out of here is in a box. (Patricia)

> What could we find that is better than this? We have an apartment here that was recently renovated. Everything is here. (Olga)

> I won't move ... They'll have to carry me out in a box. (Louise)

I asked Nina if she would want to leave here. She responded, 'No, no, no. You know they asked me to switch [apartments]. Not for anything'. For Joyce, the thought of moving was terrifying:

> I'd die if I had to move from here. I couldn't stand it. Me son wanted me to move because of this [difficult] fellow next door. He said, 'Mum, we'll get another place'. I said, 'I'd die in a month if I moved from here cos I've been here all these years'.

The length of residence, strong social ties, familiarity with the neighbourhood and local services and the cost of accommodation in the private rental sector, made the thought of moving inconceivable for almost all of the social housing tenants interviewed. A long-time resident of Millers Point, an inner-city area where public housing was first constructed in Australia, and where the state government has begun selling off the public housing stock and relocating residents (this is discussed in detail in Chapter 8), commented:

> Well, it [public housing and living in Millers Point] is the best thing I've ever known and want to know. I'm more than happy to be here. Can't see myself living anywhere else. We're close to what we need ... or to whatever medical things we have and I realise they've got them [services] everywhere too but no this suits us at this stage of life. That's right. It's different, isn't it? (Jean)

Familiarity with the neighbourhood and security were the key factors for Heather, another long-established Millers Point resident:

> I think it is the security probably ... As you get older I think you get more set in your ways and you like the security and you feel safe. I mean you know [when] you go to a new area you

don't know how safe you feel. You don't know whether there's drugs or guns next door. At least you've got a fair idea here.

Another long-established public housing resident commented:

> I just want to let your readers to know that there are people [public housing tenants] out there that love their little places. I don't mind moving but I want to move to where I'm going to die you know. Where I know I'm going to be secure and they're not going to throw me out. I know they're not going to throw me out here. (Joanne)

The few tenants who wanted to move lived in apartment blocks that had several challenging tenants. They did not want to move out of public housing but away from their troubled housing complexes. They were deeply aware of the implications of moving into private renting:

> It costs too much money. You can live on the pension if you're not paying private rentals ... No. I couldn't consider it [private rental], unless it was about $70 a week and where are you going to find a place for $70 a week. (Doris)

Older homeowners' perceptions of their accommodation

Almost all of the homeowners interviewed were deeply attached to their homes. Like the long-standing social housing residents, the longevity of residence, intense familiarity with the family home and the many memories associated with it, were significant contributors to the strong attachment many homeowners felt (Elliot and Wadley 2013; Saunders 1989). Home ownership was associated with control and independence. As de Jonge *et al.* (2011: 40) state:

> For older people, home is one of the few remaining environments where they felt they have control over their lives ... and can exert autonomy and control over their use of time and space.

Most of the homeowners could not envisage living anywhere else:

> Yes. I love my little unit and I look out on a reserve. I used to have a beautiful view of the ocean but the trees have grown

> up and hidden that, but I still see Long Reef headland and the lagoon. It's a lovely position here. (Linda)
>
> I love it. I know it is a big house for one person … I feel a bit guilty actually because one person rattling around in a house this size is a bit greedy but I love it. I really do. (Maureen)
>
> We call it paradise. Because we, I mean I'm in the back room now but if I was in the front room I'm just looking over the ocean. We watch the Sydney to Hobart yacht races go past our house … It's a full brick home. We didn't build it but it's an average nice sort of house but we're up on a hill and look over the ocean. It's a very nice neighbourhood. (Paula)

Christine and her husband lived in a regional town and had been in the same house for 22 years:

> Well I wouldn't move because I live right on the water. My husband goes fishing. We live on a lake … so my husband walks out the backdoor and catches dinner.

At the time of the interview in 2012, Lyn had been living in the same home for 53 years:

> Well, I couldn't see living anywhere else. I lived in mum and dad's home till I was 21 and then I moved in here and we haven't gone anywhere else.

Shirley moved into her five-bedroom home in 1963, the year she married. At the time of the interview her husband had passed away and her children had moved out, but she had no intention of moving:

> I can walk around this [house] at night … I wouldn't turn the light on. If I wake up during the night and I need a drink of water. I don't turn a light on cos I know exactly where I to put my feet. I can walk this house blindfolded.

For Francesca, who has four children and had been a single parent for a considerable period, owning her home was viewed as a personal triumph and gave her tremendous satisfaction:

> The thing is ... since my husband left me I had no one else ... You have to get on with life, make the most of your situation. I mean he has never paid anything to this house. I have paid for this house on my own ... I love my house ... I'm proud of myself ... I had to borrow some money but I was lucky. I was able to borrow ... but I've paid it off.

Denise had also been a single parent. She had been in the same house for 44 years and had a similar perspective to Francesca:

> Well, see my husband left me. I'd only been here in Australia 1 year and he left me here. I had a daughter who was only 6. She had just gone to school ... So I struggled to pay the house off and I think it was hard, but it is paid off and I love where I live.

The use of the space

Almost all of the homeowners felt that they needed the space they had (see Judd *et al.* 2010). Those who had spare rooms tended to use the rooms and enjoyed the space:

> We've got a spare room, which we call my room. That's where I keep all my books and music machine and stuff like that and there's the other spare bedroom which is generally a guest room and our bedroom of course ... We could do with one less bedroom ... but it is just convenient to say, 'Right, you can sleep in this room'. (Henry)

Maureen lived alone in a four-bedroom home:

> I've got a bedroom for sleeping in. I have one room I use as a study. It has got bookshelves and three computers ... I've got a lounge room, a dining room, a television room and I have a sewing room. And no, I don't use all the rooms. No, there's probably two bedrooms I don't use unless there's visitors.

Spare rooms were very important for those homeowners who had grandchildren who stayed over:

> So my grandsons come and stay and then I have a spare room, which is actually a study. I do my bible reading and stuff in there and I've got another television in there. I love my little home. (Denise)

> When the grandchildren come over and sleep over we use everything, but otherwise no. (Christine)

Having total control over their space was a source of much satisfaction.

> Like, I don't have to ask permission if I want to put a nail on the wall or if I want to repaint something. I don't have to ask permission.

Joe had a similar response:

> If I want to build another garage or I want to build something I don't have to ask anybody else except the council and I go ahead and do it and I'm the boss.

Susan's husband had been in a wheelchair. He had passed away a couple of years before the interview. They were able to do the necessary renovations so that he could continue to live at home:

> I had him in a nursing home up the road till we did the renovations ... We had to open the bedroom door. We got a builder in ... the bathroom entrance and laundry entrance and the front door we had to make that bigger.

Homeowners who had pets emphasised the importance of having their own home and adequate space: 'I need a house or something where I can have a dog, so I guess I'll stay here' (Helen).

The home as a site of activity

An important advantage that homeowners have is their freedom to work in the garden or on their home. It was a major activity for some and a source of much satisfaction:

> My garden is chock-a-block and that was important to me because I don't think I could ... live in a unit. Also the

> garden gives me something to do that's also beneficial to me you know. (Francesca)
>
> My wife actually looks after the five little gardens and she looks after them just because she likes it. No money changes hands ... She takes a lot of pride in the garden. She's always digging something out and putting something in. (Henry)
>
> We're gardeners so we have a big block ... I think it's ideal. It is on a single level, which is a plus. As you get older I think a single level is ideal. (Christine)

Joe, who was 80 at the time of the interview, appeared to constantly have a major home improvement project that kept him engaged:

> In the last year I built a new garage by myself. I also built the second garage by myself ... My next project is I'm just putting paving outside the garage I've just built. ... And after that, well I'm scratching my head ... There's always something to do ... I keep my house perfect. Every blade of grass, I keep the trees pruned. I keep it all nice. It gives me something to do.

Homeowners and ageing in place

In line with previous studies (see Levenson *et al.* 2005; Oswald *et al.* 2011), almost all of the homeowners interviewed had a strong attachment to their homes and were reluctant to move. Despite being by herself and her home having five bedrooms and requiring a good deal of maintenance, Shirley had no intention of moving:

> We worked very hard to get the house. We did you know strain against the finances ... When I retired from work I thought I'm going to start at the bedroom and I'm going through each cupboard one room at a time and get rid of all the things that I don't actually need. Well I sort of haven't finished one cupboard. So you know I'm a bit of a storer. I'm very sentimental ...

As long as they had the capacity to live independently they wanted to stay in their existing home. Linda captured this determination:

> Fortunately, at the moment, I'll be 88 in June but I'm still, I'm only a small woman but I'm active … So I'm in better shape than a lot of people you know. As they say, it takes all your courage to grow old, and I couldn't agree more.

There was a realisation that at some point moving may be a sensible option. Frances lived by herself and had various health issues. Although she loved her apartment, she was considering her options. She was deeply concerned about being a burden:

> If you're a spinster and on your own you may have a supportive family but they might live in other parts of the country so you know, are you being responsible if you stay in your own home? I don't think you are. I think you're better off being in a hostel where you are self-sufficient. Where at least there are other people around there who can help if you need help and they are on site. Whereas here there are people who can help me but it might take them 2 days to be able to get time to come and help. So I think you've got to look very carefully at that. At people who are alone without any family support and who have aged friends because if you have aged friends you don't want to give them the responsibility of looking after you.

The location of the home was another factor motivating homeowners to consider their options as regards to ageing in place. Joy, 84 at the time of the interview and still driving, said she would have to consider moving if she could no longer drive:

> I'm comfortable here and the only thing that would really make me consider moving would be if next year when I go for my driver's licence again at 85[31] … If I became dependent on public transport and couldn't drive any more that would make life very difficult because you know the public transport is within walking distance but not for my age.

The steepness and size of the block were issues for Helen:

> It is on a fairly steep block ... It only worries me if I get unwell and it is ... quite a big block but I do get a lawnmower man to come and mow fortnightly normally ... The house itself isn't very big but you know I could live in a smaller house easily and it would be nice to be on a nice flat block somewhere.

For some homeowners, especially women living by themselves in a freestanding house, security was an issue:

> I've got an alarm on in the house. I've got the dog as well. He can't do much ... but if anybody comes in they won't go out. I've got bars on the door. I've got security windows and I've got the shutters ... (Susan)

At the time of the interview, Irene's daughter and her partner lived with her. However, they were planning to move out of her large home and she was apprehensive about the impact and whether she would manage living alone:

> I don't know how I'm going to feel when Madeleine completely moves out because at the moment she comes and goes and I come and go as I wish and I do enjoy having my odd days just to myself. But when she moves I will be completely alone again rattling around in this. Do I want that?

Interviewees were concerned about the cost of moving:

> You can't just pick up your house and move. You've got to go through the process of selling and moving on and whatever and if I sold up today, well it is going to cost me around $30 000 to do it and that's just to walk out the door ... ... Each time you move you're up for at least $30 000 with government, agent fees, legal fees ... and everything. They've all got their hands out. (Doug)

There was also a concern that if there was a substantial surplus after selling the family home and purchasing elsewhere, this could impact on the fortnightly pension:

> And also cos if I sell this house and bought a unit the difference in the price of this house and the unit, if the unit was say $100 000 less than this house I'm going into a one-bedroom unit and just for argument sake … I would suddenly have $100 000 in my bank. Centrelink would then use it to decrease my pension. (Joy)

Downsizing

The few homeowners interviewed who had decided to downsize were pleased with their decision. They felt that they had been able to purchase a home that was appropriate for their situation. Thelma was divorced and was living by herself:

> Yes, I bought a villa which is freestanding. So it is just like a house but has a very small yard that I can manage. I'm a keen gardener so I needed the dirt. Maintenance-free as possible because I have no family living up here.

She had thought carefully about the future when she bought the villa:

> I deliberately chose when I bought the house. I chose the house that was on a bus route so that when I can't drive I still have transport and one that's only got three steps. It's not on the ground but three steps front and back.

A couple had downsized because their poor health meant that they were no longer able to maintain a large home:

> Where we were it was quite large. Yeah. You had grass to cut, walls to paint, roofs to clean and that sort of stuff, so it all became very difficult. I was okay then but I was just starting to deteriorate [health-wise] so now it'd be virtually impossible … Too many years of smoking. (Henry)

Downsizing was not necessarily a wise choice. Lorraine had sold her home in Queensland and moved to a one-bedroom apartment in

Sydney to be close to her son. She deeply regretted her purchase and was thinking of selling her apartment and moving to a retirement village:

> I'm finding it awful living there to be honest. It is sort of too much ... I just find it [the security] oppressive. Every time I go out of my door there's a camera there and ... there are other issues. I thought one bedroom would be enough ... but it's not big enough ... I miss, coming from Queensland, I miss the morning sun siting out on the veranda. Little things like that ... Yes, I think, I know I have to move. I know that I must do that ... I guess I want to move back to fresh air and a bit of grass. I know that sounds crazy. When I bought my unit I thought this is lovely and those balmy afternoons I can sit back and enjoy the harbour breezes. [However] it is so dusty. It is revolting and I actually have these floor to ceiling louvres and I thought it will be so lovely but it just scoops everything up and all the restaurants around and all the smells.

Downsizing often meant moving into a unit. Besides units costing nearly as much as houses, interviewees were concerned about strata fees. An interviewee in a regional town commented:

> I know we're a lot cheaper than Sydney. I mean I would get $300 000 for my house but you can't get a unit, even a two-bedroom unit would be $290 000. Well, by the time you've paid all the government fees and everything you couldn't do it ... I like my home. I'll stay here. I keep thinking I'll get a two-bedroom unit somewhere and it'd be a lot easier but then it isn't because you've still got to pay [strata] fees. (Doreen)

Conclusions

The chapter has illustrated how housing tenure and financial resources impact on accommodation quality and possibilities. The older private renters were determined to live in decent accommodation and a number had succeeded in accessing reasonable housing, but usually at great cost. Their disposable income after paying for the accommodation was often negligible. Many had not succeeded and were living in inadequate, and in some cases squalid, conditions. Their capacity to access adequate accommodation was determined by their resources and where they were located. Thus private renters in Sydney were more likely to find themselves in dismal circumstances due to the high cost of rental accommodation. There was a good deal of contingency. Some had found reasonable accommodation and their landlord had been generous and had set the rent at what appeared to be below the market rent.

Moving was viewed with enormous trepidation. It was costly and emotionally and physically draining. Their endeavours to access social housing were characterised by uncertainty and frustration. They rarely knew what their chances were and a few commented on being shown totally inappropriate dwellings.

In contrast to the private renters, almost all of the older social housing tenants were pleased with their homes. Their guaranteed security of occupancy and adequacy of their accommodation meant that they felt settled and were able to create a home in which they felt comfortable (see Chapter 8). Most were deeply appreciative of their housing and spoke of how fortunate they felt. They saw their future as being in social housing and had no desire to move. The private rental sector was viewed as an unthinkable option. Social housing tenants located in public housing complexes that had several challenging tenants expressed some dissatisfaction. Dealing with these neighbours on a daily basis was difficult (see Chapter 9 for a detailed discussion). However, even these tenants vehemently rejected the private renting option.

Almost all of the homeowners interviewed felt settled and their home was the fulcrum of their lives. The intense familiarity and the knowledge that this was their space with which they could do what they wanted, made the home a key source of wellbeing. Besides providing subjective solace, it also provided a basis for much activity. Gardening, maintenance and general pottering around, meant that home ownership and the home was viewed as richly rewarding. There was certainly concern around the future and the capacity to age in place. This was especially so for interviewees who were living by themselves in large homes and/or in locations that meant you needed to be able to drive to remain in touch. Some homeowners had downsized but most had no intention of moving. The thought was overwhelming and life was relatively easy in their present home.

6
'My social life is down the drain': housing tenure, social ties and leisure

Introduction

There is increasing division between older people who can choose lifestyles, neighbourhoods and engage in leisure activities and those who do not have the resources to do so, and have to make do with whatever their situation (Phillipson 2007). This chapter focuses on two groupings with minimal capacity to choose their residence or neighbourhood – older renters in the private rental market and in social housing – and a third group, older homeowners, who have varying capacities to choose. It examines the respective situations of these three groupings in and outside of the neighbourhood and illustrates how housing tenure has the potential to shape their social ties and leisure activity. This is an important focus as research indicates that social ties and activity are potentially important contributors to wellbeing and successful ageing and that older people who are isolated are more likely to suffer from depression, poor health and are at increased mortality risk (Berkman 1995; Lawton 2000; Uchino 2009).

Globalisation and increases in affluence, inequality, diversity and mobility have certainly altered many neighbourhoods in cities in developed economies (see Bounds and Morris 2005; Slater 2009; Watt 2013). Wellman and Leighton (1979) coined the phrase 'liberated community' to capture the dynamic that propinquity is no longer necessary for social contact. However, despite our social contacts being spread throughout the city and beyond, it is recognised that the neighbourhood potentially continues to have an important influence on social ties and quality of life (Arthurson and Jacobs 2006; Ellen and Turner 1997; La Gory *et al.* 1985). The neighbourhood is usually more important for older residents than it is for the general population. Besides no longer being in the workforce, in many cases older people's limited mobility and resources mean that their activities and social ties are often restricted primarily or solely to the local area (Bowling and Stafford 2007; Scharf *et al.* 2002). Also, as discussed in Chapter 1, length of residence is more pronounced for older residents. A 1989 UK study found that 70% of people aged 55–64 and 73% of people aged 65 and over had not moved for 10 years. In contrast, only 45% of people between 35–44 had not moved for 10 years (Coles 1989, quoted in Heywood *et al.* 2002: 78). Another UK study found that in the 39 'New Deal for Community' areas,[32] 43% of residents had lived in their neighbourhood for less than 5 years and only 22% had been resident for more than 20 years. However, in the case of older residents, 79% had lived in their neighbourhoods for at least 20 years and close to half had been resident for 40 years or more (Phillipson 2007). The HILDA Survey indicated that for older social housing residents, the average number of years resident in their current residence was 13.6 years and for private renters it was 6.7 years (Naidoo and Morris 2014). In the case of homeowners, in 2007–08, 44% of outright homeowners had spent more than 20 years in their home. Many of these would be aged 65 and over (ABS 2009). The implication is that for many older people their identities and social ties and activities are closely bound up with the neighbourhood where they reside (Rowles and Ravdal 2002) and relocation, especially if it is not voluntary, can be destabilising, whereas stable residence can have a positive impact on quality of life and disposition (La Gory *et al.* 1985; Lawton 1985; Scheidt and Norris-Baker 2003; Wiles *et al.* 2009).

The role of housing tenure in shaping social ties and activity has received limited attention in Australia. A study in Adelaide concluded that residents of community housing generally had stronger ties with their neighbours than did public housing tenants (Ziersch and Arthurson 2007). This was primarily due to a greater need for residents in community housing to cooperate around running the housing association. In a study of housing tenure, social networks and employment outcomes, Ziersch and Arthurson (2005: 437) found that in public housing, security of tenure and length of residence were 'seen as promoting connection to neighbourhood and the development of supportive social networks'. Another Adelaide based study found that public housing tenants were involved with their communities and proud of their neighbourhood (Palmer *et al.* 2004).

Of course, a range of factors usually lead to social isolation. Victor *et al.* (2005), drawing on existing research, identify 'five sets of factors [that] have been shown to be consistently associated with loneliness' among older people – socio-demographic attributes (living alone, having no children); material circumstances (poverty, low income); health resources (disability, mental health); social resources (having a confidant, social network) and recent events such as bereavement. Although housing tenure is not mentioned, it is evident that housing tenure directly impacts on three of these five factors: material circumstances, health resources and social resources. Also, older private renters and social housing tenants are far more likely to be living alone.

'Like I know all the people and we've become really good friends': Social housing tenants, social ties and leisure

In the case of public housing estates, there is a tendency to portray them as dangerous, bleak and devoid of community (Arthurson *et al.* 2014; Flint 2006; Jacobs *et al.* 2011; Palmer *et al.* 2005). There is no doubt that there are many older people in social housing who are lonely and isolated (Fine and Spencer 2009). In Australia, most older social housing tenants live alone and a proportion do have emotional and/or physical issues that make social contact difficult. Mavis lived in a small public housing complex and was lonely. She rarely went out and nobody came to visit her:

> Tuesday and Friday I go to the people at the end of the housing [complex]. They're both missionaries and we have a bible study or something like that. That's 2 days a week and

> then I go to church on Sunday. That's my whole social life ... I don't get visitors. You're it kiddo ... I don't like being on my own. It's very lonely because these other tenants they've got their husbands or their own lives to live and so they don't mix and so I look at four walls.

However, in regards to the social housing tenants interviewed, Mavis was an exception. Certainly, what this section illustrates is that for most of the social housing residents interviewed, their housing tenure meant that they had the disposable income required to participate in leisure activities and their immediate neighbourhood provided them with a social and physical context that facilitated social activity and the forming and maintenance of social ties (see Bowling and Stafford 2007). Almost all of the social housing tenants interviewed appeared positive and enthusiastic about engaging in the world and sustaining social ties.[33] Many had strong or moderate social ties in their immediate vicinity or in the neighbourhood and a number were active in their residential complex. In the public housing complexes, the concentration of older tenants, the longevity of residence, proximity of fellow residents, the community bus and the existence of nearby places to meet, greatly facilitated social contact.

Joyce, who was 85 at the time of the interview, had lived in the same very large public housing complex for close to 50 years and was a fierce advocate for the complex. She describes her neighbourhood, social ties and activity in Box 6.1.

The length of residence encouraged a strong feeling of community and helped solidify social ties:

> I do like it around here. I know where everything is and I know all the people, especially in here, around these units you know. I know everyone and they know me ... This is my home, you know. This is a community, I think. Like I know all the people and we've become really good friends. I couldn't think of being anywhere else. (Kay)

Several of the social housing tenants spoke about their social ties in their complex as being analogous to an extended family. Rachel, who

> **Box 6.1. Joyce's story**
>
> Well they [challenging tenants] don't interfere with me [and] I don't interfere with them and I've got the four people that's left here from when I first moved in. We're very friendly but we don't go in one another's flats much. We might talk in the walkway or they might come down for a book and they'll come in and sit where you are. Have a little talk and I might give one a cold drink or something and that's it. There's no cups of tea or anything like that because we don't stop long enough in one another's place, but they're lovely neighbours you know. Yes, if I was in any trouble I could always go and knock on their doors or give them a ring and if I hear anything that goes on here around here like they should know, I ring one and the other rings the others …
>
> A lot of good people are living here but they never get a mention. They're very, very good people. They mind their own business and we have a talk … but you don't hear that. You don't hear the good things. You don't hear what they do at the [Community] Centre … People come and have a cup of coffee and they'll give them something to eat. You don't hear that on television. All you hear on television is people jumping over balconies and drug addicts and what goes on here. The fights and everything. You never hear the good, nice things …
>
> So there's five of us. We go over there of a day time about 1 o'clock and we sit under the trees if there's nice sun … About half past three we all come home, go in our own units and we all meet on the bus when we go shopping.
>
> I go there [the community centre in the housing complex] twice a week. I do an exercise for the elderly and I teach the Chinese [residents] English … and they're starting to teach me a little bit of Chinese … I love it … I'm taking them over to the Belvoir Theatre tomorrow [the local theatre].
>
> I travel a lot by bus. I stop home one day and go out the next. I go out every second day … The community bus comes here and takes me to the movies once a fortnight and we go shopping every Thursday. The bus takes us …
>
> I like being here … There's a lot of people I don't know and there's a lot of people I do know mainly from on the buses and the trips and things. We've just come back from the tulips up at Bowral … I like being here. I've got good friends here.

lives in the outer suburbs of Sydney in a public housing estate that has a significant number of older people, commented:

> We are so, so supportive. It's unbelievable. It's like a family. We're very bonded. Everyone is so nice. I don't think all the years I've lived here I've ever had a row with anybody … I'm really happy.

Interviewees could walk to their friends and there were usually public spaces close to their homes where they could meet. Homogeneity also facilitated social connection (see Adams and Torr 1998; McPherson et al. 2001):

> Well, it's a kind of a community. Like we all know each other because we are all around the same age. We can sit around and have a chat with each other. You see the benches out there under the trees? ... Often we just sit out there and have a yarn with each other. Sometimes ... we just drop by each other's place and have a yarn ... This community room gets used quite a bit ... It's like a little community here ... Most of us have been here for a while so we all know each other. (Alice)

Several of the social housing tenants were active in their residential complex. Some taught residents in the local community centre and/or were involved in the tenants' association. These activities facilitated, maintained and strengthened social connections:

> We have a little tenant group that meets just down the road from our block and we've probably got a dozen, mostly older people cos the younger ones don't seem to bother these days ... We do letterbox drops and I love all our little people you know. They're lovely. So we sort of stick together there. (Joan)

The concentration of older people and the availability of a community bus made organising shopping trips fairly straightforward. The shopping excursions on the community bus encouraged social ties. A public housing tenant observed:

> And service is very good. Now, every Thursday comes a bus and takes us to do shopping for free ... And once a week they take us to market for free ... We have a very good life. For pensioners, it's the best. (Nina)

Going on excursions was a regular activity. Brian was a primary initiator of trips in his community housing complex:

> Actually, I've arranged a little trip out tomorrow. It's about 10 or 11 of us. We've got a community bus. We're all going down to Rosehill Bowling Club for lunch. It's not fantastic, but it gets ten people out for a couple of hours and also just to have that contact.

The length of residence and the close proximity of fellow residents meant that interviewees usually knew several people in the housing complex:

> Well I have got a number of friends that I've made over the years and I do do things ... Once a week I go to a craft morning and I walk once a week with a friend. I can always find things to do and visit somebody or somebody will come and visit me. So I've got contact, which is important. And they are people that you've got something in common with. (Catherine)

An important consequence of the longevity of residence and proximity was the development of trust. Ralph, who was very involved in the local tenants' association, told of how older neighbours trusted and relied on him:

> I have neighbours come to me and ask, 'Can I mind their house keys', and I do this for them, do that for them. I've got another neighbour over in the other block. She's currently in hospital ... I've been collecting her mail and just making sure that her flat's okay ... I'm like an uncertified social worker ... I've told them [fellow public housing tenants], 'You're welcome, if it's a serious issue, to knock on my door any time of day or night'.

Ralph and his fellow older tenants were proud of their housing complex and the tenants' association brought people together.

The high density of the housing estates meant that tenants were usually able to look out for their neighbours:

> I'm sure that if I wanted anything they [her neighbours] would come to me. Now Ann's next door to me, and I've only

> got to sing out ... and she's at my front door. The man next door to me, Henry, he's a lovely man. He's been sick lately. All these years we would always help out each other. (Alice)

The impact of homogeneity, urban design and longevity of residence was noted by another public housing tenant:

> This type of public housing, a complex such as this with 24 units, people around about the same age, they live more as a community than they would if they were in houses along the street. Whilst they might know their neighbours, they just don't get together as often as people in a complex such as this ... We all get along very good with each other ... I think everybody is pretty happy here. (Ben)

Another important feature of some social housing complexes that facilitated social ties was national concentration. A Russian tenant in a large inner city complex with several Russian tenants, commented:

> Yes, there are many Russians here, and of the other nationalities there are also many good, kind people here. We have a community centre here where we meet. (Lada)

The Russian-speaking tenants in this block met once a week in the community hall of the complex and it was evident that there was a good deal of contact and mutual assistance.

Not all of the social housing tenants were focused on the local housing complex for their social life. Jeanette was particularly social and spent a lot of time at the local club in her neighbourhood:

> More of my friends are down at the club. Well I don't drink and I don't smoke but I, and I don't play poker machines, but I go to the raffles and I know a lot of people and they took me out for lunch on Monday to wish me well with my operation.

Those social housing tenants who wanted to be engaged in leisure activity, appeared to have little difficulty finding the resources for moderate expenditure. Olga and her husband were very active:

> We often spend time in the park. Go on the ferry, travel on the bus, or the train. Go wherever we need … We can go to Melbourne. We have friends in Brisbane. We were there recently and they came to visit us.

None of the social housing tenants said that they had had a problem paying for organised social excursions:

> We have 2 day trips a month, costing $7 [each]. We buy our own lunch. They supply morning tea. We go to places like Palm Beach, Lane Cove National Park, Wattamolla Falls. (Norma)

For more expensive outings, they were able to save:

> If you wanna go to a show, you have to plan ahead for it, you know. Anything you wanna do, you have to plan a month ahead. You gotta say, 'Right I need to save this much …' (Marion)

Engaging in leisure activity was probably more important for people living by themselves. A married social housing tenant had an interesting analysis:

> There are mostly women here who are alone … There aren't many couples. They like to go out, and they need to. They are in their houses and they get lonely. They go to cafes, drink a cup of coffee with cake, and they sit there and daydream … They hear human voices. They see people. They don't feel so lonely. That's why I understand them and don't judge them. I'm not going to go to a cafe and drink coffee. I'm not used to that, you understand. I think, 'Goodness, I have coffee at home, I'm not going to go there'. But of course my husband and I have each other. My sister is alone. Materialistically, she doesn't have difficulties, but her loneliness kills her. (Nina)

Anti-social behaviour in their immediate surrounds was a serious issue for several of the social housing tenants and in some cases it had an impact on social contact and leisure. Living in an environment where disorder is a common occurrence can have serious psychological and social implications. In her seminal study of 2482 adults in Illinois, Ross (2000: 182), found that 'People who report a lot of disorder in their neighbourhood are significantly more depressed than others'. Some of the social housing tenants coped by spending as little time as possible in their housing complex. Their days were spent at community centres nearby. Almost all the public housing tenants were too scared to venture out at night. The impacts of challenging and difficult tenants on the lives of older social housing tenants is discussed in detail in Chapter 9.

'My social life is down the drain': private renters, social ties and leisure

In contrast to the social housing residents, the social ties and leisure activities of many of the older private renters interviewed were minimal. Besides shopping for necessities and attending religious services, many did little outside of their home. The interviews indicated that the high cost of their accommodation and resultant lack of disposable income severely limited the capacity of older private renters to retain social ties and engage in leisure activities. Those private renters who had managed to find cheap accommodation, or had some savings and/or strong family connections, were usually in a better situation and, not surprisingly, had greater capacity to socially engage.

Eileen had been living with her son but after a series of disagreements had been forced to move. She spoke about how becoming a private renter had changed her social life despite her having found relatively affordable accommodation. In June 2014, her rent was $250 a week for a very small granny flat in outer Sydney:

> I'm struggling ... I'm trying to survive ... I can't go to the movies. I can't go out for dinner and things like that, with friends for lunch ... My social life is down the drain. As I said, everything has changed. I have to be very careful with my money. I can't go to the places that I used to go. I can't do things that I used to do ... My situation makes me feel lonely.

Her accommodation heightened her isolation. It was secluded and she had minimal contact with neighbours. The location and her health meant that retaining her car was viewed as a necessity. It allowed her to shop and retain some contact with friends, but it accentuated her parlous financial situation:

> Well, the next biggest expense is the car, but if I sell my car … My back is very bad and my left leg and my right leg isn't very good either, so if I sell my car I won't be able to get out of the flat to go [anywhere].

Research has indicated that, in the case of older, people having private transport can add to wellbeing and significantly lessen social exclusion (Davey 2007).

Like Eileen, the high cost of her accommodation meant that Judith did not have the resources to engage in social activity:

> Yes, if I had a cheap rent I would be able to manage well because I mean walks are free. In this country we are lucky. The climate most of the year is good for walking. I can get on a train for $2.50. I can do things, but that is a strain because I'm paying this $500 a fortnight and that's more than the pension allows.

Chris was using ~70% of his income for rent. His minimal after rent income made it difficult for him to sustain social ties:

> And the big thing is too, again, ego or vanity … you don't like telling people that I can't go to this function because I can't afford to go. So I make excuses. I ring up and say, 'I'm ill' or 'I have to go to a funeral' … and people accept that … I've become very isolated. I used to, before I had the hip [replacement], I used to play tennis, and I loved to play tennis … but I really can't afford [it].

He could not afford to have visitors: 'Well you cut out everything that's not an absolute necessity and you don't have visitors for a meal or anything like that'.

Another private renter who was having to use well over half of her income for accommodation, told of how she could not afford to take part in the social activities organised by her church:

> There's quite an active social club at the church for over 55s but I can't go to any of those [events] ... Sometimes I think it would be nice to go ... They might have an afternoon at somebody's home and you're asked to bring a plate. You see I couldn't afford to do that. (Beverley)

Marie was deeply frustrated by her inability to partake in social activity:

> I would like to go to the theatre. I would like to go occasionally to do something relaxing, but you can't go outside the door without it costing money ... And when I see all the people sitting outside the coffee lounges ... I just can't imagine how they can afford it. It's so expensive.

The most elementary social activity was carefully assessed: 'Some nights I'd like to go to the RSL and have a beer. I can't afford it' (Bruce). Despite the generous public transport concessions for pensioners, even using public transport provoked anxiety: 'So I've had to really watch [my money]. Do you need to go out today? Do you need to go on the train?' (Marie). When this interview was conducted, $2.50 represented about 1% of the Age Pension. Arieta often found it difficult to find the fare: 'I want to go out sometime; I've got no fare to go. Before it was all right. It was $1.10, now $2.50 – very hard to find it'. One interviewee told of how she had to choose between food or breaking her isolation by using public transport: 'Well, you sort of think what you can do with $2.50. That's a loaf of bread type of thing' (Beverley).

Public transport was a cheap way for older private renters to have some social contact:

> I get the train. Sit down in the train when I am bored. Then I go to Campbelltown and travel around. Have a look. Stay in the train, come back home. Few hours, couple hours, 3, 4 hours, I spend for travelling. (Arieta)

There was a realisation that it was crucial not to become too isolated:

> Loneliness is a terrible thing. It's a killer ... See I do go out. I feel sorry for people because it is hard and once you stay in, it's like crawling out of a slime pit. You have to actually. I have to say, 'Get up and go out. Go up to the shops. You know. Pretend you need potatoes or something' ... You have to. (Marie)

Religious participation was an important social activity for many private renters:

> I belong to a local church and it's been a great solace. I work there voluntarily, which is a great thing because it keeps my mind active and gives me some contact. (Chris)

For a few private renters, volunteering was a central part of their lives. James had made visiting a charity that feeds homeless people a daily activity. It gave him an interest and helped him come to terms with his own situation:

> Yeah, I just enjoy it there. I enjoy the outing. Getting on the bus and getting out ... There are people living under freeway overpasses and I see them every day. Boy, that's doing it tough. So I've got plenty of complaints but believe me ...

Some of the older private renters had no desire to socialise. Their situation had worn them down. Their anxiety about having the means to pay the rent and purchase basic necessities and their concern for the future, meant that their capacity to initiate and sustain social ties was minimal:

> Well the last 2 years have been very difficult ... Thinking virtually daily and nightly how I'm going to do something with the money and plan what I'm going to do ... It's almost as difficult as maintaining a full-time job. (Chris)

They rarely knew anybody in the neighbourhood who was in a similar situation. This compounded their isolation:

> I don't have anyone to talk to ... You sort of feel very isolated. You feel like you're the only one, but you're not ... So I do think that if there was a community of people, not necessarily living in each other's pockets, but somebody who would ring if they didn't see you around for a while or whatever that would be good. (Judith)

Noteworthy is that the couple of private renters who were in a relatively good financial position appeared to be far more socially connected. Carol earned an extra $190 a month doing cleaning jobs and this greatly facilitated her ability to socially engage. She was able to partake in activities that a private renter totally dependent on the Age Pension and Rent Assistance paying a market rent could not envisage: 'I went out to a very expensive restaurant last Saturday night with some friends'. Carol was well aware of the dangers of isolation:

> No, I am not isolated and I have made sure that I am not isolated because I think that brings more problems. You have enough health-related issues as you're getting older. I think if you isolate yourself I think you bring mental health issues into it.

Nellie who had managed to find secure and affordable accommodation was very active in the community. Her financial situation certainly contributed:

> I am able to you know to buy myself a car you know to run around in. I volunteer in the Rural Fire Brigade. I don't fight fires but I'm in the communications and it is a role that I absolutely enjoy ... and it keeps me busy. I am fairly active. Yes, I'm 74 and I'm going okay. I think doing the volunteer work makes you feel that you are making a difference you know ... I get a lot out of that and I do other things as well.

'I'm a very busy person': older homeowners, social ties and leisure

The interviews, not surprisingly, indicated that there was much variation in the degree to which older homeowners on the Age Pension engaged in leisure activities and the extent of their social ties. Some were extremely active, while others were content with their own and their family's company and did not engage in much social activity or have extensive social contacts. What was evident was that their low accommodation costs meant that most of the homeowners interviewed had the financial resources (capabilities) to partake in leisure activity and to maintain social contacts if they so desired. Many had lived in the same accommodation for an extended period, in some cases for over 50 years. For some this had resulted in them having strong ties in the neighbourhood. An important factor is that while all of the homeowners interviewed were dependent mainly or solely on the Age Pension for their income, many did have savings that they could dip into if required. This further facilitated their ability to be socially active.

Although expenditure on leisure was generally moderate, the older homeowners appeared to be content with their social lives. Maureen summed up the situation of many older homeowners, especially those living by themselves and dependent solely on the single Age Pension:

> Well I can [and] I do participate. I don't go to the opera because that's too expensive … I don't go to live shows because they're too expensive, but that's okay. I do other things. I'm a very busy person.

She lived in a spacious home in a leafy suburb and had major expenses (see Chapter 3). However, she did have some savings that gave her a bit of a buffer and allowed her to take part in social activities and maintain social ties.

The homeowners who lived by themselves usually made a big effort to be socially active. They were determined to break their isolation. Shirley explained:

> When there's the two of you, your needs are different you know. You don't need to go anywhere else for company. You've got company, whether it is good company or aggravated company or whatever. They're [the spouse] there, you know. What I mean, so when it is the two of you, you manage differently to when suddenly you're back to one.

Francesca, who had brought up four children by herself, was enjoying her social life now that her children had left home. She was certainly frugal:

> So I've got a couple of friends that sometimes we go to a movie but it is not often you know and it is $8 and then we go to McDonalds. If we get something it is just the little ice cream ... and we'll have that. Did you know that you can get a cup of tea for free if you're a senior?

Moderate social activity was not a problem:

> I'm very grateful that I do have some very close friends. We go out for morning tea or coffee or whatever. There's always somebody that I can sort of pick up the phone and ring. (Val)

Meeting up with a friend for coffee or lunch was viewed as an important activity:

> Now I think to myself you can't buy anything else now cos you've got this health fund [to pay] and this is coming up but it doesn't mean if a friend of mine said, 'Do you want to go out for lunch Denise?' and we don't go to posh places ... I'll go, because variety is the spice of life and I don't like to be miserable so we do things like that.

Older homeowners had the capacity to join clubs. For some, this was an important way to meet people and keep active:

> As far as entertainment goes, I do belong to a bowling club but that's about $75 a year or so, not very much, and I belong to several craft groups. They are not expensive so I can have an active lifestyle. (Maureen)

Choices were made and if an interviewee was passionate about something they were usually able to save and indulge in the passion concerned. Joy was an ardent theatre-goer:

> I don't travel you know ... so instead of spending money on travel I spend money going to the theatre. See I do it in such a way that I am a subscriber ... and I go to the launch of the

6 – 'My social life is down the drain'

new program in November each year and I go to that and I get the program for the year and I book for the whole year at once and that way I save hundreds of dollars ... I can pay for that in two bites.

The greater income of older couples meant that they had greater capacity. Christine and her husband appeared to have a hectic social life:

Yes, I've just played tennis today. I do Tai Chai, I read and go to meetings, Probus[34] Club activities ... and my husband's at golf at the present moment. He golfs a couple of times a week ... We belong to a Probus group which is very social and so yes, there's a lot of activities.

Henry allocated himself ~$350 a fortnight for his own discretionary spending. 'I give her [his wife] $300 and the rest is mine to do what I like with and somehow I seem to spend it all'. When he went to the pub he spent lavishly, but it was his one major indulgence:

Once a fortnight I'll go to the local hotel and I might be there 3 hours, or I might be there 6 hours. Now, it is not hard to spend $60 or $70 in a hotel; $5 a beer so you have probably ... six beers so $30 for beer and then I usually play the pokies. Not to excess – $20 or $30. Yeah, there's your $60. But that's only 1 day a fortnight ... I've got to see the mates. Life's pleasures are simple.

Susan was also extremely busy:

I do not lead a boring life. I go out with my friends. We go to different places. I go to the Blacktown Sports Club when they have a dinner and show because you've only got to pay an extra $10 and you get a nice main meal ... I don't sit around at home. That's why my daughters, they're always cranky, because when they ring me on the landline I'm never home.

Older homeowners, while certainly careful with their spending, could be innovative. Leonie explains her most recent holiday:

> So another thing we've done to have a holiday is we found in the Seniors newspaper a wonderful place up at Coolangatta ...There's half a dozen of us women. We decided we'd get the train as far as we could for nothing, which is to the Queensland border, and then we could actually walk to this place which is right near ... to where you got dropped off ... You could walk to this block of flats which is just lovely. Basic, but just lovely. I think it worked out at $30 a night.

Not all of the older homeowners were so restrained. Denise managed her pension extremely well and she saved for holidays. In the 5 years before the interview she had been to the Philippines, Norfolk Island on a cruise and when she was interviewed she had just come back from a 16-day tour of New Zealand.

In regards to social ties, neighbours played an important role for some of the older homeowners. A number had had the same neighbours for many years:

> They're very good neighbours. The ones on the right-hand side we moved here in the October [1963] and they moved here in the January [of 1964] ... We've seen each other raise family sort of thing, but we're not in each other's pockets but we're there if needed you know. They're absolutely wonderful ... On the other side, the couple that are there now have been there 15 or 16 years and they are extremely thoughtful young people so I'm very grateful for my neighbours. (Shirley)

Neighbours were also very important for Roslyn:

> I have a neighbour that's just moved in, well 5 years ago. But all the previous ones are just so beautiful. My one neighbour, if she cooks food, she often brings it in because I'm coeliac. She says she enjoys a challenge. Yeah, when I get up in the morning I pull the blind up so they all know I'm awake or alive and the man over the road brings my paper in and puts it in the front chair so I can get it when I want it. They put my bins out and another neighbour brings them in.

Not all of the homeowners could rely on their neighbours and in some cases contact was minimal. This was especially so for those interviewees who lived in homes on large grounds. Maureen had been in the same house since 2000 but had little contact with the neighbours:

> The neighbourhood's excellent, but not very helpful. I was considering getting one of those care alert tags but I'm not close enough to any of the neighbours either physically or mentally to have them come in case of [an] emergency.

An important factor shaping leisure activity was whether a homeowner had any major recurring expenses. Doug and Cheryl who as mentioned spent a good deal of their income assisting their unemployed son, had limited capacity to engage in leisure activity:

> Well my wife goes out once a fortnight with friends for a lunch. Well that's only a $10 lunch at a hotel or club or something like that. She can't afford the coffee or a drink because the coffee will cost you nearly as much as a meal so she'll have a drink of water with their meal and they get together that way. We do a bit of volunteering. We belong to different organisations. We get out a bit.

The role of family

For many of the interviewees, family support was crucial and a key source of social activity and support. Contact with family was extremely varied. Some interviewees had very close and regular face-to-face contact, while others had minimal or no contact. Many had family living a distance away so physical contact was minimal. In a few instances, interviewees had minimal or no contact with their children.

Social housing tenants

About four in five social housing tenants had contact with family. Some saw family members constantly, others mainly had telephonic contact. A Russian couple commented on the importance of their children and grandchildren:

Boris: The fact that they are near us is an enormous source of help and joy.

Alina: We have a very cohesive family, which is not unimportant for life.

Boris: It is very important.

Alina: That we have their support.

Interviewer: *How often do you see them?*

Boris: Often. Sometimes once a week, others twice a week, but not less.

Alina: Sometimes every day. Yesterday, Anna was here with the family. Today, everybody is here.

Some social housing tenants relied extensively on their children:

> My children have cars. They come here. If we need to go somewhere, they pick us up. The day after tomorrow [my husband] needs to go to the hospital. My son will come here and take him there … Our kids do everything. They take us to the doctors, and shopping … I see them often and they call often. If my son can't come, he will call. (Raisa)

Ellen worked as a volunteer in an organisation two-and-a-half days a week. She had been doing it for 30 years and ran the organisation. However, her husband needed constant care and she was reliant on her daughter's support:

> So it's a long time and it is the only outlet I have. So my daughter basically she took over the caring of my husband so that I can still do what I love doing and it is the only thing that keeps me sane.

For the social housing interviewees who did not have a car, visiting children and grandchildren could be difficult. Pointing to several framed photos in her apartment, Marina explained:

> This is all my grandchildren and great-grandchildren. I love them, but I see them rarely. I can't travel, and now taxis are very expensive. I am scared to travel by bus. My legs are very bad.

Regular telephonic contact was important. Marina spoke to her son every day during the week: 'Every morning I call him at 7.30 and tell him that everything is okay. Every single day'. Joyce commented: 'Yes, I can rely on my son. He rings me every second day and I've got a wonderful daughter-in-law'. Flo was very proud of her family and kept in regular phone contact. She saw them on special occasions:

> I've got six great grandchildren, ... five grandchildren and they've all turned out real good, real happy with them. They're married and settled down and they're working and they don't get into any mischief or anything which is a bonus. My son's a very good man. My daughter's a very caring girl.

A few of the social housing tenants had no contact with their children. Mavis had lost contact with her three children:[35]

> I think it was their idea. There was no argument or anything or disagreement. It is just that they just moved [and] ... didn't bother telling me where. So I thought they've got their own lives to live.

Private renters

Only nine of the 46 private renters interviewed said that they had no contact with family. However, there was much variation in the level of family contact. Some of the private renters had constant contact and family members helped financially and socially:

> We help each other. We support each other. My son has two children. My daughter has three. They're both single parents. Tell me when to stop. (Marie)

Elsie's rent was more than her pension and without her daughter's assistance she would have been in a desperate situation. Fortunately her daughter had the means to support her:

> I couldn't live. My two sons they sort of know [my situation] but they haven't got any idea cos I don't like telling. I don't really tell my daughter. I try to work it (her finances) out some way, but I can't. It's an impossibility ... My daughter just says to me, 'Mum I bought you some groceries'. I say, 'Thank you, darling'.

Helping with the grandchildren was a primary activity for a few of the interviewees. Jan, who lives in a regional town, commented: 'I have my granddaughter here now. She comes here after school and waits for one of her parents to pick her up'.

John and his wife spent a good deal of their time looking after their grandchildren:

> Our week tends to be taken up with a couple of days of voluntary work and helping ... my daughter with the kids ... My daughter has had two children recently ... and that's been exciting. So we've been helping her as much as we can and she's about 5 minutes away at the moment.

Siblings, and sometimes a combination of family members, helped keep private renters in contact:

> Well, yes, I've got the family. Both my sisters live up in Mount Druitt which is only about 20 minutes drive away from here and she's got all her kids and all their family and I go up there quite often. (Paul)

Pam was close to her family all of whom were very supportive. Her daughters helped her with large items and her sister was generous. Having a sister who was a homeowner, middle class and supportive was clearly extremely helpful:

> Ah yes. I've got my sister. She's over at Brighton Le Sands. Well I go to her place every Saturday and Sunday. We spend the weekend. It's quite good. And everyone else lives in the country. But I've got nieces that I do see and they come here.

Private renters whose family members were also struggling found the financial demands from these family members difficult. Bruce had a daughter who would come and stay every second weekend. He was anxious about how spending money on her would impact on him and was also concerned that he did not have the resources to entertain her adequately:

> And that is a worrying thing too cos when I have my daughter and I'd like to take her to the club and she gets off the train and she's hungry and I feel remiss if I can't take her to get something for her but at the other end I've got to bear the cost somewhere.

Malcolm appeared to have a reasonable amount of contact with his 18-year-old daughter. She usually contacted him when she needed money:

> And, as I said, she rings me up when she needs me. The most common thing is money, and I say, 'Well I haven't got any so you're going to have to whistle'.

Judith told of the difficulty of entertaining relations who were visiting from the United Kingdom (UK):

> And I've just had visitors for 2 or 3 weeks ... It has been difficult just to take them to town or buy lunch or to say it's my turn, you know, and it's been very, very difficult. I'll pay the price for weeks to come ... And I don't want people to know just how bad it is to buy three sandwiches instead of one. You know, three cups of coffee instead of one.

The lack of finances certainly made retaining family contact more difficult. Anne, who had moved into social housing a few months before the interview, when asked, 'Is your relationship with family members affected when you haven't got any spare cash?', responded:

> Tremendously. From being in a position where you are the main provider for them to all of a sudden turn around and say, 'I'm sorry. I can't help you', is I think one of my biggest hurdles that I had to overcome. It was heart-breaking.

A few of the private renters had little or no contact with their children. James, who was divorced, had minimal contact with his daughter. He felt that his accommodation was too wretched to have her come round:

> We have a daughter. She's now 22 .... No way can she visit me. There's no way she can visit me where I live. Not possible to bring her there.

Chris had no contact with his one daughter:

> I have two daughters and one I don't have anything to do with really. She lives locally, but my other daughter who lives in the Southern Highlands, I do, and she's been supportive in as much as she can.

Of course, being estranged from one's children is not a function of housing tenure. However, there is little doubt that the desperate situation older private renters found themselves in gave them little financial or emotional capacity to resolve family disputes. Also, many of the older private renters were reluctant and embarrassed to ask their children for financial support. A common sentiment was that their children were also struggling.

Older homeowners

Among homeowners, spending time with family was common especially if they lived in close proximity. Only four of the 33 older homeowners interviewed said they had no family contact. A key factor is that many homeowners had the capacity to keep in touch with their family. They had the financial means, they drove and their homes were big enough to entertain. Wilma's two sons lived nearby and she saw them and their families regularly:

> They visit quite a lot ... I think the main thing is when you're getting older is keeping friends with the children and hopefully they won't all work overseas as so many of my friends' kids do.

Denise was close to her daughter. She saw her and her family at least once a week:

> My daughter and her husband and children come for dinner on a Sunday … Yes I'm content. I'm very content. My daughter, as I say, she's given me two beautiful grandsons.

Siblings were also important for some. Linda is a widow and had her two sisters living nearby. The quote also illustrates how older homeowners have some capacity to choose their neighbourhood:

> Well it is such a lovely spot here and one of my sisters lived nearby and that was partly why we chose to come over to Pittwater [a suburb on the coast in Sydney] and then another sister who was a widow lived up in Maitland [in the Hunter Valley] and she sold up there and she bought a unit near me so it is very nice having the three of us near one another. We are all very good friends.

Shirley had a large number of family members in close proximity:

> My husband came from a family of six children so there's lots of them around and they live in Sylvania, which is the next suburb, so I have family all around me. My nieces and nephews are there too. So you know I would say that I have a fairly good social life.

Grandchildren for some homeowners took up a good deal of time. Their financial resources certainly enhanced their capacity to engage with their grandchildren:

> I think as you get older and you are retired they [the grandchildren] help you because you know like the children have concerts at school you have to go to the concerts because mum and dad are working. That gets you involved with their life and things like that … At least you're not made to feel like that you could possibly be redundant. (Christine)

As discussed in Chapter 5, older homeowners usually had spare bedrooms. This facilitated contact. Grandchildren stayed over and in a few cases, children spent time at home. Joy's son came to stay every second weekend:

> My youngest son, who lives up in Campbelltown, comes down and stays over the weekend cos he has a long weekend. He works a 9-day fortnight, so he comes down and helps me in the garden and does other bits and pieces. Like when I can't lift something he comes to do that.

Pets

Pets, especially dogs, played an important role in the social lives of some interviewees. This is not surprising. Research has pointed to the positive impact pets can have, especially for older people (McNicholas *et al.* 2005; Parslow *et al.* 2005). The social contact facilitated by dogs has been recognised as having significant health benefits (McNicholas and Collis 2000). Judith, an older private renter, was fairly isolated and deeply stressed by her situation. However, her two dogs played a central role in making her life bearable:

> Every morning I go out just to, there's a park which is too far to walk, but it's dog friendly. And having the two little dogs I can put them in the car and I can have an hour and a half, 2 hours walk sharing with the dogs and that is my, well for me that's quite important, sharing with my dogs and for me health-wise it's good. Yes, that I can do.

In a second interview, 10 years after the first (she had managed to access community housing in the interim and one of her dogs had died), Judith told of how her remaining dog still played a crucial role in her life:

> Yes, you've got a choice. It's strange. You either live alone and you sit there and you don't do anything but if you've got a pet, like in the morning I have to get up. I think well it's not too hot, got to get up and take the dog for a walk, so it does make you sort of, keep you active if you like.

Helen, a homeowner, also walked her dog every morning. She drove down to the beach and walked with a friend. Usually she had a coffee afterwards. The walk was the highlight of her day:

> I walk him every day and I usually meet someone and they come for a walk with me so that's my little social outlet for the day. If I can have a walk along Mountain Road ... and have a coffee afterwards with my dog and my friend or sometimes just on our own and come home and I'm happy then to stay home ... I love it.

A public housing tenant who had serious health problems and limited mobility, relied on her dog for company:

> She doesn't like other people taking her out. She thinks she's been taken away from me. She's a good little dog but she's got to be around me ... I'm home all the time. (Dorothy)

There is a negative side to pet ownership. Expenditure on pets was potentially a substantial part of the budget and sometimes meant that owners had to restrict themselves:

> I have to be very, very careful because there's not a lot left and as you know the cost of living has gone up for everyone and I have the little dog so I have to be extra careful as I may need a vet to look at the dog. (Judith)

Conclusions

Endeavouring to unravel the impact of housing tenure on social ties and leisure is difficult. It is evident there is no necessary relationship. An older homeowner can be more isolated and restrained in their leisure activity than an older private renter. However, the interviews did strongly suggest that housing tenure can, and does, play a central role in shaping the capacities of older people on the Age Pension to maintain social ties and engage in leisure activities. Interviewees who were in secure and affordable housing had greater capacity to engage socially (Bartlett and Peel 2005; Bowling and Stafford 2007).

Older private renters' lack of financial resources, combined with their minimal security of occupancy and general anxiety around their situation, meant that most found pursuing social contact and leisure activities difficult. Day-to-day they were preoccupied with trying to survive and minimise expenditure. The rent they had to pay was a crucial determinant of their capabilities, as were savings and family support. Those private renters who were totally dependent on the Age Pension and had no savings or support from family were certainly the most likely to find themselves in a vulnerable social situation. The few older private renters who had found affordable and secure accommodation were more likely to be socially engaged. They had the financial and emotional capacity.

In contrast to the older private renters, most of the social housing tenants interviewed had solid social ties and were able to engage in a range of social activities. As illustrated, this was due to several inter-related factors. The low and predictable cost of their accommodation meant that they had the financial capacity to engage in modest social activity. Second, because their security of occupancy was guaranteed, they were able to focus on living a decent life and were not constantly preoccupied with what was going to happen to them. Third, for almost all the older social housing tenants, the immediate neighbourhood was critical for them having the capacity to develop strong social ties and engage in social activities. Many of their neighbours were fellow older renters and common histories and interests and longevity of residence contributed to the building up of trust and supportive networks (see Scheidt and Norris-Baker 2003). There were usually safe spaces in the immediate vicinity where they could meet with fellow older residents. In the bigger complexes, the gardens and the community centre were easy and important meeting places. The weekly shopping trips were important, as were the longer leisure-orientated excursions. A final factor was the activism in some housing complexes. Older people who were involved in the tenants' associations or were on the tenants' committee of their CHP were in a position to develop social connections with like-minded residents.

The social ties and leisure activities of older homeowners varied significantly. Some were not particularly interested in social activity or social connections. However, the interviews indicated that, in almost all instances, they had the financial capacity to engage in social activity if they so desired. Their low accommodation costs gave most of them the financial capacity to socially engage, albeit modestly. Holidays (local and abroad) were not uncommon. Most were able to run a car and this certainly facilitated their capacity to maintain social ties. Couples were in an especially good situation.

For all three housing tenure groups, family ties were potentially an important source of social activity. Again, there was much variability. For some interviewees, the family was central and there was little desire to make connections outside of the family. Family support was particularly important for some of the older private renters. Those older private renters who had children or siblings who helped them financially and otherwise were generally in a far better position to engage socially than their counterparts who had limited or no family support.

7
'I really have thought this can't go on': housing tenure and health

Introduction

This chapter examines the relationship between the housing tenure of interviewees and health. It shows that the cost, condition and location of their housing, the perceived security of occupancy, and the quality of their family and social connections all contributed to the health status of the interviewees.

As discussed in Chapter 1, there is consensus that housing can influence health status, and older people in poor quality accommodation are particularly vulnerable (Howden-Chapman *et al.* 1999, 2011; Phibbs and Thompson 2011). The impact of housing tenure on health is a more complex and contentious relationship. In the first Australian study of the contribution of housing tenure to health inequalities, Waters (2002), drawing on the National Health Survey conducted by the Australian Bureau of Statistics in 1995, found that renters reported a significantly higher number of serious health conditions than did homeowners. They also made more visits to their doctor and were more likely to smoke. Noteworthy is that 'Housing tenure was found to be independently associated with self-assessed health status' (Waters 2002: 2). A more recent Australian study concluded that 'People in precarious housing had, on average, worse health than people who were not precariously housed' and that 'the more elements of precarious housing people experienced simultaneously, the more likely they were to experience poor mental health' (Mallett *et al.* 2011). A major study by

Engelhardt *et al.* (2013: 1) based on the Health and Retirement Study, which interviewed close to 25 000 Americans aged 55 and older in 2010, concluded 'Older renters have almost double the number of limitations in their ability to conduct daily activities relative to homeowners'. On both physical and psychological measures older homeowners had better health. An important longitudinal study (1985–2009) by Howden-Chapman *et al.* (2011) of 10 308 British civil servants concluded that over time renters had poorer mental health than homeowners, and difficulty paying bills and problems with housing quality were important determinants of mental health.

Of course disentangling causality is extremely difficult (Connolly 2012). Is historical low income the cause of poor health and, if so, what role does housing tenure play? Do renters enter this housing tenure with poorer health or does renting have a negative impact on their health? As will be illustrated, what the interviews strongly suggest is that when people are dependent on the Age Pension for their income, housing tenure has the potential to shape health status. Not surprisingly, the interviews indicated that if an older person is in adequate, affordable and secure housing they have far greater capacity to maintain their health. Key factors are security of tenure, the capacity to sustain social ties, have a healthy diet, purchase required medication and pay for services not covered by Medicare.

Mental health was a major issue, and the interviews indicated that the housing tenure of a person on the Age Pension potentially had a significant bearing on their mental health. A crucial difference between the circumstances of older private renters, the social housing tenants and homeowners was the level of control. Most of the private renters felt that they had limited or negligible control over their present and future housing circumstances. They lived in constant feat of being asked to vacate or being subject to an untenable rent increase. Everyday life was characterised by a lack of control due to their limited resources and the landlord–tenant relationship and was often enormously stressful. In contrast, the interviewees in social housing and the homeowners could usually control their budgets and their present and future housing situation. Research indicates that a sense of control is crucial for subjective wellbeing (de Quandros-Wander *et al.* 2014) and is particularly 'important to wellbeing and even longevity in the elderly' (Aldwin 1991: 174). Rothbaum *et al.* (1982) distinguished between primary and secondary control. The former refers to the ability to attain what you desire and the latter to an acceptance that not all desires can be met. Although primary control does decline with age, it remains crucial for subjective wellbeing. The interviews indicated that many of the older private renters felt they had limited primary control. It is evident that psychological wellbeing is very much an individual phenomenon, and there were private renters who remained positive. As Lawton (1983: 356) concluded in his seminal article on the impact of the environment on older people, 'the world is full of older people who live in very stressful or very deprived environments, yet manage to remain 'up' in every other way'.

There is consensus that social isolation can precipitate poor mental health in older people (Aylaz *et al.* 2012; Singh and Misra 2009). Of course, poor mental health can be a precursor to increasing isolation. As illustrated in Chapter 6, the stress associated with being an older private renter, and their lack of financial resources, contributed fundamentally to many being isolated and socially disengaged. In contrast, the social housing tenants and the homeowners generally had the capacity to engage in leisure activities and sustain social ties.

A major factor shaping health status is the capacity to pay for medical requirements. Despite Medicare and the Pharmaceutical Benefit Scheme (PBS), the cost of health care for many Australians is substantial.[36] The Household Expenditure Survey (HES) found that in 2009–10, households spent on average $65.60 a month on medical care and health expenses. This expenditure 'is net of any refunds and rebates received from Medicare, private health insurance companies and employers' (ABS 2012c). As people age, invariably they require more medical intervention (AIHW 2007; De Nardi *et al.* 2009).

Medical expenses were a concern for many of the interviewees. The level of anxiety around health costs, not surprisingly, was influenced by housing tenure and health status. Interviewees in the private rental sector were particularly concerned, and those who had chronic health conditions and had to take several medications often had to cut back on other necessities. Although prescription drugs are heavily subsidised for older Australians dependent on the Age Pension, COTA found that for a proportion of older Australians who have chronic health conditions, maintaining their required drug regime can be difficult and older people use a range of strategies to reduce the cost:

> These included reducing the dosage of medications e.g. only taking a medicine every other day instead of daily, dropping some completely, and sharing medications with other people. (COTA 2014: 3)

The cost of dental care was also a common concern. This is not surprising because dental care is not covered by Medicare. A national dental survey established that about one in four older Australians (65 and over) with an income under $40 000 avoided or delayed visiting a dentist due to cost (Chrisopoulis *et al.* 2011). Saunders *et al.* (2007) found that 46.3% of respondents who were clients of welfare agencies said that they could not afford dental treatment if needed. The underfunded public dental health system is hopelessly overstretched. A COTA submission on health to government at the end of 2012 concluded:

> Many older people are now missing out on dental care with public dental hospitals and clinics either not accepting any new cases or reporting waiting lists of well over 12 months. (COTA 2012)

Other items not covered adequately by Medicare include glasses and less traditional treatments such as physiotherapy. Another potentially substantial medical expense is specialist services. Although most general practitioners bulk bill patients who are dependent on government benefits for their income, many specialists in the private health system do not. The cost of specialists can be extremely stressful (see Wesley Mission 2015: 10).

This chapter focuses on the impacts of housing tenure on health, more especially mental health, and interviewees' capacity to pay for medical expenses. The nature and quality of the accommodation and neighbourhood and its potential impact on health is also briefly examined. The issue of healthy diet has been discussed in Chapter 4. This chapter discusses private renters, social housing tenants and homeowners in turn.

The health impacts of being an older private renter

Minimal security of occupancy, financial stress, inadequate accommodation and inappropriate neighbourhoods contributed to many of the older private renters being plagued by high levels of stress. There is consensus that, although individuals' ability to cope with stress varies, chronic and high levels of stress can precipitate a range of health problems (McEwen 2008; Sweet *et al.* 2013). Sweet *et al.* (2013), drawing on a longitudinal study of 8400 young adults, established that high levels of financial debt relative to assets resulted in high levels of stress and depression and also impacted on physical health.

Judith's situation captures the impacts of high accommodation costs on mental health. She had decided to move from Sydney to the central coast and live in a caravan because she thought this would resolve her accommodation and financial situation. However, she found the environment in the caravan park unbearable and, after a couple of years, decided to move back to Sydney when her son, who had separated from his wife, asked her to help him look after his child. She found a rental property nearby but had to use a large part of her Age Pension to pay for the accommodation and was constantly having to dip into her savings to get by. Her housing situation appeared to have contributed directly to her depression:

> Yes, I'm on medication for depression … I don't know which came first, the chicken or the egg, because when I was living in a caravan park I became depressed, and then so I got something for the depression, and moved here, and now I'm anxious so, it's a bit of a vicious circle. But I think that it's helping [the medication], just to keep me going. Otherwise I'd become quite suicidal really.

She was battling to cope and was terribly fearful of the future:

> It's [living in private rental] a battle that can get you down. I think I'm quite a strong reasonably intelligent woman and I do reason quite well. I think I'm fairly grounded, but it's [the insecurity and financial stress] still getting the better of me. You know, rather than me getting the better of it, it's getting the better of me and I don't want that to happen. I don't want to fall down in a screaming heap, for want of a better way to put it … I try not to really think of the future and that's awful isn't it? That's a dreadful thing to say really … So now of course I'm losing that ability to have any way of earning an income. And yes, so that's where it's frightening. My costs are more than my income, even being very careful. They're still more than my income.

Elsie was not coping with her situation. Her rent was more than her pension and she was only able to survive because her daughter stocked her fridge:

> I usually ring Lifeline when I feel that I want to commit suicide. To tell you the truth there's somebody there and everyone who talks to me says the same thing you know. I don't want anyone to know [my situation]. I've got too much pride for that … At the moment I'm a burden on everybody too that's why I think when … people get to 65 and they're on a Centrelink pension [and in private rental] they should be entitled to take their life if they wish to and if they don't do a good job if perhaps they could help them you know with Nembutal. That's the way I look at it.

Raelene and her husband had lost their home a couple of years before the interview and were now dependent on the private rental sector. They were in their eighties and not well. She was despondent about their situation:

> Sometimes I think I'm too old for this. Maybe I'll be dead in a year's time and we wouldn't have to worry about it. All the stress … I said to my doctor, 'Why keep us alive when there's nothing there for us?' I said, 'There's no help for us' and she

agreed with me ... I told her we couldn't get into a retirement village or even buy a caravan, or mobile home. We couldn't even buy that. So we have a little bit of money but we can't do anything with it. It's not enough to help us.

For some of the private renters their situation evoked a feeling of shame:

I'm very surprised at the psychological impact on me. Feeling ashamed and feeling like a failure. Like I must have made a mistake somewhere. I must have done something wrong, is what I feel like. (Faye)

Having to depend on charity was deeply humiliating for many of the older private renters:

I feel terrible. You know you feel you're like somebody going with a begging bowl or something like that, but I mean when the time comes that you just don't have quite enough to pay your electricity or your phone, well rather than get it cut off, well they'll help you out. (Beverley)

Peter became seriously ill during his search for affordable rental accommodation. After his partner died, her daughter gave him 6 months notice that his rent was to be increased to a 'market rate' of $500 a week (See Chapter 5). He could not afford the market rent and was forced to look for alternative accommodation. His search, outlined in Box 5.2, was fruitless and the phenomenal stress triggered what appears to have been a heart attack:

It was so desperate [the search for affordable accommodation] that I went down with a heart thing and I was rushed to RPA [hospital] and I was operated on and I never woke up for 3 days. That was the pressure that you're under ... It's like a pressure cooker. You don't know where to go [or] what to do.

When Faye was asked 'What would you say are the health impacts (physical and mental) of being on the Age Pension in the private rental mark?', she responded:

> For me, I find a loss of a sense of continuity. I don't feel inclined to decorate [my cottage] in case the lease isn't renewed. I hesitated even to connect my internet in case it was short term. My children and grandchildren have been affected by the enforced move and the stress. I am not so badly off because I mostly can still think clearly and my physical health is improving but any form of faculty loss places us in a very vulnerable position when the home base is insecure, expensive and/or unsuitable. I see a corrosive thread of fear amongst us [older private renters] and exhaustion, combined with shame and loss of dignity.

Several private renters were staying in accommodation and/or neighbourhoods that were not conducive to their health. James was convinced that his accommodation (see Box 5.1) had contributed to his poor health. It was a stressful environment:

> It [the accommodation] causes a lot of anxiety and [a] lot of tension and you know you're always feeling a bit under pressure. It's not a relaxed environment. You know people should be able to go home and relax. In my situation, I go home, shut the door and won't open it for anybody and you're constantly listening for things that are going on around you.

Phyllis was in a particularly difficult situation. She had been forced to move back into private rental after separating from her partner. Interviewed in 2015, she was paying $270 a week for a tiny one-bedroom cottage in an outer suburb and her accommodation was presenting a range of challenges. Besides the lack of space, she was terribly isolated. She could not afford a car and was dependent on an erratic public transport service:

> I go to the shops, go to the clubs occasionally. That's about all. I don't know anyone my age around here cos I can't settle and it makes it really difficult to get interested and involved with anything because of where you live. The transport and things like that cos I don't own a car, as you know. Yes, with the bus service I try and get down there occasionally but I

have a lot of difficulty cos I'm frightened of falling and the buses only run every so often ... It is very isolating so therefore it doesn't do your health any good ... It is having an emotional impact. My doctor is quite concerned about my situation. She's written several letters herself filling forms and everything to the Housing Commission to try and get me in quicker.

The private renters who had a positive disposition were generally in relatively well priced and secure accommodation. A good example is Nellie. Interviewed in 2015, she was living in a regional town and had a pleasant garden cottage for which she was only paying $120 a week. She had an excellent relationship with her landlords, a couple who lived nearby, and they had given her a 10-year lease. Nellie was highly engaged in the community, volunteered extensively and had a busy social life.

The health impacts of being in social housing

Many of the social housing tenants had health concerns, but the interviews suggested that the security of occupancy and the reasonable and predictable cost of their accommodation had a positive impact on their physical, and more especially their mental, health. The stress, anxiety and depression so common among the older private renters interviewed, were rarely noted.[37] Almost all of the social housing tenants interviewed had a positive disposition. Research has indicated that having a positive outlook appears to have positive health outcomes (Pressman and Cohen 2005; Wu and Schimmele 2006). The low cost of their accommodation and guaranteed security of occupancy meant that they felt in control. The intense security of occupancy certainly contributed to relaxed dispositions. Daisy was very clear about this link:

> I feel secure and I feel very safe, and, you know that someone [the housing authority] is there. It's a big thing, isn't it? I'm not anxious about anything.

Jeanette said that she felt relaxed about her situation: 'The only anxiety I get is when I have to go for an operation and things. No, I'm not worried about anything'. Patricia 'loved' her home and felt very settled: 'I think as I've got older I've got more outgoing and I'm enjoying life more'. Boris and his wife felt totally secure and they were adamant that this created the foundation for a good life: 'We're not scared of tomorrow. We feel good, like we are set for the rest of our lives'. John commented, 'moving into public housing has got me off the alcohol'.

Dan felt that being a social housing tenant created a foundation for a decent life and impacted positively on life expectancy:

> When you know your accommodation is right, this is especially when you're older, you can pursue other interests. You're more relaxed and I do feel, I really feel, you're in for a longer life you know ... When you get older you're so vulnerable to any type of change at all and you just can't, you haven't got the nervous energy to you know to sort of fight back and little things stress you out so quickly ... When you're young you sort of get up and just start again. You can't when you're older.

When Dan was asked, 'So is there anything you think which would improve the quality of your life?' he responded:

> Look, I've got to be quite truthful and say, 'No. I don't think so at all' ... I'm quite content and I think it's just wonderful that the government does supply these houses.

He was then asked what would have been his health trajectory if he had been living in the PRS:

> I suppose I would [be around] but I would probably be living right out in the bush or something you know and probably be very miserable.

The sense that she had security of occupancy was enormously significant for Mavis. She spoke of being at peace after a difficult spell as a private renter:

> I'm happy with that peace ... It's [the security] is worth more than all the money in the world ... Well they know I'm here for as long as they let me and there's nothing for them to stop me. I think the only thing that will stop me is passing on and

then they pass it on to somebody else, which is fair enough. Life's got to go on.

Patricia was a long-term public housing tenant. She was content and felt her life had been successful and that public housing had provided a vital foundation for her and her family's success:

> Well I get by quite well. I've got no complaints ... I'm in the fortunate position of having brought up three children that weren't a problem. And so far, out of my grandchildren, I've got nine, and five of them are beyond school age and they're all doing quite well and pulling their weight ... In general I'm pretty happy with my lot in life.

In response to my asking whether having affordable housing had been positive for her health, Jeanette responded:

> Yes, wonderful. I mean because I couldn't afford [private rental]. I've got friends that pay a lot of rent and ... they're always complaining that they haven't got any money ...

Their housing situation gave older public housing tenants the capacity to be active in their community. This activity was conducive to good health as reflected in Norma's comment. Despite being 85, Norma was highly involved in her housing complex and had a very positive disposition:

> They appreciate the voluntary work that I do you know and I want to keep doing it because it keeps me active. Teaching English keeps my brain moving and there's no good looking after the physical area if you don't look after the brain area. You've got to look after both.

John was very active in the local tenants' association and his role gave him enormous satisfaction:

> I find a great amount of pleasure in coming home, having an early dinner, sitting down and watching the news and that's the end of my day in most cases you know. Most days I feel, well, I've really fulfilled something.

Brian played a central role in organising social activities in his community housing complex. He had a positive outlook:

> I like to see people laugh ... Because you're old and you're incapacitated for some reason, it doesn't stop you from enjoying life.

Even Doris, who was living in a challenging public housing situation due to difficult fellow tenants (see Chapter 9) and stated that she 'hated' public housing, was able to take control of her life. Her security of tenure and moderate rent allowed her to participate. She went to a local community centre every day where she had close friends and was active:

> I live here [at the community centre] every day. I'm on the committee here and I do things every day. This is my home, my family. Everybody is friendly with everybody. We have outings and things ... I'm very busy. I play bowls and go walking. Things like that. Very active here and I've never had a nervous breakdown since I've been here. I keep busy. I haven't got time to worry about things.

Although they were not living in social housing, the Kings were living in a comfortable apartment heavily subsidised by their son. Like social housing tenants they had a strong security of occupancy and an affordable rent. They had a positive outlook despite failing health: 'We're very, very fortunate. We've got nothing to really complain about' (Eleanor King).

Perhaps the most powerful illustration of the potential impacts of housing tenure on health are the interviews with people on the Age Pension who had been in the private rental sector but had ultimately managed to access social housing. Nancy had moved out of private rental into community housing 2 months before the interview. The move had totally transformed her disposition and outlook:

> I feel very differently ... I only pay $100 a week and that stress is gone. I feel a different person ... I am so happy here ... I've sort of relaxed here. I'm a different person. At least

> you've got a roof over your head and you know that you're not going to be thrown out ... Yeah, it's [private rental] a worry all the time ... Yes, I was a nervous wreck before I moved. Absolute nutter. You don't sleep. Every time you wake up, you start worrying again. Yeah. It's always there, always there. Yeah, I don't feel that now. Whatever happens, happens.

Anne had moved from the private rental sector into social housing a few years before the interview. I asked her, 'How did it change your life?'

> Immensely. I started cooking again. I started gardening again. I started being involved in the community at different levels. I didn't stay with the revival church. I started socialising with others within the complex where I was living ... I had a base. I had a secure private place that was mine.

I first interviewed Judith in 2005 when she was a private renter and interviewed her again in 2015. She had managed to access social housing in 2009. She vividly described the impact of moving into social housing on her mental health (Box 7.1).

Gloria, who had also moved from private rental into social housing, spoke of how her life had been transformed:

> My wellbeing has dramatically changed since moving from private rental to affordable community housing. I am more ebullient and laugh more frequently with neighbours and our local shopkeepers. My general health and hypertension has improved dramatically. I can also focus quality time on creative writing and I look forward to sharing garden interests with other residents.

Noteworthy is that the social housing tenants interviewed in Millers Point were extremely stressed and anxious.[38] As mentioned the state government has begun relocating public housing residents from the area. Heather was deeply troubled:

> **Box 7.1. Judith's passage**
>
> Well it [moving into social housing] gave me a great sense of relief because at that point in time I felt like I was under the umbrella of being looked after, if you like, rather than out there on my own. Because in private rental you're battling with working people and families, and of course the older you get the harder it is to battle for a place when you're on your own and on the pension because the rents are so high. So it gave me peace of mind … More because I'm 76 now. So now I've not got the fear of not being able to manage if you like until my time's up … I mean you do feel quite secure cos you know that they can't [over]charge you, you know like in private rental where the rental goes up and if you can't pay it, 'Well sorry, somebody else will' … [In social housing] you know exactly what little bit of extra you've got or not as the case might be … You know that your rent is paid which is your number one. Your rent and your food of course and I get my electricity taken out every 2 weeks … So at least I know that I've got a roof over my head and I can put the TV on if I want to and I'm covered so yes, it is a great relief to have that.
>
> *Do you think moving to social housing has enhanced your health?*
>
> Yes, certainly my mental health.
>
> *Do you want to elaborate?*
>
> Well because I felt I was so fearful before.
>
> *What would have happened if you had stayed in private rental?*
>
> I don't know what would have happened. I really don't know how I would have, well I couldn't have managed … I had to go and find somewhere. I know they said to me once you reach 80 which I'm not far off now they [the state housing authority] have to find somewhere for you. But I really, I could not have managed because they [landlords] don't say, 'Well look you're an older person and you haven't got a lot of money. We'll cut the rent', and in Sydney of course, because less people are able to purchase their own home there are more people looking for rentals.
>
> *So when you received the news that you had got into Community Housing did you open a bottle of Champagne?*
>
> I was absolutely, well I sat down and cried. I literally sat down and cried because I felt like well at least I had the protection of the Department of Housing whereas before of course I didn't have any of that. I had no protection whatsoever … My children were having children so they couldn't [take care of me]. They're just working-class people and so they couldn't care for me … So consequently I couldn't see any future at all until I got the word from Housing that I have got somewhere.

I mean this is bad enough with stress and anxiety here. The not knowing you know … I've always said you can take a house away you know but it is hard to take a home away. A house and a home are two different things. So a home is where your family are and your kids. You've brought them up. Your grandkids come and stay and all that sort of thing.

The health impacts of being an older homeowner

Besides the low cost of their accommodation, the interviews indicated that the key advantages of being an older homeowner were their guaranteed security of occupancy, control over and adequate space, financial security, a capacity to make their home age friendly if need be, some capacity to choose the neighbourhood they wanted to live in and the sense that they had an asset they could leave to their children. These benefits, in combination, created a foundation for good health. This resonates with the findings of Kearns *et al.* (2000) who, in their study of the psycho-social benefits of home ownership in West Central Scotland, found that 'At least four out of five owner occupiers derive feelings of privacy, refuge, safety, freedom and control from their homes'.

Nussbaum (2003: 33) states, 'If we ask what people are actually able to do and to be, we come much closer to understanding the barriers societies have erected ...'. In the case of older homeowners, their tenure position meant that they generally had far fewer barriers than older private renters and social housing tenants (the gap between older homeowners and social housing tenants is generally far smaller), and thus greater capacity to determine what they were able to do and be, which in turn meant a greater likelihood of them having a positive disposition and better health. It is important to note that for older homeowners their present home may not be appropriate or be viewed positively. It can be a lonely place, present barriers to ageing in place and be a space that is imbued with bad memories (see Sixsmith and Sixsmith 2008). However, most interviewees concurred with Oswald and Wahl's (2005: 23) conclusion that 'an elder's home might be a comforting, familiar place despite the fact that it is becoming burdensome to maintain and unsafe (and therefore a source of anxiety)'.

Val lived in an apartment with a sea view. She was asked whether being a homeowner has been beneficial for her health and, if so, in what ways:

> Owning my own home gives me a feeling of security and comfort. It's hard to be lonely because of a lovely view. I've

> just got to look out the window or go for a short walk to feel happy and content. It can be a worry [getting old and living by oneself] and sometimes I consider a retirement village but not for long. Maybe a day or two. Another important thing is that it is open house for my children and grandchildren … So far I haven't needed financial help but if I live long enough I could get a reverse mortgage.

For many of the older homeowners their home was a source of great pleasure. Frank forcefully articulated the link between having a comfortable, welcoming home and good health. He described his home in the following way:

> You walk in and you feel comfortable. You just feel at home. Everything's just great. It doesn't matter which room you go into … you've got the sun in the right direction and the wind in the right direction and you've got nice views in all directions and it's on a corner block and it's a nice big block. A nice garden surrounded by roses, flowers, vegetables. Nice veranda on back and front and it's just homely and comfortable.

Her home was a source of enormous pride for Denise and it was evident that it contributed fundamentally to her positive disposition:

> I'm very happy …My home is my joy …They say in England, 'An Englishman's [sic] home is his castle' and I feel that this is my home and I love it and I have to look after it and I want people to come into my home and feel happy and content just as I am and make them feel warm and comfortable … I've worked all these years for it and it is mine and that's what I always wanted. The sense of security of not having to [hear], 'Oh Mrs Smith we need the house. You've got to move on'. And that's something that I don't think I'd cope very well with.

The intense security associated with outright home ownership was mentioned by all of the homeowners. Shirley had had several stressful events occur in her life and was prone to depression, but she viewed being a homeowner as hugely beneficial for her health:

> Well I think it is a sense of security. It is a great thing because, as I said to you, irrespective of what happens or what doesn't happen it just means that now, at the time that I need it, I have that sense of security that I will always have a home to live in irrespective of whether it is here [or] somewhere else … I will always have a home to go to so that in itself I think is a great thing to have as a standby. Having the pool has been an advantage because I do swim as much as I can and because I have a back problem that's a great asset … But I think more than anything, you know, the sense of security of having a roof over your head and I do think that has got a good impact on your health.

Paula also highlighted the impact of security on her wellbeing:

> I couldn't say that we've been without stress in our lives. Everyone has some amount of stress but when you own your own home and you feel quite settled and you're not moving often from one place of accommodation to another … and the rent's not going up … So there's got to be a certain peace in owning your own home.

When Francesca was asked what are the main advantages of being a homeowner, she highlighted the guaranteed security of occupancy, the freedom to do what she liked in the space and the capacity to choose to not live with challenging tenants. Control over the space was a common theme and was viewed as a major contributor to health:

> No one will tell you, you have to leave. You can do what you want in your own home.

Edward had a similar analysis to Francesca. Besides the issue of affordability, he also emphasised the centrality of having control over his home:

> You're better able to live on a pension. You don't have to play around with landlords. If I was to change anything [in my home], which I don't, if I wanted to change anything I'd be at liberty to do it … More freedom, unrestricted … You're in

control. You don't have to ring up the agent and seek approval to do anything. It is yours.

The importance of having control was also highlighted by Joe (80). When asked, 'What would life be like if you were a private renter?' he responded, 'I don't think life would be worth living'. When asked to elaborate he emphasised the freedom and control that comes with being an outright homeowner:

> I like to be able to do what I want to do when I want to do it and I don't want to be responsible to anybody else. If you are renting a house well you've got certain obligations haven't you? So I'd still be around but I wouldn't be as happy as I am now, put it that way.

The low cost of their accommodation meant that homeowners usually had the resources to avoid social exclusion. Not having to worry constantly about finances and being able to participate in the world created the basis for a good and healthy life:

> Christine: I could think of nothing worse than having to worry about when the telephone bill came in or the utilities came in and you know and then I've got to [decide] what do I do first? Do I have to pay my rent? Do I eat? Do I pay my bills? No, no, [homeownership is a] very different situation.
>
> Interviewer: *Right. So you're basically able to lead a life that you value?*
>
> Christine: Yes. An extremely good life I think.

A major advantage of homeownership is the possibility of ageing in place (Sixsmith and Sixsmith 2006). Besides not having the threat of eviction, homeowners usually have the capacity to adapt their home to accommodate a disability. Susan was able to move her husband back from a nursing home.

> There was the big garage but I had to open up the garage and make it a dining room because of my husband in a wheelchair

so I needed more space ... I had him in a nursing home up the road till we did the renovations ... We had to open the bedroom door ... The bathroom entrance and laundry entrance ... and the front door we had to make that bigger.

Tina's husband had Parkinson's disease. They were able to adapt the house so that he was able to move around the house and access the outside.

We've made it age friendly with the help of the government interest-free loans that were available ... We put a walkway and a ramp to the front deck and a ramp from the front deck into the front door and inside there are little ramps into the other rooms.

The importance of her supportive neighbourhood was also emphasised by Tina:

He (her husband) has at times floated the idea of moving into a village but we are very fortunate that we live in a little cul-de-sac. We're on the corner and people are so friendly and supportive and just so nice. Why would you go into a place where everybody is the same age?

Paula (80) also mentioned the health benefits of having supportive neighbours:

I would like to stay in this block, having lived here for quite a long time I've become quite friendly with the people in my block and because I'm old I actually quite depend on, potentially depend on them and so that's worth an enormous amount to me.

Some of the homeowners were living by themselves in large homes. However, they were determined to stay put because they felt comfortable in their home and neighbourhood (see Wiles *et al.* 2009). Most had no intention of moving, and adapted the space so they could age in place. Jennifer lived by herself in a large double-storey home and was adapting the space to make life easier:

> Yes, in the main bathroom (upstairs) I'm going to set up a little mobile table cos there's plenty of space in the main bathroom. And I'm going to set up a main table with a cooking plate, an electric jug and a toaster so that I don't have to go downstairs if I'm working on anything. So I don't have to go up and down the stairs every time I want to have a tea.

The capacity to work on one's home and in the garden was viewed as a major health benefit. Joe (see Chapter 3) spent most his day maintaining and enhancing his property. Thelma could not contemplate living in a home without a garden:

> I love my little garden so when I'm a bit down and out or depressed … an hour outside is all it takes to fix me up.

Frank regularly pottered around in his garden:

> Well it is very relaxing to walk out and have a go at the garden when you want to and walk back in and sit on the veranda, have a cup of tea or whatever.

Convenient and lively locations were viewed as having major health benefits:

> The flat is also incredibly well-situated. There is a bank, a post office, there are loads of shops and cafes. It's lively and you know there are two bus routes that are extremely good … I mean that's worth a lot to me. (Julia)

Not all homeowners were in convenient and appropriate locations. Marlene owned her home but she could only afford a home in a small village in a remote area. She was isolated and far from medical facilities:

> We must have variety and, as I said, something to look forward to especially when you live on your own … When I moved here it was a very happy little village with some nice people. They've died or moved on to nursing homes and the houses have been sold cheaply to a rougher kind of element.

> People who wouldn't be able to live anywhere else and I'm not at ease with these people so I can't make friends with them so there is quite a bit of isolation.

Her isolation was a concern, but she kept herself busy. The security of homeownership and being in control gave her the capacity to endure her situation:

> It [home ownership] has relieved a lot of anxiety. If I was renting privately, I would be feeling anxious about how long I could stay there. Would the owner sell the property? Would something happen to make me need to move? I hate being uprooted. ... It [home ownership] just gives you security. You know it's your home. You can do whatever you want. You can paint it pink and purple if you want to. It gives you freedom of expression ... Your home is an extension of your personality. When people walk in the door here, they don't expect to find what they do behind the simple cottage front. But then after they've been here a while the comment is often, 'This is very you', and that pleases me because I feel it part of me because home is very important even though people don't often think about it, voice it or realise it. Home is the most important thing.

Paying for medical expenses

The capacity of private renters to pay for medical expenses

The older private renters who had to take several medications struggled to cope with the additional expenditure. Carmel had a serious heart condition, was a diabetic and was having to take over 20 tablets a day. It was an enormous financial burden. The day she was interviewed she was upset because she had had to ask St Vincent Du Paul (charity) for financial assistance as she did not have enough to pay for all her medications:

> When it comes to a big batch like here, when I had to buy seven [different medications] that really knocks the budget up. I can't even add it up but that's seven times $6.10 and that makes it

extremely difficult. And there's other things in between that aren't on the chemist thing [PBS] that you still need to get … I know people that don't even go to the doctors or when the doctor gives them something (a script) don't get the scripts for it. Mine are heart things. I've really got to take them.

For Chris, paying for medications was a major challenge and provoked much concern. He relied on the goodwill of his local pharmacy:

I sort of rely on having a very understanding pharmacist where I have an account, and I'm going to have to pay them when I can. And what happens now … I've rung up Centrelink. There's an availability of $500 that they give in advance, so I'll get that and I'll go and pay my pharmacist's account, and a few other bills and things.

Like Chris, Bruce was also dependent on his pharmacist's willingness to give him credit:

At the moment I owe the chemist about $76 and it has been going on for 2 months and I haven't had the money to pay it. She's patient … I like to pay my way and you see I feel guilty because sometimes I can let go on some extravagance and then find it's either feed myself or pay the chemist. I just run short.

Arieta spent $40 to $50 a month on medication and at times this had contributed to her having no money for food:

Sometimes my friends come and bring some [food]. My son might come and give me some food. One fortnight I am very broke. … I need to buy the food. Then my son will go and buy the food for me.

As mentioned, the major limitations in Medicare are spectacles, dental care, treatments that are not mainstream and specialists (they rarely bulk bill). Older private renters struggled to pay for dental care[39] and tended to delay treatment for as long as possible:

> But you know I've got something I'd like to do with my teeth but the last time I went it cost us, even with the health fund, it still cost $600 so you delay that sort of thing because of the cost. (Thomas)

Thomas was one of the only private renters that had managed to keep up his private health insurance. Judith had had to dig into her savings to pay for dental treatment:

> Yes, I paid $500 and something for dental treatment just a few months ago. I was lucky that I had that little bit of money to be able to do that because I've always had a thing of wanting to keep my own teeth …

Rob was concerned about anything going wrong with his dental plate:

> Dental [support] is non-existent, … false teeth $1400 … so I'm very careful you know what I eat, what I chew. I'm all false teeth so it's not too bad and super glue[40] is not bad actually.

The expansion of government dental care services in some area had lessened the problem for a couple of interviewees:

> But before we discovered it [the government dental services] that was about 2, 3 years ago, it was a huge part of the budget. It was really stressful. Every time you'd got to go to the dentist you're literally spending your whole pension with one visit and then he says, 'Come back in a fortnight'. That was a killer. So having discovered the government service, you get it for nothing. That was a major, major benefit for our budgeting. (Greg)

Greg was fortunate. In May 2012, it was estimated that 650 000 people were on the waiting list for publicly funded dental care and people were having to wait for up to 5 years to see a dentist (ABC News 2012). Also, there are very few locations where people can access public dental care. It may involve extensive travel that may be beyond an older person's capacity.

Although visits to the optometrist are covered by Medicare, spectacles are not. The New South Wales Government does have a spectacles program and people who are dependent on income support from government can apply. In order to be eligible, you have to have assets of less than $500 if single and $1000 if a couple. Recipients are restricted to one pair of glasses every 2 years. For some of the interviewees, the cost of glasses was a substantial burden:

> Well they say you get glasses free, but like I had to get three pairs of glasses ... And Visioncare[41] they'll cover the cost of ordinary glasses but anything above that you pay for ... In the last 12 months, I've had three pairs of glasses because of this eye. I've had a lot of trouble with this eye ... so I have to keep getting the lens changed all the time. (Pam)

Chris was apprehensive about having to find the money for new glasses:

> I don't know how I may be able to get these [glasses] modified, but I've only just had this cataract done ... and I've got to wait 4 weeks before I have to find, you know, $700 or something.

Thomas delayed going to the optometrist: 'I keep getting letters saying my glasses are due for [renewal] you know. It's been a couple of years and you put that off because you know it's going to cost you more'.

Medicare covers a maximum of five sessions of physiotherapy annually. Pam, against her doctor's instructions, had curtailed the number of times she went to physiotherapy:

> So when I have to go to physio you get so many treatments free, then the doctor says I need another 3 months of physio, but that was $45 a visit. I was supposed to go three times a week. I could only afford to go once a week.

For older private renters, going to see a specialist was stressful as many specialists do not bulk bill:

> And specialists, they charge through the nose. You know you only get a certain amount back [from Medicare] … It is very hard. I always ask, 'Can I just pay the difference? Do I have to pay the whole amount up front'? … I say, 'I'm in a situation where I can't really pay that money on a pension'. Sometimes they will [be accommodating], sometimes they won't. So I cancel the appointment in the end. (Susan)

I asked Susan if she avoided going to see a specialist because of the cost. She responded, 'Yes. There's a lot of people out there that do that'.

Gloria told of how the move from a private rental situation to social housing had enabled her to save money for medical costs:

> Now in Community Housing, within 9 months I have been able to save $2000 toward emergency medical costs – my goal is to have $4000 by end of 2015.

The capacity of social housing tenants to pay for medical expenses

There was certainly concern among social housing tenants about medical costs. However, there was not the same degree of anxiety as displayed by the older private renters. Thus, the social housing tenants interviewed who had chronic conditions that required that they take several medications found it difficult, but they appeared to manage. None said that they cut back on or did not pick up prescriptions:

> We pay for medicine. My husband takes a lot of medicine. Every day my husband takes a bunch of pills twice a day. Morning and night, every day. (Lada)

> But see when scripts went up to $5.30 each, that was a bit of a drain because I'll go to the chemist, such as last week, three scripts, that's $15, $16 just about, just on those three scripts. That's $16, I, you, could've bought something else with. But, medication is vital. If you don't get the medication, you

probably won't need anything else. You'll probably be passing on. (Graham)

Like the private renters, Lorraine and Judy also relied on understanding pharmacists. Both had chronic conditions and had to take several medications:

> I have quite a few tablets that I get … The chemist down here where I live is very good and I have a bill there and I pay it. I manage to pay it. I went yesterday and paid half of it for this month and then the other half, well I'll pay at the end of the month. (Lorraine)

> And sometimes at the end of the fortnight you don't have enough [money]. Luckily, I've got a chemist who can help me out. If I didn't have that I'll be in trouble. (Judy)

There was also much concern about the cost of dental care:

> Dental care is very expensive. It's very hard. I mean dentists charge the earth. One of the ladies I know, 84 years old, had to have a tooth removed and a few other things done, $600. Now she's a lady who has no extra income … so she had to use what they call a $500 loan from Centrelink. (Betty)

> They're [dentists] are very expensive … It is a big problem. I wish you could have it in Medicare. (Evelyn)

> I really think, the only thing that I perhaps would have done if I'd been in [a better financial] position, I would have kept up private health insurance[42] … You need your glasses and you need your teeth fixed. That sort of thing. (Catherine)

Catherine insisted that if she had to go to the dentist or needed new glasses, she could afford it.

Social housing tenants who had a range of medical conditions and resultant expenses battled with any extra medical costs. Asked whether she was able to afford dental treatment, Louise, who had numerous medical problems, responded:

No. No dental work at all.

Interviewer: *So when you have a toothache or*

You just heal it yourself. I always keep a thing of toothache drops in the cupboard just in case.

The cost of specialists induced anxiety:

You just gotta cross your fingers that you don't have to see a specialist. Like I had to just go in for an operation in June. Thank God … that he bulk billed. Thank God, I didn't have to pay anything. (Marion)

Medicare's good as long as you're in an area that you can get bulk billed but specialists, there's not many specialists that bulk bill … It's very hard for people … and you've suddenly got to have something that's got to be dealt with and you've got to go to a specialist and they want 50 bucks just to say hello. That 50 bucks is nothing to you but it might be for me. (Betty)

When you reach a certain age you need surgeons and specialists and a lot of these are charging gap fees. I think it is a terrible thing what they're doing … I really believe that it is a terrible thing. If it was a set $50 gap fee you could accept that but you get to $120, that's very difficult …[43] (Ann)

The cost of specialists resulted in Ann delaying treatment for a serious eye condition and waiting for an appointment in the public system:

When the optometrist told me I had the problem with both my eyes, he said, 'You're going to need injections … Go to this specialist'. To go to that specialist I needed $800 for the first visit and it had to be paid there and then … I never went to that specialist because I think that's terrible that senior [older] people have got to pay all that money up front and … then I met one of the community members who said he's going to the Eye Hospital[44] so I went in and saw them and they've given me an appointment for April. (Ann)

In the case of social housing tenants who had ongoing medical expenses, the low cost of their accommodation meant that they were usually able to save to cover their expenses:

> The only thing is I have to go and see a specialist and you have to find the money to pay them up front and … the first one that I've got to go and see … is $160 you know and I've been putting away so much each fortnight which I've managed to get all the money together so I think I'm very lucky. If I was private renting I'd think, 'Oh my god, where am I going to get that from?' (Kate)

Edna had a serious lung condition and various other ailments and took several vitamins to supplement her diet:

> I think that Nature B has supplemented any deficiency in my diet … And you finish up paying about $200 … because you buy it in three monthly amounts. You came here to see how I manage with my money. I don't know how I would manage if I were not in here [social housing].

Older homeowners' capacity to pay for medical expenses
Although older homeowners expressed concern about health costs, they generally appeared to have the capacity to pay for medical expenses. Their more middle class location historically meant that several had had private health insurance for many years and the low cost of their accommodation meant that they were able to hold on to it. This relieved much stress around medical expenses:

> I've still got the health fund, which I've been very tempted to pull out of but I've been in it all my life and I think why pull out now when I need it the most probably and I had a hip replacement 7 months ago and despite being fit I had a pretty bad recovery and actually I've just come out of hospital. (Thelma)

> I'm with this very good [health insurance] company ... I [need] glasses. I need my teeth and ... if I have to go to hospital I want private. I don't want to go in a ward with a lot of other people. (Denise)

Paying for private health insurance was difficult for some of the homeowners, but there was a reluctance to relinquish it. Many homeowners, especially those with ongoing health problems, saw it as a necessity:

> Well the one thing we do have which is a very big expense is that we're in a health fund ... We feel that we can't afford not to be in it. A lot of people say to me [they] can't afford to be in a health fund, cos you're paying about $55 a week. It's a lot of money out of the pension. But we feel that's what we've got to do. My husband had shoulder surgery this year. He's had heart surgery in the last 2, 3 years and it means for us if there's something that needs doing we can have it done. We don't have to say, 'We can't afford it' and wait.[45] (Paula)

Besides health insurance, most of the homeowners had some savings that they could draw on if necessary. For example, Jennifer had about $40 000 in shares that she said she would sell if need be. It was comforting: 'I always think if I have a medical issue I can sell them and I've got something there'.

Edward made sure he had money available for all expenses, including medical emergencies:

> I have to maintain a cash flow. I've got to have say $5000 at all times in the bank account to pay MasterCard, rates, hospital fund, Telstra, lights, gas.

Val had private health insurance but was relieved she had some savings:

> As you get older you do less ...so I don't know that you need quite as much money but you do have expenses. I'm on three medications every day and they are all on the cheap list like

> but you know you might go to a podiatrist whereas you used to cut your own nails and things like that ... [so] I would hate to be dependent entirely on the pension.

A couple of the interviewees had had to borrow money to pay for expensive medical procedures. Frank borrowed the money from a Christian charity:

> For urgent medical things you've got to pay money upfront or whatever ... With this eye surgery it cost me about $3000 and I didn't have the $3000 but they loaned me some money towards it and I paid that back fortnightly.

Noteworthy is that the one homeowner who was finding medical costs particularly difficult was Doug, the homeowner who was having to support his unemployed son in the private rental sector. He and his wife had several health problems but he was considering letting go their health insurance:

> We've got that [private health insurance], but we're thinking very seriously about having to get rid of it. It is due to go up again and that takes about $200 a month out of our pension and without that [expense] it would be a lot easier but my wife's had a knee operation and eye operation and so we don't know whether she's up for them again in the next 12 or 18 months so you're sort of, the devil's got you by the balls you may as well say ... If you keep it, you've got to pay the first $500. If you give it up, you might have to wait 3 or 4 years to get your operation... and I've got to have a colonoscopy and tracheotomy or whatever it is ... and there's a 12 to 18 months waiting list.

Dental expenses were a concern but most of the homeowners appeared to be coping. When Marlene was asked whether she could afford dental care she responded: 'Yes, only because I live frugally and I make sure I've got savings for emergencies that pop up'. Jennifer said she had little problem paying her dental and osteopath bill:

> I go to the dentist twice a year. It costs $160 a time for a check-up and at the moment I'm going to the osteopath. I've got a bad back and he's $80 a time. That's a bit iffy, but I'm managing.

Sylvia had taken out medical insurance specifically for dental work: 'I'm in a dentist scheme. I pay so much a year and I get a reduction through that … but just for dental so I'm sort of managing with that'.

Major dental work could be an issue. Christine had contacted the public dental service but realised her husband would have to go to a private dentist:

> Somebody suggested to me that I ring the government dental place which I did. I was amazed that they either give you a filling or take the tooth out and my husband had a cap that was broken and we needed it repaired. Well, they don't do that. It's either [an] extraction or filling, no other. Cos they said to me, 'That's cosmetic work', and I said, 'Well no, it's not'. I think the government should do more as far as dental goes … Just because we're older it doesn't mean that we don't want to have nice teeth.

Conclusions

The interviews indicated that the housing tenure of people on the Age Pension does potentially impact on health. Perhaps the clearest indication of this was in regards to mental health. The older private renters were certainly more likely than homeowners and social housing tenants to experience acute and ongoing stress that was a direct result of their housing situation. Those older private renters who found themselves in expensive and insecure accommodation were constantly fearful about their situation. Their minimal ability to control their present and future situation was a source of much anxiety and several interviewees in woeful circumstances in the private rental sector appeared to be seriously depressed.

Their ability to look after their physical health was also compromised. They were worried about having the financial resources to cover everyday expenses and any unexpected expense was a serious issue. Medical expenses were seen as a serious burden by a substantial proportion of older private renters and it was evident that there was a tendency to avoid health services not covered by Medicare.

In stark contrast to the older private renters, the intense security of occupancy of the social housing tenants and the fixed and predictable rent created the foundation for a positive disposition. Almost all of the social housing interviewees appeared content. Even those who were living with challenging fellow tenants were generally able to create a safe space for themselves within which they could lead a decent life. Medical expenses were a concern, but they tended to manage. The power of strong security of occupancy was reflected in the interviews with residents of Millers Point. The few Millers Point residents interviewed who at the time of the interview faced eviction, were clearly suffering from severe stress.

The homeowners felt in control of their space and they had the necessary resources to cope with medical expenses. Their housing situation generally laid the basis for a positive outlook. Many felt that their home and their status as outright homeowners were absolutely central to their health and capacity to lead a decent life. They felt secure and in control. Almost all said how much they appreciated and loved their home. Another key aspect of homeownership that was beneficial to their health was the capacity to age in place. Most of the homeowners were determined to stay in their homes for as long as possible.

8
'I won't be here that long because they are waiting for the right price': landlord–tenant relations

Introduction

The landlord–tenant relationship is invariably an unequal one (Hulse and Milligan 2014; Izuhara and Heywood 2003; Morris 2009; Mowbray 2015b). This is especially so in Australia's moderately regulated private rental sector (Hulse *et al.* 2012). A survey of over 500 renters conducted by the Tenants Union of New South Wales found that 77% of respondents 'put up with a problem or declined to assert their rights as a tenant because they were worried about adverse consequences' (Cutcher and Patterson Ross 2014). Older private renters dependent on the Age Pension are particularly vulnerable because often they will not have the financial, emotional or physical resources to move out of an unsatisfactory situation and will be hesitant to request anything from the landlord in case s/he retaliates by putting up the rent or makes life difficult in other ways (Izuhara and Heywood 2003; Means 2007). In the UK, Izuhara and Heywood (2003: 216) found that 'malpractices by private landlords caused stress, anxiety, ill health (both mental and physical) and sometimes loss of home to older tenants'. In NSW, landlords can ignore tenants' requests, as they are aware that there is little likelihood of them being sanctioned. As discussed in Chapter 2, the *Residential Tenancies Act 2010* does potentially protect tenants against landlord retaliation and the NSW

Civil and Administrative Tribunal can declare a termination notice void if it concludes that it was premised on retaliation (see Mowbray 2011). However, it does mean that the tenant has to go through the arduous bureaucratic process of applying to the Tribunal and on any account the latter can rule against the tenant, even when it finds evidence of retaliation.

As outlined in Chapter 2, there are substantial differences between the levels of security of occupancy for older private renters and social housing tenants. The legislation protecting older private renters is minimal. Once the fixed term of the written lease ends, the landlord has the *de jure* right to increase the rent as they see fit and to give tenants written notice to vacate for a range of reasons or, indeed, no reason at all (Tenants Union of New South Wales 2015). The capacity of tenants to fight rent increases and eviction is limited. In contrast, although there has been a winding back of the rights of tenants in social housing (see Fitzpatrick and Pawson 2014), older social housing tenants usually have a written lease that goes for at least 10 years and, *de facto*, as long they pay the rent, their tenure is usually life-long. However, in New South Wales, in certain localities, the historical relationship between public housing tenants and the state housing authority has been torpedoed by the state government's intention to sell off public housing stock in certain areas. The case of Millers Point in inner Sydney is the most contentious contemporary example.

The chapter first discusses landlord–tenant relations in the private rental sector, covering security of occupancy, maintenance and creating a home. It then examines landlord–tenant relations and creating a home in social housing. It concludes by outlining the situation in Millers Point.

'I won't be here that long because they are waiting for the right price': older private renters and security of occupancy

Secure occupancy in the private rental sector is defined by Hulse and Milligan (2014: 6) 'as the extent to which households who occupy rented dwellings can make a home and stay there, to the extent that they wish to do so, subject to meeting their obligations as a tenant'. There is good deal of contingency in the private rental sector and the interviews indicated that there was no standard relationship between older private renters and landlords/agents. Some tenants had a good and trusting relationship with their landlord. These landlords kept the rent manageable and responded in a timely and competent fashion to tenant's requests. However, many of the older private renters interviewed felt insecure and anxious about their future and had little or no idea of their landlord's intentions. Maintenance was done reluctantly or shoddily or not at all.

The importance of guaranteed or secure housing for 'ontological security' is well established (Dupuis and Thorns 1998; Hiscock *et al.* 2001; Hulse and Saugeres 2008; Padgett 2007). Ontological security refers to a deep-seated feeling of consistency in everyday life. Anthony Giddens (1991: 54) defines it as:

> the confidence that most human beings have in the continuity of their self-identity and in the constancy of their social and material environments. Basic to a feeling of ontological security is a sense of the reliability of persons and things.

Dupuis and Thorns (1998: 29) argue that a key aspect contributing to housing being a source of ontological security is that the home needs to be 'a secure base around which identities are constructed'. The sense of being persistently insecure was deeply felt by many older private renters: 'I became so aware of my insecurity that I lost the capacity to laugh' (Gloria). When Rhonda was asked what it was like to be a private renter, she responded, 'I hate it because you're more or less at somebody else's mercy all the time'. There was a deep fear of being asked to vacate and homelessness:

> I never get behind in my rent because when I go to the bank I have to pay it fortnightly. That's the terms and conditions. So I just go to the bank, draw out the money and go straight down and pay it and the only way I'd ever get into trouble is if somebody snatched my bag. But I pay it. That's the first thing I do is pay the rent, because there's a roof over my head. (Beverley)

Asked what she would do if her rent was increased, Beverley responded: 'I don't think about it. I don't want to think about it.'

Deep and constant insecurity about their security of tenure was a common theme:

> You don't go through 24 hours without thinking of it. I mean you can't totally put it aside ... I would say that's the biggest stress my wife and I have. (Thomas)

> I do think a lot about that but there is nothing I can do ... There is nothing I can do about it ... You know if the landlord decides to sell the house you know and tells me that I have to get out, I have to get out. (Eileen)

Judith was extremely anxious that the small cottage she was renting would be sold:

> These are the last four houses and they're just waiting for the right price and they'll be gone. I mean I won't be here that long because they are waiting for the right price ... They've already been offered. Yes. They've already been offered, but they didn't accept the offer.

When asked what she would do if she had to move Judith tearfully responded: 'I don't know. I don't know. I really don't know. I don't know'.

Being forced to vacate because owners wanted to sell or because of a rent increase or for another reason, was not uncommon:

> I've moved about five times in the last 6 years because people wanted to sell their house so I got turfed out. Well, when the lease expired I had to go and that put me at some stages in a very difficult position. (Robert)

Marie told of how she had shared a large home with her children and grandchildren but had to move when the owner decided to rebuild:

> We had a huge house. My son and my daughter and the five children all lived in it and we split it into three ... But the owner pulled it down and this is the risk you take ... So that was difficult. And then we rented separately, which was much more expensive, but we couldn't get another house big enough.

8 – 'I won't be here that long because they are waiting for the right price'

At the time of the interview, Marie was living by herself and was anxious that she might be asked to leave her present accommodation:

> But he [the landlord] did say the other day, he's got a little place down the coast, he was going on about this land tax and they were talking of selling. And he said, 'It won't be for about a year'. So I'm not really secure. No, I'm not. I'm not.

An increase in the rent to an untenable level was probably the most common source of insecurity. Even though Nancy rented an apartment from a couple she was acquainted with, she always felt insecure. Eventually the rent was increased and she knew she had to find another place:

> And I knew I couldn't afford [to pay] any more so I just had to get out and look. … I was expecting it [being asked to vacate]. I mean I didn't ever feel very secure there because … I knew it was worth a lot more.

After four rent increases in 3 years, June had become very concerned about the future and her ability to stay where she was:

> At the moment I'm in private rental and I have applied to Housing where I've been on their register since 2002. Now at the moment I'm paying $190 per week. I've been here since February 2005 and this was the fourth rental increase and in November it is increasing to $210 per week which I'm finding it very hard to afford.

For many of the older renters, the slightest rent increase was enough to generate an untenable situation:

> And it's upsetting, the security and my landlord sort of, he was very good and I was able to keep paying him all the time. At the moment I think I'm 2 weeks behind … But he sort of got a little you know, edgy about it, and then he's now sort of saying, 'Well there hasn't been an increase for a couple of years and we're really looking to increase it'. So I just couldn't [pay]. If he put it up, I'd have to go. There's no way in the world that I could do it. (Chris)

Another reason for having to move was the owner wanting to move into the property. This is what happened to Paul:

> Well I was living in a house over in Bankstown, but the owner he was getting married and he wanted to move into the house himself. So he gave me, you know, told me to get out. He was quite nice about it ... and what happened was, I asked for emergency accommodation from the Housing Commission and they said, 'No. You'll have to wait for about 6 months or something', and I said, 'Well I've got to get out within 6 weeks'.

The minimal timeframe for finding a new place as illustrated in Paul's quote is not unusual. Beverley had found herself in a similar situation: 'Where I was living before the unit was sold and I had ... about 2 weeks to find somewhere else to go'. Fortunately, she was living with her son at the time and he helped her find alternative accommodation.

In instances where tenants had a lot more *de facto* security there was still anxiety about the future. Even though Bruce had been in his present accommodation for close to 8 years, he was still constantly fearful about the possibility of being asked to vacate:

> Well, I think I've been reasonably secure here but every time I get a letter from the landlord's agents I'm a bit horrified to think they might want to get rid of me. So there is no sort of security here for an older person.

Greg had been renting from the same landlord for 14 years. When asked if he felt secure he responded:

> Not secure in terms of tenancy that you can rely on. Living here year after year, you've got to renew your lease every year and that's a bit stressful. But in terms of the relationship with the landlord there's nothing wrong with that but being a renter you're never secure. You never feel 'this is my home and this is where I'm going to stay till I die' sort of thing. You always wonder when the axe is going to fall and you start

looking for somewhere else you probably can't afford. There is the stress factor in our life. That single issue.

Raelene and her husband had managed to find a house owned by what appeared to be a very accommodating person. The landlord had assured them that as long as they paid the rent they could stay as long as they liked. Despite the landlord's assurances, Raelene was still uneasy:

> I think I would like to be in something that we were renting permanently and know that you're there till you expire, but at the moment I feel as if we could be tossed out of the house or something, but Gwyn [the landlord] assures me we can stay here as long as we like but you never know what's around the corner. They might have to sell the property some time … because they have young families as well coming up you know. You don't know what's in the future for you.

As mentioned, some interviewees had been fortunate and had empathetic and supportive landlords. Pam had an especially good relationship with her landlord. She felt secure, the rent was relatively low and she had a good deal of *de facto* security. She was confident that any rent increase would be reasonable. Her apartment was linked to a shop run by her landlords and she kept an eye on the premises. Daily, they checked up on her:

> They've been good to me … They've even got to the stage where they sort of wouldn't come in here to check, but now if they don't see that my slippers are at the top of the step [the apartment entrance was through the landlord's shop] … they try and ring up and if I don't answer, well then they'll come up and have a look in case something's happened to me.

Fred felt that his landlord was fair and receptive: 'I've told him that I'm a pensioner and I said, 'I hope you don't put the rent up.' So he's left it alone now since January last year'. The spatial location of the accommodation can be an important factor shaping the tenant–landlord relationship. If the properties are adjacent there appeared to be a greater chance of a healthy relationship developing. Besides proximity, Faye felt that her know-how and extensive experience of being a private renter had contributed to the good relationship she had had with her last two landlords:

> The last two properties that I rented the owners actually lived on the property and I've rented a small cottage and I've been very close to both ... But I've been fortunate in that but I'm also very careful about where I rent. As I said, I've rented my whole life so I have some skills and I find the older ones who haven't rented their whole life don't have the skills and they can go in a little bit naively.

Thomas and his wife had been in the same house for 10 years and felt very secure:

> We have a great relationship with the landlord. In fact he said to us only yesterday that you know he has no thoughts of selling the place but if he did he'd be happy to offer it to us ... I generally take care of all the maintenance of the house like lawns and that sort of thing so I do that for him. Yeah, so I see him as a good landlord and I think he sees us as good tenants.

One private renter who had been particularly fortunate was Nellie (see Chapter 7). As mentioned, she had been given a 10-year lease and her rent, $120 a week, in 2015, was relatively very low even for a regional area. The landlord was looking for a tenant who would keep an eye on his elderly relatives who lived in the house in front of the rental property. Nellie explained:

> I'm in a little house ... My family happened to see this property under private rental and as it turned out I have elderly people living in front of me and the people who own it ... wanted someone in this house that would be compatible with these elderly people in the front ... So it was a case of well look we want a particular sort of person that would be compatible with these elderly people and look it just worked out absolutely spot on. They are very elderly but they fill a

void in my life and we get on. You know I sort of look after them in any way that I can. Like the lady is 97, the gentleman is like 85 but they are delightful people and so they made a difference to my life as well.

Maintenance in the private rental sector

Landlords have a statutory responsibility to maintain the premises (Division 5, NSW *Residential Tenancies Act 2010*). Nevertheless, the way landlords or agents responded to maintenance issues and conveyed to tenants that they could approach them with concerns, varied significantly. Some landlords were responsive; others made little or no effort. Rhonda felt that she could not trust her landlords, a husband and wife team, and after having her initial requests ignored, could not ask for anything:

> The day I came up to look at it [her rented property] I had my two sons with me and yeah we thought it was a good place … And then I had to come back a couple of days later to sign the lease and I was on my own that day and the bathroom cupboards were all water-damaged and all that and I had spoken about that and they said they were going to have them fixed and the day I came up to sign the lease … I said, 'When will the bathroom cupboards be fixed?' And they said, 'We're not going to do that'. And I said, 'Well you said you would'. And they said, 'No. We didn't say that'. And I said, 'Look, I'm on my own now here but when you said it my two sons were here'. And I had no other option but to sign the lease because at that stage I thought I was in a bit of a tight corner … So I sort of right from the word go I thought, 'Well I can't trust these people because they're not telling the truth'.

She made the important point that for older renters proper maintenance is more important due to frailty and the risk of falling:

> You know there's things that probably wouldn't worry other people but worry you when you're aged. The path that goes out to the gate, well the whole fence and gate is falling down

> ... and the gate doesn't swing properly. It scrapes on the concrete path so that you've got to really struggle to open the gate and shut the gate after you. And the path has got moss on it and when you're walking on it, when you're old you're frightened you're going to fall over and break a hip.

Pamela was loath to ask her real estate agent or landlord for anything:

> Like the light in there goes on and off and I'll mention it to Theresa (her daughter) rather than mention it to the agent cos I know what he'll say, 'We'll get in touch with the landlord', and take 3 months to do so.

A few landlords were extremely remiss and appeared to fit the definition of slum landlord. Valerie's landlord owned several houses in her inner-city area and was extremely reluctant to do any maintenance. As described in Chapter 4, her house was in an appalling condition when she moved in:

> I guess he just knows that it's going to appreciate ... so he doesn't want to do anything much to it and so the only thing I was able to achieve was to force them into steam-cleaning the carpet ... deodorising other areas. Most of the work I did myself.

Lesley's landlord refused to fix up a major leak:

> Well it is a 150 year-old house. There's three houses together and it was built in 1850 but for the whole of the 16 and a half years I've been here we've had a leak and it can be pretty bad ... It has never been fixed and never will be fixed and it has got old pipes. It is just very difficult to get the real estate agent to get the landlord to do anything and we've got a new landlord ... and he's doing even less than the previous landlord.

Part of the problem appeared to be that many of the landlords were small investors who either did not have the money or were not prepared to spend money on maintenance (Mowbray 2015b; Seelig *et al.* 2009).

Bruce's two-bedroom flat in outer Sydney needed a fair amount of work. The carpet was dirty and there were sizeable strips of plaster coming off the walls:

> This plaster always seems to come undone but I don't think he's a fellow [the landlord] who'll end up with a lot of money but he does what he can. You can see the carpets want replacing and they did an inspection the other day. He said, 'It was perfect', so there we are … The last time I said, 'You've told me all about these expenses. What about giving me a screen door and a few of these basic things that you keep telling me about' … and he said, 'Well I can see you need a new carpet but I can't guarantee you this and that'.

Another private renter whose landlord was a small investor observed:

> They keep saying it's a charming family home. Well it once was, not so well-appointed these days. The things have gone you know. They won't replace the cooker so of course I got cranky and got an electrician to take it out because I was fed up fighting for one and generally they haven't bothered with the cottage. … I never reneged on the rent once in 16.5 years. When I asked for something to be done it was like trying to get blood out of stone. (Gloria)

The lack of maintenance was potentially very stressful. Gloria had serious concerns about the electrical connections in her cottage and the possibility of a fire:

> I said, 'It's your responsibility', and the people who were managing the property wouldn't deal with it and [they said] it was all the tenant's fault and that was probably destroying me more than anything … This sudden like attempt to make me responsible for a 70-year-old cottage. It was awful.

In some cases, in exchange for a low rent, the tenant was expected to be responsible for all the maintenance, even though such an arrangement would be void under the law (Section 219, *Residential Tenancies Act 2010*). In a regional area, Faye had found a place for $150 a week. She was very pleased with her low rent but there were conditions attached:

> But it also means that's [the low rent] on the grounds that I attend to all repairs and maintenance. The owner won't be [doing maintenance]. He intends to pull it down in about 10 years. He just doesn't want any problems with it.

Many interviewees feared that if they complained and asked for repairs to be done, their rent would be increased or they would be evicted: 'If things don't work, you think if I ask him, he'll put the rent up' (Marie). Lesley had a similar sentiment. She was reluctant to complain too vigorously about the leaking roof:

> Well it is for that reason. If we complain, the rent goes up for a start and I don't want to be turned out and have so many weeks' notice and have to find somewhere else …
>
> It is just depressing knowing that I feel helpless. That I can't do anything about it and I've got addresses for the tenants' representative and a lawyer but I'm afraid to go. I don't want to go … We feel powerless and the back fence is falling down and it is just plain rotten and nobody wants to know. Nobody wants to come and have a look. Nobody will fix it.

As discussed, often the slightest rent increase was unaffordable so private renters were prepared to endure living with items that required repairing. There was also the fear that complaining may annoy the landlord and encourage eviction. Landlords of boarding houses appeared to be particularly difficult:

> They tend to be very unsympathetic to everybody. Several I've found can become quite belligerent … You can't complain to them. If you make a complaint about something then it gets to be real bad news sometimes. (Malcolm)

Tenants complained about landlord insensitivity and failure to consult before embarking on actions that had serious consequences.

Gloria poignantly recounted how the trees in the back garden were cut down without any consultation:

> I could not bear to watch my beautiful trees in the back garden being demolished by the owners. This murderous act has completely devastated the garden plants they were shade plants, now burnt to nothing! ... They cut the trees down in preference to ensuring fans and lights work! They still have not had the necessary electrical maintenance done on this old wiring problem and that's 2 months now.

The interviews suggested that landlords were more likely to be responsive when they knew the tenant and had a relationship that was not defined purely by the landlord–tenant relationship. Faye had had a good relationship with her landlord: 'By the end of 4 years they're almost like family. That makes a big difference and they've been good with maintenance'. Paul had an amicable relationship with his landlord:

> He's quite a nice bloke ... He's given me his home phone number. He's given me his mobile phone number and he said, 'If you've got any problems just give me a ring and I'll be over'.

In cases where the landlord or a family member was a good handyman, it appeared more likely that the maintenance would be acceptable:

> She's a nice lady ... Her son does all the maintenance ... He's an affable character ... You can ask him things and he will look at them. He's a hands-on man. (David)

If an interviewee was renting in a 'respectable' block, it appeared that the maintenance was more likely to be adequate. Beverley lived in a solid and reputable apartment block. The managing agent was efficient:

> I must confess anything that has gone wrong, which hasn't been very much, you know I ring up today and the fellow usually comes the same day. It's usually things that have to

be done anyway, like perhaps a toilet might keep running, well that has to be fixed, but they've been very good.

The ability of older private renters to make a home

The ability to make a home requires that tenants feel in control of their home space and free from unnecessary landlord scrutiny (see Easthope 2004, 2014). In NSW, private renters need the written permission of the landlord to make any modification to the property. If it is deemed a minor alteration, the tenant can appeal to the Tribunal for a ruling if the landlord refuses to agree to the request. Landlords are entitled to prohibit any major alteration such as painting the walls or adding a window (NSW Government 2010). Although few private renters experienced overt interference by landlords and agents, there was a sense that it was not their home and they could not do as they pleased. Rhonda was particularly agitated:

> Well, you can't really do anything because you've got to get permission to do everything. If you want to put a nail in a wall cos where I'm living there's no wire door on the front and the back wire door is very bad. It's got holes in it and it doesn't meet properly and the blow flies and everything underneath the sun comes in.

However, in regards to making a home, the big issue for older private renters was not so much surveillance or interference by their landlords but rather the lack of resources to do anything, a perception that it was not worth doing anything as it was not their property and they may not be there for long and the fear that expending energy and money 'making a place feel like home' could enhance the quality of the accommodation and lead to a rent increase.

Eileen was reluctant to spend money on making her granny flat more of a home. She did not feel secure so was not keen to use her minimal finances on a place that was not hers and that she may have to leave at any time:

> I only got a few pots of plants and things like that. I'm starting to collect them now. It was a little bit too hot to do it

but now I've got a few plants and I try to make it look nicer but then I don't like to do too much because it is not my place.

Raelene used to be a keen gardener when she was a homeowner but had little enthusiasm to invest in the garden of her rented accommodation. Also, she could not afford to purchase plants:

> I can go out and do a little bit of weeding if I feel like it cos I used to love my garden, I had a beautiful garden … I like flowers but I don't bother so much now.

Based on past experience, Bruce was concerned that if he improved his apartment, his rent would be increased. He also did not have money to make improvements:

> The other thing too is I have been tempted to make certain improvements to the place and all that but in the past when I did all this only to find the landlord … put the rent up … And I'd have to spend my own money which I don't have a lot of.

Endeavouring to make their accommodation more of a home by spending money was viewed as risky. Gloria told of how after she made several improvements her rent was 'hiked so high, I had to leave'.

James's found it impossible to create a sense of home in his studio apartment. Besides the damp, it was too small. Even cooking was not possible:

> Not even toast because toast if you get toast fumes and whatever it'll set off the fire alarms. The only thing good about the place is it has got plenty of fire alarms and there have been quite a few fires in rooms so the alarms go off pretty regularly so I haven't been killed by fire yet. That's about the only advantage I can think of here.

In a few instances, significant landlord interference made it exceptionally difficult for tenants to make a home. Leonie had had a particularly bad experience:

> I would just dread when she [the landlord] … came up for weekends. I dreaded when I'd see her out the back, gardening. She'd move pots. If I put a pot outside you'd go out and the pot would be moved where she wanted it. It was a rather insidious, creepy sort of situation. She'd say comments like, 'Were you hanging stuff up on the walls? I heard you banging around you know'. It might have been like 6 o'clock in the evening, and no, I wasn't banging around. I was quite within my rights … all this and sort of someone watching me all the time. It was very frightening that and you had no rights as a tenant but you were scared, because I never knew when she'd say, 'Get out' … She was bullying me which is a horrible situation to be in.

In her present rented accommodation Leonie had a good relationship with her landlord and felt secure and had been able to create a sense of home: 'It almost feels like it is my own place …'

Private renters who had strong *de facto* security of occupancy and supportive landlords were in a far better position to create a sense of home:

> Like he said, 'You can do whatever you like to it' [the apartment]. And a couple of times there was a couple of things I wanted done, and he said, 'We'll come up and do it. Just yell out'. So I've got no worries. (Pam)

Carmel was extremely proud of her home. She had been in the same accommodation for 10 years and felt totally secure:

> Look, it is really a dear little place. I've got real pride … It is a darling little place. It looks elegant and lovely. I've got nice little bits of furniture and things in it. It looks really nice. It's really home.

Sophie was the most established private renter interviewed. She had been in the same apartment for 43 years: 'You have it like you want it and you can walk around with your eyes shut'. Lesley's *de facto* security of occupancy (see Hulse and Milligan 2014 for a discussion of *de facto* security) had encouraged her to invest in her apartment. She was also motivated by her landlord's reluctance to do anything:

> Well it is reasonably okay because I've done a lot. So I put tiles down and a carpet and painted inside and out. I've done quite a bit to make it look nice and clean and everything.

Social housing tenants' perceptions of security of occupancy

The social housing tenants interviewed had a strong sense of rootedness. Tuan (1980: 8) defines rootedness as 'a knowing that is the result of familiarity through long residence'. The knowledge that their rents were fixed and accommodation guaranteed for as long as they pay their rent and did not cause significant disruption was extremely comforting and empowering. Almost all of the social housing tenants said that they envisaged being in their present accommodation for the remainder of their lives (see Chapter 5).

Raisa spoke of how being accommodated in social housing brought 'peace': 'We can't lose it [the house]. We live here and I can't lose it … It gives you peace'. Lada emphasised the sense of being in control and settled:

> The main thing is that … we have settled in. We can buy whatever furniture or whatever we need. We don't need to worry that they're going to kick us out tomorrow. We are settled.

Dan was passionate about the sense of security he had in public housing:

> The Government is the best landlord that I've ever had. They're very responsive. They leave you alone and as long as you pay the rent, they don't interfere and so on and so forth so I do feel that there is a terrific lot of security here …

When Catherine was asked what was the most positive aspect of social housing, she also emphasised the intense security of occupancy:

> Well, the positive aspects are mainly security. When I say security, I mean security of the tenancy. You're not going through that getting notice to quit … All that type of thing.

Also, because the rent is set at 25% of income, there is no possibility of being forced to move because of an untenable rent increase. Marie had lived in public housing in a regional area but lost her foothold in this housing tenure when she moved to Sydney. She yearned for the security of public housing:

> With the Housing Commission … it's like my own home. I don't feel as if I can be put out in 6 months. They're very fair when they put the rents up. They maintain them … You know … I know people abuse Housing [NSW], but to me it's the next best thing to buying your own home.

An important spin-off of guaranteed security of tenure for older people is that if you know you are secure it is much easier to sustain social ties and organise care if need be (Petersen 2015). Gloria, who had been in the private rental sector for many years when first interviewed in 2013, had subsequently been able to access community housing. She was very conscious of this issue:

> Security of tenure is very important … Now providing I keep myself in good health, I can die in that place because I can get people to come in and look after me.

Some interviewees were unsettled about the state government's intentions in regards to the sell-off of public housing: 'Well we don't know what the government wants to do? We get rumours … that they want to get rid of housing commission' (Evelyn).[46]

Social housing tenants and maintenance

There is a formal expectation that the state housing authority and CHPs promptly and efficiently respond to tenants' maintenance concerns. The NSW state housing authority has a 24 hour hotline and its website states, 'Our specialist staff provide excellent support and advice and are able to make decisions on the spot about what needs to be done'. In the public housing complexes there were varying views on the quality of the maintenance. Many interviewees said the state housing authority was doing a 'good job':

> Two years ago the government fixed up our kitchens, gave us fantastic bathrooms, changed everything for us, and it didn't cost us anything. In that respect, things are excellent. If something breaks, the electricity or the windows, or other problems with the water you just call them and they come and fix it. (Lada)

> And every time some renovations need to be done or some repairs, they always do it. Sometimes you need to wait 2 or 3 days … If something breaks they always come and do everything. All you have to do is ask. Our window broke accidentally, and the next day they came and changed the frame completely and changed the glass. That's how it is. Not only with us, the whole building. (Olga)

> If somebody calls [on the intercom], we need to run down from the eighth floor to let them in. This is a problem. Everything else is fine. No problems. We can't complain. Our housing commission is very good, very good. (Nina)

> Look, I'll tell you what I found that they've been very good all through. Yes, there's no worries there. Anything that needs fixing and that they put you on the list and very quickly it's all sorted. Very professional, and so on and so forth. (Dan)

Tenants tended to be philosophical about the slow turnaround with minor repairs: 'I've got no complaints. The only complaint I have is they're very slow with their repairs, but who isn't … If anything goes wrong, major, they fix it straight away' (Patricia).

Interviewees who were involved in tenants' associations commented that the funding cuts combined with the bureaucratic procedures in place for maintenance requests meant that the response was too slow and unpredictable. A resident of a large inner-city public housing complex (over 500 apartments) who was very involved in the local tenants' association, argued that the government's funding cuts were having a serious impact on maintenance. John was interviewed in 2006:

> The Federal funding has really declined to the point where they can hardly afford maintenance. Maintenance is a very big issue. ... It [the complex] needs a lot of fixing and maintenance doesn't work properly. If I have a leaking tap I ring up about it. Well, you'd think, they'd give you a timeframe ... They give you a timeframe, if your hot water's not working well. That is urgent. They do that within 24 hours. Leaking taps will be a week to a fortnight. The way the work is organised, it all goes through a maintenance call centre. From there it goes out to the head contractor who subcontracts you know and the point I'm getting to is this is where a lot of money is wasted because they'll come out and they'll fix my tap but instead of doing all these repairs as a block they do it individually.

He felt that tenants were often not treated appropriately by state housing personnel when they reported a problem:

> A lot of tenants have the same feeling about their local office. They feel that they're sort of being attacked in a personal way and of course the older people are scared of any type of authority you know.

A tenant representative from another inner-city area had a similar view: 'They [housing personnel] try to put you down. Intimidate you, treat you like an idiot' (Betty). She felt that 'The Department of Housing is under-resourced, under-staffed and has problems'.

In the large public housing complexes, a common sentiment was that the public areas could be better maintained: 'They help with the apartment and we look after it well ourselves. But the building ... Don't confuse the apartment with the building. The building needs to be looked after better' (Alina). Some tenants were scathing:

> It used to be increasingly difficult to get them [the state housing authority] to listen to anything, to do anything, probably still is. I've given up, so I don't bother. If I can't do it myself I don't bother saying anything. I just do what I can do and leave it at that. (Joan)

> Some people haven't had their places painted for 10 years and this room is just falling apart. It's a shame cause it's a lovely room, but the water is getting in the ceiling. I don't know how many times they've come out. I don't even think they're tradesmen. … They've got no idea. Unbelievable. (Daisy)

Tenants in apartment blocks with a large number of difficult tenants and high rates of vandalism, were generally negative about maintenance. When Doris was asked whether the block was well maintained, she responded,

> No, you've got to beg them all the time. Things like the door at the entrance doesn't work so therefore that's open and that's not very nice to have it open of a night time.

As is discussed in Chapter 9, looking after the common areas is challenging due to vandalism, drug-taking paraphernalia and littering by some tenants and visitors.

The relatively small number of homes the CHPs are responsible for appeared to give them greater capacity to be responsive and supportive landlords.[47] Interviewees in community housing were very positive about the quality of the maintenance:

> And [name of housing provider] is a superb landlord you know. I ring up and I have a problem, a couple of days later it's fixed. Totally unlike the private market. (George)

> They've started coming out twice a year now and they sit down with you and they go through every room in the house and ask you if you have any concerns or if anything needs to be repaired or [if there's] anything you can't do that needs to be done. (Anne)

This CHP appeared to go out of their way to help:

> I mean at Christmas time my hot water decided to not warm up … so I rang [name of housing provider] and they organised somebody to come … They got somebody and

sent them the same day and fixed it all up for me ... They do what they can. (Jeanette)

Social housing landlords and pastoral care of tenants

Besides maintenance, social housing landlords were involved in varying levels of pastoral care for their tenants. In public housing complexes, there were some endeavours by the housing authority to go beyond the traditional landlord role. Some of the larger housing complexes have community development workers to whom tenants can turn for assistance and who help organise events. Tenants' associations represent the interest of residents and in the large public housing complexes meetings and events are held in the local community centre. They bring older people together: 'We're trying to make sure elderly people are looked after in the community centre here' (Joyce). Joyce had lived in the same complex for over 40 years and was very involved in the events in the community hall. Another long-time public housing tenant spoke about the activities in her neighbourhood:

> We've also got a community centre around at Millers Point. At the moment I'm getting Meals on Wheels from there but you can go around there for a meal and they have outings ... They're having a big Christmas party next weekend they send buses to pick you up and bring you back home and we've got a social worker there which helps ... There's lots of things to do if you want to and also we get taken shopping. (Dorothy)

If a housing complex has a large number of tenants of a particular nationality specific events are organised. One public housing complex in inner-Sydney had a large number of Russian residents:

> We have a calendar of events. They gather us together to speak on certain themes. Sometimes a doctor will come, other times, someone from the bank. We got together for the 8th of March recently [International Womens day – a big celebration in Russia]. We get together and sometimes they hire musicians and pay them some money. Then we have a light lunch and tea and coffee. (Lada)

The CHPs appeared to be more involved in their tenants' lives than the state housing authority responsible for public housing. Again, this is probably due to the smaller housing stock they have under their control. The community housing tenants interviewed felt that their housing provider made an active attempt to enhance their quality of life by encouraging participation and having events and meetings that encouraged contact between tenants:

> They are an exceptional landlord. They're very involved and they, you know, they want happy tenants ... I've actually got involved in the meetings that they run for tenants as well so I'm getting to meet some other tenants ... It lets me know what's available to me as well. (Anne)

The endeavour to build a sense of community was greatly appreciated:

> It's quite a lot different from say public housing. They're [CHP] ... concerned with building community. How you relate to your neighbours. That your life isn't just stuck in there watching *Days of our Lives*. They offer you opportunities. (George)

When asked if her housing provider was a 'good landlord', Jeanette responded:

> They are. They make sure you're okay. They're very good. We're involved in a lot ... We're on different committees. We made the calendar this year and last year and the year before and then we go on days out and things like that. It's really good. There is always something to do.

The ability of social housing tenants to make a home

In the case of social housing tenants, their guaranteed security of occupancy, longevity of residence and low rent meant that they had the resources and the motivation to make their accommodation feel like their home. There was a strong sense of ownership. 'I am at home here. This is my home' (Raisa). A long-established public housing resident felt totally at home:

> It's home. It is my home. Like I said, I've got a couple of dogs there. I've got all this stuff growing in the gardens. It's where my roots are and that's me sort of thing. I've been there for 41 years so I guess it's pretty well-established. It's home. (Graham)

A community housing tenant, who had been a private renter for many years before being offered a place in community housing, explains the transformation in meaning of home: 'I have a base. I have a secure private place that is mine' (Anne). The social housing tenants generally had a strong sense of place: 'I am happy. I am very happy. My place is clean, nobody bothers me … I have everything' (Marina). There was a sense of ownership and control:

> We treat them as our homes. Where a lot of people think, 'Oh, Housing, it's not mine so why should I look after it?' For me, you're living in it. It's gonna be yours for however long, so you look after it. (Marion)

Having a sense of control was important. Mavis had recently moved into public housing. Previously she was a private renter in somebody's home:

> And see living in someone else's house you tend to hold back a bit cos you don't want them to think you're going to take over their house and so you hold back a bit … Yeah, I can control things here. I can do what I like. I even said to them, cos I got a lot of family photos, I said, 'Can I put photos up?' They said, 'You're going to be living there for the next 10 years, so it's up to you'. But I still hesitate cos I don't want to put holes in the wall.

A resident of Millers Point had been in the same house for over 30 years. It was tastefully furnished and in excellent condition. She had clearly put a lot of effort into the aesthetics of her home and was extremely proud of it:

> We looked after our homes. I mean they were never our houses but I think a home is a home. A house can be anything

> and we just looked after it and maintained it. … It is [in excellent condition] because a lot of love goes into it and care and I think if you're given something you look after it … and I really appreciate it. To go out and pay full rent there's no way I could do that you know … So when you get public housing I think it's great … (Heather)

Jean (84) had lived in Millers Point for most of her life. She described how residents saw their homes:

> People took great pride in their houses. They looked after their houses. Every day they were out throwing buckets of water on the front veranda and washing that down, polishing the brass and I know because I was made to do that. They were some of the chores I had to do of a weekend. So people took pride in their houses and the basis for this was the attitude of the Maritime [Services Board].[48]

Long-term social housing tenants spoke of their familiarity with and investment in their home: 'We are used to this place. We have invested a lot of our effort into this apartment' (Alina).

For those social housing tenants who lived in a house with a garden, gardening was an important part of creating a home:

> I think most people look after their own gardens. It gives people something to do you know. It makes the place look nice with the gardens around here. It makes the places look like home you know. (Kay)

Dorothy lived in a ground floor apartment and had won an award for her garden:

> I've got a little garden … and I grow vegetables for the caterpillars to eat and I do get some out of the garden. But just well even where you are just sitting, just looking out into the garden, it's quite pleasant. It's more peaceful even than looking out over the sea. It's nice. I love the views but I think here you are. To me it's [her apartment] like a little cottage.

Not all social housing tenants felt at home and in control. For those living with challenging tenants, it was difficult to develop a sense of home. Doris commented, 'When I was in my house [she had been a homeowner], it was mine, but this is not mine'.

The undermining of guaranteed security of occupancy in public housing: the case of Millers Point, Dawes Point and the Rocks

Over the last decade there have been increasing signs that state governments are keen to offload their public housing stock (Pawson *et al.* 2013). In most instances, this has involved shifting public housing stock to CHPs (see Chapter 2). However, a far more ominous development has been the selling off of public housing stock in the open market to private individuals in areas that have become highly gentrified. The most dramatic case in Sydney is Millers Point, Dawes Point and the Rocks (henceforth referred to as Millers Point): an area that has been dominated by public housing for over a century.

Millers Point has a rich history. It was the site of Australia's first public housing development. Most of the men worked on the wharves (by the late 1800s there were 16 wharves in the area) and lived with their families in housing built and controlled by the Maritime Services Board. In many instances homes were transferred from one generation to the next. In the 1970s, the area was threatened with redevelopment and was spared after massive resistance and the 'green bans' imposed by the union movement. The green bans meant that no construction workers were prepared to be employed in the redevelopment of the area. In 1986, the Maritime Services Board handed over the homes they owned to the Department of Housing (now called Housing NSW), the State Government's housing authority, 'as part of a deal to preserve the character and worker housing of the area' (Mazzoldi 2014).

In March 2014, the New South Wales Government announced that the approximately 400 public housing properties in Millers Point were to be sold on the open market and the residents were to be relocated over a 2-year period. The Government justified the sale on the basis that the homes are too expensive to maintain, are inappropriate for older tenants (too many floors and stairs) and that the revenue generated by the sales will be used to augment the social housing stock (the government has said that 1500 public housing dwellings will be built with the proceeds from Millers Point) and thereby partially alleviate the critical shortfall of social housing. Pru Goward, the Minister responsible at the time, stated:

> The sale of public housing properties in Millers Point is the right one to ensure this state has a sustainable social housing system to provide a safety net for those who need it most. (Goward 2014)

It later emerged that the state government ignored a report it commissioned on the social consequences of the sale and references 'warning about an increased risk of death were either removed or altered' (Hasham 2014). The report drew on a Swedish study by Danermark *et al.* (1996) that examined the mortality rates of 22 579 older people who had moved or not moved. The authors found that there was no difference in the mortality rates of people who had moved voluntarily and those who had not moved, but they did find 'an increased risk of death among those who are exposed to urban renewal, both in the case of temporary evacuation and permanent moves' (Danermark *et al.* 1996: 216).

There is no doubt that the threatened sell-off has evoked enormous distress in the community (see Mowbray 2015b), more especially for the long-term older residents as this quote attests:

> If we knew something and they could say something in writing and we were secure that would be fine but it is very anxious times … Terrible stress, yeah. Not sleeping, angry, tired all that sort of thing goes with it. Trying to be nice. Trying to be happy, but underneath it is anxious moments. (Heather)

Millers Point adjoins the iconic Sydney Harbour Bridge and is in walking distance of the Opera House, making it extremely desirable real estate. It also adjoins the new Barangaroo luxury development. In 2003, the NSW government announced that the 22 hectare Barangaroo site that was formerly part of the Sydney wharves and shipping infrastructure was to be redeveloped into an upmarket urban precinct. When complete it will house approximately 3500 residents and 23 000 office workers. No doubt the developers and future residents of Barangaroo are keen to see Millers Point gentrified. The latter has become one of the most expensive neighbourhoods in Sydney. The chief executive of McGrath, one of Sydney's biggest real estate companies, named Millers Point as his 'top pick' in his companies 2014 Annual Report (Johnstone 2014). The first public housing terrace was sold in August 2014 for $1.911 million. Security for the sale was tight and only vetted potential buyers were allowed into the auction space. In September 2014, a five-bedroom terrace (public housing) in Millers Point sold for $3.95 million, a record for the suburb (Johnstone 2014). The first five sales of public housing in the area generated just under $13.7 million. In June 2015 the home that had been bought in May 2014 for $1 911 000 was resold for $2.5 million, generating a $590 000 profit (Anderson 2015). By April 2016, the Millers Point sales of 71 properties had generated $189.95 million (New South Wales Government 2016b). The sell-off of Millers Point has generated substantial resistance from residents, especially the older residents and in April 2016, 2 years after the announcement, 67 residents had refused to move. The City of Sydney and the opposition Labor Party have declared their support for the residents. However, there has been no indication that the Government is reconsidering its decision. The concerning question is whether the sell-off will be extended to other areas. Heather was determined to stay:

> I know it is not my house but it is a home… I've still got the copy of the Maritime [Services Board agreement] before it was handed over to Housing. We were to stay here till the end of our days.

The vignette in Box 8.1 is an extract from an interview conducted with Jean, an 84 year-old Millers Point resident in August 2014. She has lived in the area for over 50 years. Her husband worked on the wharves.

Box 8.1. Jean's view of Millers Point and the government's relocation plan

My husband took this place and ... so we settled in here nicely ... and it is an area where we grew up ... We had a great time here. Walked over the bridge. No, first of all we'd get the boat over to the Olympic pool and we'd save a couple of pennies for a little ride in Luna Park and then we'd walk back over the bridge ... I played basketball, learned to do knitting up there in the playground and to crochet and do pottery ... All the things that the kids don't have nowadays to keep their minds occupied, and then I got a job. Left school on the Friday and my father said, 'Well you don't have to go to work'. He said, 'You can help your mother', and I thought, 'Well I'll never get out and I'll never have any money, so I am getting a job'. So I left school on the Friday and had a job on the Monday. That's how we were brought up. If you wanted something you had to go and get it and I wasn't sitting at home with mum with no money and I wouldn't be able to go anywhere.

... And then when bath time's on we had to light the fuel copper, carry the water down eight stairs and my brother, being the youngest one, and there was still warmth in the tub copper so he could sit in there and have a bath. It was all good times you know and we were happy to stay here. It was our life.

We all had jobs to do. I worked, as I say, at Bushells, met my husband there, got married and then he went on the waterfront ... I only ever wagged school once and met my dad the second time. If we did anything wrong ... my mother would know what we were up to before we'd get home and she didn't have a telephone. It was a community. They kept an eye out on everybody, 'Don't do that otherwise I'll see your father and let him know about this'. So you know we were under observation from everyone that knew the family you know ... and you could leave your door open.

Maritime [Services Board], when we were tenants of theirs, they'd do the little handy jobs that had to be done. Water and gas or whatever. My husband done everything else. He painted this place, standing on this handrail here till I bought him a ladder and I had to say, 'You missed here. That's wrong and that's wrong'. And he had his little bit of garden down the back with the lawn ... He wasn't in for growing flowers. Tomatoes was the only thing..... He liked the yard to be kept tidy and he'd paint the veranda and do this and that ...

And of course since he's gone ... all of this upset [threat of eviction] hasn't helped in any way. I just feel at this age that I should be able to relax .... I think it is definitely [wrong] to move us old people around like we didn't matter ... It is just so distressing and all we want to do is to stay here. We maintain what we have ... Where do they get away with saying we [the state government housing authority] spent $144 000 on each property. Not here, they haven't. All

(continued)

> they've ever done is maybe if the tap needs a washer, or electrical … They've done nothing, but I've never had much bad feelings with the Department of Housing until recently. This past couple of years more or less.
>
> When one woman told me from the Department that I was getting cheap rent I was furious. I thought how dare you talk to me like that. I pay the rent, a percentage of my pension. I don't know anyone that lives around here for $5 a week or even $50. I mean they're making us out to be wasters. That we're not deserving of living here because we don't have plenty of money, but even if we did I'd still want to live here. You know this is our home. This is our area. We maintain it …
>
> I was a sandwich hand, shop assistant. The hours were perfect but we didn't think to start putting it [money] away, not that we ever earned big money to buy a house or a block of ground. We thought we'd be right here cos there was generations of people here … Hello, look at the predicament we're in now.….
>
> The Maritime Services Board always said that you pay your rent and keep your nose clean you are here for life and there was never, you know, an issue about having to move on and of course the community kept us here … When I get up of a morning, one of the facts, I can look out that window and think how lucky I am.
>
> And when the girl [from Housing NSW] came to interview me she said, 'Oh well, you may struggle with all the stairs', and I said, 'Well I'll bring the bed down here. Get rid of the lounge and bring the bed down'.
>
> I really don't want to go. I tell you, I don't want to go. I don't see that we should have to … I haven't gone to view [alternatives]. I'm too emotionally drained. I mean I don't want to be sitting there crying like a big sook. I just can't visualise myself being anywhere other than here …

Conclusions

This chapter shows the very different situations of older private renters and older social housing tenants in regards to security of occupancy, maintenance and the ability to make a home. Many of the older private renters were in situations where their security of occupancy was tenuous. The lack of security was often accompanied by minimal or no maintenance. The power imbalance between landlord and private renter meant that private renters found it difficult to assert themselves and push for adequate maintenance. Their deep vulnerability meant that many older private renters were fearful that a complaint may lead to a rent increase and/or result in their relationship with the landlord souring and that they be asked to vacate. A primary concern was ensuring that neither occurred. Although several private renters had been fortunate and had found secure and affordable accommodation and supportive landlords, there was always the fear that circumstances could change and the landlord could decide to sell or increase the rent to an untenable level. For most of the older renters, the slightest rent increase had the capacity to precipitate a crisis.

In contrast, social housing tenants, with the exception of those resident in neighbourhoods threatened with a sell-off of public housing, felt secure. This strong sense of security created a fundamental foundation for a decent life. Maintenance and pastoral care in community housing appeared to be particularly strong. The situation in public housing was more variable. Many interviewees were satisfied with the maintenance of their homes and housing complex; others felt that the process was slow, cumbersome and not reliable. Within some public housing complexes, there were community development workers and events that helped create a sense of community. In the larger complexes, the community centres play an important role in facilitating social connections (see Chapter 6).

When it came to making a home, many of the older private renters did not feel at home. The insecurity and power imbalance were too overwhelming. Many simply did not have the resources to make any improvements and they were concerned that if they spent money on making their accommodation more attractive their efforts could result in a rent increase. They were also concerned about spending their limited resources on a property that was not theirs and that they may have to vacate. The interviewees in the PRS who had had the good fortune to find amenable landlords and felt secure were more able to make their accommodation a home.

Almost all of the social housing tenants felt that they had made their accommodation a home. They were proud of their homes and the guaranteed security of occupancy meant that they were prepared to spend money on enhancing their homes. However, the sale of public housing in Millers Point has evoked enormous distress for the tenants in the area and sent shock waves through the public housing sector. Older social housing tenants, especially those in areas that have become highly sought after, were feeling less sanguine about the future.

9

The increasing residualisation[49] of social housing and its implications for older tenants

Introduction

Historically, most social housing households were low-income working families and it was often a stepping-stone to home ownership (Hayward 1996). In the last two decades, the household composition of social housing has changed fundamentally. Thus in the year ending 30 June 2013 only ~6% of new allocations were to couples with children, about half were to single people and 30% to sole parents with children (AIHW 2014). The dire shortage of social housing and the low turnover rate has made it exceedingly difficult to access this housing tenure. In NSW, the setting for this study, at the end of 2014 there were 59 500 'approved applicants' on the waiting list for social housing (New South Wales Government 2014). Thousands more have dropped off the waiting list due to a realisation that they had no chance of being allocated social housing. If you are employed, it is highly unlikely that you will be eligible: 'The provision of social housing and housing assistance more generally has moved away from focusing on low-income worker families to targeting the most vulnerable in society' (AIHW 2013a: 9). Many of the more recent social housing tenants are single, unemployed and severely disadvantaged. A worrying proportion have a psychiatric disability and/or substance abuse problem (Atkinson *et al.* 2007; Jacobs *et al.* 2010). In the financial year ending 30 June 2013, 63% of new allocations in the social housing sector had special needs (AIHW 2014: 54). Special needs refers mainly to disability but the definition also includes being aged 75 or over. The proportion of new social housing tenants in 'greatest need' increased dramatically in the last decade, from 36% in 2003–04 to 77% in 2012–13 (AIHW 2014). Households in greatest need are defined as:

> households that, at the time of allocation, are either homeless, in housing inappropriate to their needs, in housing that is adversely affecting their health or placing their life and safety at risk, or households that have very high rental housing costs. (AIHW 2014: 52)

The proportion of the social housing population that is unemployed has continued to rise despite consistent economic growth since the early 1990s. Nationwide in 2013, only 8% of households in social housing had employee income as their main source of income. The most common source of income was the Disability Support Pension (29%) followed by the Age Pension (24%) (AIHW 2014: 37).

The implications of social housing now being a housing option available almost solely to people in greatest need and/or with special needs, has increased the possibility that a proportion of tenants will be difficult co-residents. This chapter examines the ways in which older public housing tenants[50] conceptualised the shift in the profile of public housing tenants and how they viewed and managed its impacts. The impacts are certainly uneven and it is difficult to generalise. However, the interviews showed that the increasing residualisation of public housing means that many older public housing tenants are having to cope with challenging fellow tenants. Wacquant (2008: 11), drawing on his research on public housing estates in France and the USA, comments that some urban spaces become 'mere warehouses for supernumerary populations that no longer have any identifiable political or economic utility in the new polarized capitalism'. It can be argued that, in Australia, increasingly public housing estates are being conceptualised and treated in this way. They are being used to house the most vulnerable citizens, often with little support.

The quality of the immediate environment in regards to neighbours, security and amenities is crucial for older people. Age-friendly neighbourhoods encourage '… active ageing by optimising opportunities for health, participation and security in order to enhance the quality of life as people age' (WHO 2007: 1). This chapter illustrates that, for many older public housing tenants, residualisation has had serious implications. In varying degrees, it has weakened a sense of feeling at home and the immediate environment has become challenging and less age-friendly.

In 2014, about one in five public housing tenants were aged 65 or over (New South Wales Government 2014) and they are perhaps the group that has been most affected by residualisation. Most are long-term tenants and were thus able to discuss the changing composition and the impact of residualisation on their own lives. The chapter first considers the narratives of older tenants around the changing composition of public housing. It then examines how older tenants view the impacts of residualisation and the ways they cope.

Older tenants' narratives around the changing composition of public housing tenants

There was consensus that the composition of public housing has changed fundamentally over the last three decades. However, the way this shift was described varied. Not surprisingly, the extent to which the shift had had an impact on the interviewee concerned shaped their portrayal.

A common sentiment was that not only had the profile of their public housing complex changed fundamentally over the last couple of decades but that many of the more recent tenants were 'difficult'. Interviewees observed that when they first entered public housing nuclear families were dominant and most of the men were employed in stable, albeit low-paid jobs. They contrasted this to the contemporary period where many of the more recent residents are not in the labour force, live by themselves and a substantial number have mental health and/or substance abuse issues.[51] Gaby had grown up in Millers Point. She was deeply upset by many of the newer public housing tenants in the area:

> As I said, everybody knew everyone else and you know it was a self-regulating community too because being brought up like that in close proximity to everyone else ... It was always

> impressed upon you that you had to be mindful of your neighbours ... as opposed to when the Department of Housing took over they just started moving in the most antisocial people that I think I've ever come across. They weren't all like that but there were a hell of a lot of them ... They don't think anything of having loud parties till 3 and 4 in the morning with music blaring and they've got antisocial dogs who bark all night and that didn't happen with my growing up. I mean people were very mindful of each other.

A tenant who at the time of the interview had been in public housing for over 30 years emphasised the inward movement of people with 'problems':

> Around where I live ... we have a lot of people with problems ... When I first came here, it was more for low-income earners ... My husband was still working and my son was still at home doing an apprenticeship. There were a lot of people like that. (Catherine)

Another long-standing tenant had a similar view:

> Ah yes, when I first moved in, it was very nice. You had couples ... elderly couples like me, but then because they moved into better places, with their family and that, and so then the other people came in ... Like single people and people that have lots of problems, and they don't know where to put them so they put them in my building. (Doris)

A major concern identified was drug dealing. There was a general frustration that not enough was being done to deal with the issue. It was viewed as primarily responsible for a range of problems, most notably vandalism, intimidating behaviour and noise:

> And one of the things in public housing, we all know we've got dealers but does the Department of Housing do anything about it? No. 'We need proof', they say. Unfortunately, Department of Housing officials go home at 4.30 pm in the

afternoon. They come back at 8.30 am in the morning. Guess when everything happens? (Betty)

It is not unusual for working-class households to make distinctions between themselves and others (Watt 2006). In the case of older public housing tenants interviewed, there was probably a tendency to romanticise the earlier period of public housing and present it as devoid of difficult individuals. This resonates with Ravetz's (2001: 177) study of public housing estates in the UK. She commented on how 'virtually everywhere older tenants speak of a golden age when their estate "used to be lovely"'. Noteworthy, is that unlike the UK or the USA, where race is viewed as a significant factor (see Watt 2006), none of the interviewees spoke about race, ethnicity or religion when discussing the changing social composition of tenants.

Interviewees often employed what Hastings (2004) has called a 'pathologising discourse'. A common narrative when talking about the more recent tenants was that a substantial proportion had serious mental health problems and that this explained their anti-social behaviour:

> It used to be working families ... but nowadays it's people with special needs. It's families with problems, or singles with problems ... Alcoholism, drugs, disabilities, mental health is a really big problem. Public housing ... was increasingly being used to house people with serious mental health problems ... The requirements to be ... eligible for public housing now are very strict. Low income is not enough. You have to have other needs as well and so you're getting more and more problem tenants. (Betty)

Dorothy had a similar analysis:

> They are moving so many mental health people into the area that sometimes it makes it (maintenance) very difficult. They're using it now mainly for mental health and transients.

A tenant who had been in the same apartment for close on 20 years and was active in the local Tenants' Union, argued that the Richmond

Report (1983),[52] which recommended deinstitutionalisation and led to the closure of many mental health facilities, was a turning point for public housing:

> Since the Richmond Report ... there's nowhere for the people to go ... So what they're doing, they're putting the majority ... into public housing ... The people with the drug problem they need rehabilitation ... which they're not getting, so they just wander around aimlessly and it's like a network you know. If there's a drug dealer out there ... everyone seems to know the contact. Consequently ... they finish up with about half a dozen people or more sleeping on their floor. (John)

A common view was that if public housing was to be used to accommodate people with serious psychiatric and/or substance abuse problems, it was incumbent upon the state housing authority to takes responsibility for ensuring that these tenants are given adequate support:

> It puts a lot of pressure on particularly older residents when you get tenants who don't take their medication and the mental health services can't cope and it's really, really hard at times ... with tenants with mental health problems. When they're taking their medication they tend to be okay ... What needs to be done is mental health patients need to be looked after a lot better and not dumped in public housing ... If they're going to be in the public area for heaven's sake they need support systems. (Betty)

Noteworthy, is that the interviewees were generally empathetic. Most did not construct these difficult tenants as 'bad' and 'undeserving' (Marston 2004). Rather, they felt that they should be given the support necessary so that they could be 'good' tenants and neighbours. They accepted that they were entitled to social housing, but there was a strong view that the provision of affordable housing should be accompanied by adequate support. In their classic study of 'Winston

Parva' (Winston Parva is the pseudonym for an outer suburban area of a large town in central England), Elias and Scotson (1994: xviii) argue:

> Exclusion and stigmatisation of the outsiders by the established group were ... powerful weapons used by the latter to maintain their identity, to assert their superiority, keeping others firmly in their place.

There is little doubt that several interviewees perceived that they were superior and tended to stigmatise the new arrivals. However, the interviews suggested that most older residents were accepting of newly arrived residents if the newcomers respected them and their housing complex.

The concern with challenging tenants was reinforced by the constant movement of tenants. Historically, the life-long leases meant that the movement of public housing tenants was minimal. This encouraged strong social ties and cohesion because tenants knew and trusted their fellow residents. Interviewees spoke of how in the contemporary period, especially since the introduction of short-term leases in New South Wales in 2006, there was far more movement of tenants. The persistent inward movement of new tenants meant that it was difficult to get to know fellow tenants and develop amiable relations. An interviewee in an apartment block summed up this new situation:

> People come and go ... and you don't know who you've got ... You wouldn't know your neighbour. In the old days you did, but not now. You wouldn't know who is at the top or at the bottom. (Doris)

Residualisation, anti-social behaviour and its impacts

A common view was that many of the new entrants, especially young men, did not adhere to what is generally regarded as acceptable, neighbourly behaviour. They did not subscribe to what Rose (2001) has called the 'grammars of living', which broadly prescribes what is viewed as 'acceptable behaviour'. Almost all of the interviewees commented that there had been a substantial increase in behaviour that caused them distress. The main anti-social behaviours identified were excessive littering, noise, threatening behaviour, substance abuse in public places and vandalism.

Previous research has shown that, for public housing residents, local issues such as crime, drugs and vandalism are of great concern (Arthurson and Jacobs 2006; Dalton and Rowe 2004; Mee 2007; Palmer *et al.* 2005). However, there were significant variations in how interviewees responded and were affected. The extent to which anti-social behaviour was a feature of the everyday experience of older tenants varied greatly. As Wacquant (2008: 172) eloquently argues we certainly cannot presume that residents in public housing have common experiences, interpretations and perceptions:

> What appears from the outside to be a monolithic entity is experienced by its members as finely differentiated congeries of 'micro-locales' – centred on buildings and even on different stairwells inside the same building. People from the northern cluster of the project want nothing to do with their counterparts of the southern cluster, whom they consider to be 'hoodlums'.

Not surprisingly, interviewees who perceived that their apartment blocks had experienced significant residualisation and tenant movement were more likely to have experienced and been affected by anti-social behaviour. The latter had several impacts: a perception of not being secure; an invasion of privacy; degradation of the physical environment and the disruption of social connections and leisure. In varying degrees, these contributed to stigmatisation and 'spatial alienation and dissolution of place' (Wacquant 2008). It destabilised the ability of interviewees to feel comfortable in their homes and the immediate vicinity. The impacts are discussed in turn.

A perception of not being secure

A key feature of a sense of home for older people is that it is a physical space 'where one feels secure, both psychologically and physically' (Despres and Lord 2005: 326). Many of the interviewees had had encounters with fellow tenants that had made them anxious and fearful. Interviewees felt safe in their homes; the issue of security was mainly confined to the common areas – the lifts, corridors, foyers and the spaces around their apartment blocks or homes. The sense of not being safe and the intimidatory and unpredictable behaviour of some tenants was a concern for many of the public housing interviewees. The nights were especially bad:

> [Older tenants] … go down to the main entrance … The older people sit down there and these young hoodlums bang on the door, 'Let me in; let me in. I've lost me key' or whatever you know … and if the older people don't get up and let them in they get all the f's and c's bordering on physical violence you know. (John)

Interviewees were worried that they if they confronted or reported a troublesome tenant, there could be retribution:

> I'm just saying you have got to be wary. If I rile him, it does make your way of life not so good because they then go out of their way to be nasty. (Dorothy)

Joyce (85) told of how she felt intimidated by her next-door neighbour who has a serious psychiatric disorder:

> I'm not happy with the fellow next door … He's a dreadful man but there's nothing that they can do about it. … There's nowhere to put him, see. He slams the doors and … floods his unit out. He's a man you can't help. If you offered him anything he'd swear at you … If he's coming one way, I go the other.

Fear that something untoward may happen meant that older tenants tended to restrict their movements to daylight hours:

> You'll find people here will not venture out of a night-time. It's in their own interests not to go out unless they're escorted by somebody. (John)

Interviewees in highly residualised apartment blocks and neighbourhoods were constantly fearful:

> I keep my door locked and do not open it for anybody. It's so bad. I feel threatened ... I have security. I have bars across the windows. ... And I have a security door. As soon as it starts to get dark, I'm home. I'm in with the door closed and that's it. It's scary. (Doris)

Another resident had a similar strategy:

> Yes, I feel safe. I lock me door of a night. I've had the locks put on properly by my son, deadlocks and I feel safe here cos I don't go out of a night. If I do go out [during the day] I'm home at 4 o'clock. (Joyce)

Although most of the interviewees were able to maintain their usual routine, many did not feel at ease in their immediate environment. There was a constant wariness and in the evenings most would not dare venture out. This certainly had had an impact on the age friendliness of these areas. As Phillipson (2011: 284) has observed, 'The experience of crime and the fear of being a victim of crime can act as direct barriers to the maintenance of a normal daily life for many older people'.

An invasion of privacy
An age-friendly neighbourhood implies a context where older people feel that they are in control of their personal space both within their home and immediately outside of it: 'Home as privacy ... means the possession of a certain territory with the power to exclude other persons from that territory and to prohibit surveillance of the territory by other persons' (Somerville 1992: 532). The invasion of privacy can take various forms. Physical breaching of the home is the most acute form. In the case of the public housing interviewees, this was rare. What was common was the invasion of privacy by excessive noise. Noise can be a major contributor to dissatisfaction with the neighbourhood (Shon 2007). Many of the interviewees mentioned

that excessive noise was a serious issue. 'Yes, from the fights and the arguments. Yes, that kind of thing ... You don't get a proper night's sleep' (Doris). Drug and alcohol use were seen as the main precipitators of unruly, noisy behaviour:

> They tend to get up in the middle of the night, and run up and down the corridors and yell and scream ... They bang on the security doors because they've forgotten their key or they've forgotten the flat they're trying to get into so it can be very disturbing. (Betty)

A common intrusion was the screams of drug-users:

> Every morning between four and six you can hear screaming and ranting and raving from people who are coming down off highs. (John)

In some apartment blocks, domestic violence also contributed to the making of a noisy, unpredictable and difficult environment:

> I haven't got very good neighbours ... There's six floors and I'm on the fifth floor and ... they ... throw their furniture over the balcony ... And how would you like to be in bed and at 1 o'clock in the morning, someone starts throwing the furniture over the balcony from the next floor and half of it lands on your balcony ... That's very scary. (Doris)

Degradation of the physical environment

The creation of orderly and pleasant public spaces is viewed as an important component of an age-friendly environment. The outside environment has 'a major impact on the mobility, independence and quality of life of older people' and affects their ability to age in place (WHO 2007: 12). Research suggests that older people who find themselves in an environment characterised by decay and neglect appear more prone to depression and isolation (Scharf *et al.* 2002). Interviewees complained that residualisation had been accompanied by an increase in public drug use and dealing, vandalism and littering:

> The fire escape is where the drug addicts go and do drugs and leave their syringes. And they urinate there and leave a terrible smell. What can we do? ... We have many drug-addicts. (Lada)

Vandalism was a serious concern for interviewees:

> You can go through those glass doors sometimes and you'll find one smashed or they've broken the gate where the cars come in. They smash that because they've got nothing better to do ... (Norma)

The older public housing tenants were generally proud of their complex and were demoralised and angered by the persistent vandalism:

> You're probably aware of the upgrading we're going through at the moment ... but I pointed out at a meeting last week that while all this upgrading is going on the rest of the place is deteriorating. All the garbage bags disposals have had the doors pulled off ... and graffiti is being put through our building. (John)

Ironically, in some cases anti-social behaviour had had a positive impact. In some of the housing complexes, anti-social behaviour had helped mobilise older residents and was the central focus of the tenants' association. The large number of older residents in these organisations encouraged social connections and inclusion and helped them cope with challenging tenants.

Disruption of social connections and leisure

The impact of anti-social behaviour on social connections and leisure was uneven. All of the interviewees said that they had friends in their housing complex and, in most instances, residualisation had not seriously constrained their social ties or activity. Unlike the findings of a study in Adelaide, where public housing residents were 'too fearful to even open their front door' (Palmer *et al.* 2005: 400), there were few instances of older tenants not interacting because of being overwhelmed by fear. Interviewees were careful, but in most instances they were not anxious about venturing out during the day and in most complexes the public spaces (gardens, community centre) were well used by older tenants. The strong social connections and the persistence of safe spaces were crucial elements in the ability of older interviewees to cope with difficult neighbours. In some complexes there was a perception by interviewees that there were no safe spaces. Some of these interviewees coped by spending their days in a community centre in an adjoining neighbourhood:

> This is my home [the community centre] ... I see more of these people than I see of my family ... They [the public housing tenants] fight all the time ... It's not a very nice atmosphere, so I only go home to sleep and I'm up bright and early in the morning. (Doris)

Stigmatisation of the neighbourhood

A few interviewees felt that the anti-social behaviour of some of their fellow tenants had resulted in their housing complex and the surrounds being stigmatised. They told of how their family and friends were reluctant to visit. Doris had the following analysis:

> It's (the housing complex) got such a bad reputation, the place now, that ... my relatives and that, they don't like to come now because there's graffiti everywhere and we've got damage to property all the time and it means that a lot of people don't want to come here and even I suppose myself [don't want to be here], that's why I come down here [the community centre].

This resonates with Loic Wacquant's analysis of cities in the USA and France. He argues that certain neighbourhoods become stigmatised due to a concentration of what he calls 'advanced urban marginality'. These areas are 'perceived by both outsiders and insiders as social purgatories, leprous badlands at the heart of postindustrial metropolis where only the refuse of society would agree to dwell' (Wacquant 2008: 237).

Although stigma was partially due to the media representations of these housing estates (see Arthurson *et al.* 2014; Palmer *et al.* 2004), the interviewees felt that the actions of some of their fellow residents certainly made it easy for the media to construct these areas as 'dangerous'.

Conclusions

Increasing residualisation is certainly a feature of public housing in Australia. Although it is perhaps not as pervasive or deep as in some of the housing estates in France, the UK or the USA, the data indicate that a growing proportion of public housing residents are permanently shut out of the formal labour market. Certainly the interviewees were acutely aware of the residualisation phenomenon. Older residents who historically have been 'good citizens', now have to coexist with an increasing number of unpredictable and intimidating residents (mainly young males) who are unemployed and may have serious mental health and/or substance abuse problem. As Young (1999: 12) powerfully concludes in his discussion of marginal young men, these '... young men are bereft of social position and destiny. They are cast adrift ... locked in a situation of structural unemployment ...' It is not surprising that many of these men engage in anti-social behaviour; 'Being denied the respect of others they create a subculture that revolves around masculine powers and 'respect'' (Young 1999: 12).

The interviews indicated that the perceived increase in anti-social behaviour has, to varying degrees, altered interviewees' sense of home. A proportion did not feel secure in their housing complex, especially after dark. There were significant variations in the neighbourhoods and public housing complexes reviewed. The intensity of residualisation, tenant movement and anti-social behaviour was far greater in some apartment blocks and these were not age-friendly. In other housing complexes, older residents were able to create enough space between themselves and difficult fellow tenants to lead a decent life and view their complex as home despite the challenges posed by increasing residualisation. The large number of older tenants in these blocks and well-resourced and safe community centres, made it easier for residents in these locations to maintain an age-friendly environment and cope with difficult tenants. They had rich social ties with fellow residents and during the day were able to use the public spaces in their complex and there was a high level of place attachment. A number were active in the local tenants' association. This contributed to giving older tenants a sense of control over their space. They felt part of a collective endeavour to improve their housing complex.

Notwithstanding residualisation and anti-social behaviour, all of the interviewees were determined to stay in public housing (see discussion of moving in Chapter 5). They were acutely aware of how privileged they were relative to older private renters. The alternative housing tenure, the private rental market, was unthinkable due to the high rents and insecurity of occupancy.

Making public housing primarily the domain of people with complex needs has serious implications. Living in a housing complex with individuals who are unpredictable and threatening can be difficult and unsettling. Residualisation potentially creates a challenging governance environment and anti-social behaviour, if not dealt with in a considered and effective manner, can over time create untenable social spaces (Flint 2006).

An interesting finding was the empathy that many interviewees had for difficult public housing residents. Difficult residents were viewed as victims of a flawed system. The policy implications for the interviewees were clear. They recognised that challenging residents needed secure and affordable accommodation but there was a strong sentiment that if public housing is to become a major site for accommodating people with complex needs, government should do all it can to ensure that residents who require support are given the assistance required so as to improve their wellbeing and their capacity to be 'acceptable' neighbours. To a minimal extent, this has been recognised by the state government in NSW. In 2003, the Housing and Accommodation Support Initiative (HASI) for people with mental illness was established. The HASI initiative accommodates people with serious psychiatric disorders in public and community housing. In the first rollout of HASI (HASI 1), each client was provided with intensive support, a support worker for half a day. The support worker helped their client deal with everyday life. The program was remarkably successful (see Muir *et al.* 2008), illustrated most starkly in a substantial drop in hospital admissions. By March 2011, HASI had 1135 clients receiving varying levels of support (Bruce *et al.* 2012).

Wacquant (2008: 9) makes the important point that 'urban space is a historical and political construction'. In Australia, the present policy of making public housing a scarce resource and limiting its access overwhelmingly to people with complex/special needs will necessarily accentuate public housing's stigmatised and marginal status.

10

Conclusions: where to from here?

The study illustrates that the circumstances, dispositions, capabilities and social exclusion of older Australians vary dramatically and that housing tenure is often the key factor responsible for these variations.

The interviewees dependent on the private rental sector for their accommodation were especially susceptible to social exclusion, deprivation and a lack of capabilities. There was much contingency in their lives. Some of the older private renters interviewed had been fortunate and had found secure and reasonably priced accommodation. However, most were having to spend a considerable part of their income on accommodation and were constantly anxious about their security of occupancy. After paying the rent, they had little left for necessities and for some ensuring adequate nutrition was a major challenge. Social exclusion was severe. Their lack of funds meant that their capacity to participate in society was seriously constrained. They had little or no capacity to engage in leisure activities and maintaining social ties was financially and emotionally challenging. Their circumstances had a deleterious impact on their health. Many were anxious and depressed about their situation. The constant anxiety around their financial situation, security of occupancy and future wore them down. Even those who had found reasonably priced accommodation were constantly stressed because they were aware that there was always the possibility that their rent could be increased or the dwelling sold. Their limited income meant that their ability to choose their accommodation was constrained and a number had to endure totally inadequate and inappropriate accommodation. This was especially so for older renters in Sydney. Once older renters found accommodation they tended to stay, however dismal the conditions. Moving was viewed with great trepidation, due to the emotional, physical and financial costs involved. Their vulnerable situation meant that they were reluctant to ask anything of the agent or landlord. There was a feeling that they should not do anything that may upset the landlord. An analysis of the rental market in Greater Sydney by Anglicare found that, of the 13 939 properties available for private rent for the weekend of 2–3 April 2016, for a single person dependent on the Age Pension for their income not one property was affordable and for couples on the Age Pension less than 1% of dwellings were affordable (Kemp *et al.* 2016) An affordable rent was defined as a rental property where the rent was less than 30% of income. A similar analysis by Fairfax Media of advertised rents in Sydney in 2015 found that, for workers earning the minimum wage, only 0.1% of properties were affordable within 40 kilometres of the CBD (Bagshaw 2016).

Besides the psychological stress, renters found it difficult to pay for medical expenses not covered by Medicare. Despite medication being heavily subsidised, older renters who were required to take several drugs found it difficult to maintain their drug regime.

What was crucial for older private renters was family support. Those who had family support were invariably in a better situation: in several instances it made it possible for the older renter concerned to have a decent life.

It is likely that the situation of older private renters, especially those living in Sydney, is becoming more desperate. In the year ending June 2015, Sydney recorded its biggest annual rise in house rents in 5 years. The Sydney median house rent rose 3.9% to $530 a week. In the Eastern suburbs, the median rent rose 8.9% to $975 (Robb 2015). The more recent interviews with older private renters, especially those living in Sydney, revealed tremendous difficulty finding adequate accommodation that was remotely affordable. The only way they could remain in Sydney was by moving into accommodation that was woefully inadequate. Also, the private renters living by themselves were far more vulnerable than couples.

The situation of the older social housing tenants interviewed starkly revealed the enormous potential benefits of affordable, secure and adequate housing. The social housing tenants said they were able to cope on the Age Pension. They had to budget carefully but were able to cover basic necessities and engage in inexpensive leisure activities. They were highly appreciative of, and generally satisfied with, their accommodation. Many lived in housing complexes where there were several older people. The length of residence, proximity and similar circumstances meant that they often had strong social ties with fellow residents. This added to the quality of their lives. It was evident that social housing provided the basis for them having the capabilities to lead a good life. They felt secure and in control of their lives. They knew what their rent was going to be and could budget accordingly. There was no anxiety around their future housing situation and, besides the Millers Point interviewees, all were confident that they would be in their present accommodation until they passed away.

The dramatic impact of social housing on older people's lives was starkly revealed by the interviews with older social housing tenants who had had to endure the private rental sector for an extended period of time. Accessing social housing changed their lives profoundly. Interviewees spoke about how their intense anxiety dissipated dramatically. They felt reinvigorated and were once again able to engage with the world. The interviews with the social housing tenants in Millers Point, where public housing tenants have been told they will be moved, revealed the intense attachment older public housing tenants have to their homes and neighbourhoods. The stress of the Millers Point residents interviewed was acute and they were determined to fight the state government's edict to the bitter end.

The circumstances of homeowners varied substantially. A few were struggling on the Age Pension. This was most evident in the case of homeowners living by themselves in large homes who had minimal or no savings. Insurance and maintenance were substantial costs. Homeowners who were still supporting adult children were also struggling. However, all of the interviewees were able to cover the necessities and most felt that they were able to lead a decent life, more especially interviewees who received the couple Age Pension. Their ability to decide in most cases when and what maintenance was to be done meant that they were able to control their accommodation costs. The capabilities of older homeowners who were healthy and did not have any major ongoing expenses were generally extensive. They were able to pursue a healthy lifestyle and many led active lives. This was helped by many having a financial buffer. Unlike the older private renters, who usually had exhausted any savings they may have had, older homeowners on the Age Pension were able to hang on to their superannuation/savings. Their savings, although generally modest, gave the older homeowners concerned a comforting buffer and a greater capacity to consume than their social housing and private renter counterparts.

The study gives credence to Kemeny's (2005, 2006) thesis. To recap, Kemeny argues that in welfare states where homeownership is dominant, it is likely that the Age Pension will only be adequate if you are a homeowner or a renter in substantially subsidised accommodation. These contexts are characterised by what Kemeny calls a 'dualist rental market'. In a dualist rental market, of which Australia is a prime example, the social housing sector is confined to poor households and the regulation of the private rental sector is minimal. The implications for older private renters dependent on the Age Pension for their income are severe. As indicated by the interviews, it is highly likely that the Age Pension will not be adequate for a decent life due to the high cost of their accommodation and security of occupancy will be minimal.

A related argument of Kemeny's is that in countries where the social housing sector is large and home ownership is not viewed as an overriding aspiration, the non-profit rental sector will, to a large extent, shape the contours of the private rental sector. In what Kemeny calls the 'integrated' rental market' there is much regulation. Rent increases are controlled and tenants have a good deal of power. The social housing sector in these contexts is not confined to very low-income households, but is also occupied by middle-class households. Renting is viewed as a sensible and viable lifelong housing tenure option (Hulse *et al.* 2011).

The impact of the cost of accommodation is revealed by the before- and after-housing-poverty rate of people on the Age Pension. As Yates and Bradbury (2010) indicate (see Chapter 1) the minimal housing costs of a large part of Australia's older population does mean that although the before-housing-poverty rate is one of the highest in the OECD, the low housing costs of most older Australians and the guaranteed government Age Pension means that Australia has one of the lowest rates of poverty after housing costs.

What is of major concern is that at least 100 000[53] older Australians in the private rental sector are at present living in dire circumstances. Not only is their financial situation desperate, but their minimal security of occupancy means they are persistently anxious about their future. Even more concerning is that the present policy nexus and the data around population growth and housing affordability, indicate that the proportion and absolute number of older private renters will grow substantially in coming decades. Jones *et al.* (2007: x) estimate 'The number of people aged 65 and over living in low-income rental households is projected to increase by 115 per cent from 195 000 in 2001 to 419 000 in 2026'. Yates and Bradbury (2010) conclude that the proportion of older homeowners will drop by at least 10% by 2046. It is clear that present policy will ensure that the social housing sector will not be able to accommodate the increasing number of older non-homeowners and almost all will be dependent on the private rental sector. We can thus confidently predict that at least 15% of older (65 plus) Australians will be dependent on the private rental sector by 2040.[54] The Australian Bureau of Statistics (ABS) has three estimates as to the size of the older population in 2041, depending on the total fertility rate (TFR), life expectancy and net overseas migration. The most conservative ABS estimate is that 9 million Australians will be aged 65 and over by 2041 (ABS 2013b). If 15% are in the PRS this translates into 1.35 million older Australians.

The notion that the PRS should accommodate older Australians dependent on the Age Pension for their income is not an acceptable policy option at present. If the PRS is to be a viable option for this group there needs to be a radical rethink of the present subsidy and legislative arrangements. At present, Commonwealth Rent Assistance (CRA) is pegged at a maximum of $64.20 a week. The data indicate that CRA does make a significant difference. An analysis of an Australian Government Housing Data Set by the Australian Institute of Health and Welfare (AIHW) concluded that on the 1 June 2012, before CRA, 60% of CRA recipients aged 65 and older were using

30% or more of their income for rent; and after CRA the proportion dropped to 27.3% (AIHW 2013a: 38). There was no regional breakdown of the data. What is evident is that, nationally, rents in the private rental sector vary dramatically. In Greater Sydney, the median weekly rent for a one-bedroom dwelling in December 2015 was $465 a week. In Cessnock, 150 km from Sydney, the median rent was $195 (New South Wales Government 2016). A major policy issue is that the CRA does not take account of locational differences in the median rent. Thus private renters in Cessnock are entitled to the same level of CRA as renters in Sydney. This is clearly an issue. Far more low-income private renters in metropolitan Sydney will be in housing stress than in regional NSW. Ideally, the CRA in any particular area should take account of the median rent in the locality concerned.

The other area of policy that needs to be rectified is security of occupancy and levels of rent increases. If the PRS is to become a major source of housing for older Australians, it is imperative that the legislative framework around private renting is changed so that it gives older private renters the capacity to lead a decent life. They need to be given long-term leases and a guarantee that annual rent increases will be in line with the consumer price index (CPI). Globally, this is not unusual. In those countries with an integrated, rather than dual, rental market there are regulations in place that give tenants security of occupancy and control the degree to which rents can be raised. In an integrated rental market the differences between the non-profit/social housing sector and the private rental sector are not substantial (Hulse *et al.* 2011; Kemeny 2006).

At this time in Australia, the chances of the PRS being reined in and regulated more tightly are remote. The 1.3 million small investors in the private rental market makes any endeavour to restrict the power of landlords highly politically charged. The possibility of making the private rental market a more attractive tenure has become even more remote in Sydney. The massive increase in housing prices since mid-2012 means that new investors are not inclined to keep rents low or support any proposals that seek to increase the power of tenants, impose restrictions on rent increases and enhance security of occupancy. An analysis of the Sydney rental market in June 2015 concluded:

> The combination of surging prices and increased supply of rental properties has crunched the annual rate of return from rent that new investors make on a Sydney house to 3.4 per cent, the lowest level since 2005 ... (Yeates 2015)

This does not mean rents are low; rather it means that rents are low relative to prices paid for housing.

Perhaps the worsening housing affordability crisis will force government to step in and endeavour to strengthen the non-profit rental sector. A major social housing construction program reminiscent of the 1985 to 1995 period, when 115 000 public housing dwellings were built (see Chapter 2), would be a sensible government intervention. Besides providing affordable housing, it would provide tens of thousands of jobs and stimulate the economy. If housing is viewed as a human right, this may lead to a policy shift over the long term. Numerous international conventions view affordable, adequate and secure housing as a right. The Universal Declaration of Human Rights states, 'Everyone has the right to a standard of living adequate for the health and well being of himself and his family, including food, clothing, housing and medical care'. In 1991, the Committee that has the responsibility of monitoring and implementing the International Covenant on Economic, Social and Cultural Rights (ICESCR) elaborated on what defines a right to housing with the passing of General Comment No. 4. The opening paragraph of this Comment declares:

> The human right to adequate housing, which is thus derived from the right to an adequate standard of living, is of central importance for the enjoyment of all economic, social and cultural rights. (United Nations 1991)

A key conclusion is that the right to housing extends beyond:

> merely having a roof over one's head ... Rather it should be seen as the right to live somewhere in security, peace and dignity ... [and] the right to housing should be ensured to all persons irrespective of income or access to economic resources.

A primary argument is that housing should be adequate. Adequacy has several components:

> Adequate shelter means ... adequate privacy, adequate space, adequate security, adequate lighting and ventilation, adequate basic infrastructure and adequate location with regard to work and basic facilities – all at a reasonable cost.

Noteworthy is that affordability is viewed as a fundamental component of adequacy:

> Personal or household financial costs associated with housing should be at such a level that the attainment and satisfaction of other basic needs are not threatened or compromised. Steps should be taken by States parties to ensure that the percentage of housing-related costs is, in general, commensurate with income levels. States parties should establish housing subsidies for those unable to obtain affordable housing, as well as forms and levels of housing finance which adequately reflect housing needs. (United Nations 1991)

Security of tenure is also viewed as a central feature of adequate housing:

> All persons should possess a degree of security of tenure which guarantees legal protection against forced eviction, harassment and other threats. (United Nations 1997)

The notion that an Australian Government may view housing as a human right and act accordingly may be a pipe-dream, but what is evident is that, as long as a virtually unregulated market is viewed as the primary way for low income households to access housing, an ever-increasing number of older (and younger) Australians will be destined to live in inadequate, unaffordable and insecure housing.

Appendix A: methodology employed in the study

Pierre Bourdieu (2002: 1) in his superb co-authored book *The Weight of the World: Social Suffering in Contemporary Society* notes, 'We are offering here the accounts that men and women have confided to us about their lives and the difficulties they have in living those lives ...' Bourdieu and his contemporaries used in-depth interviews to gather the rich data presented. *The Australian Dream* has a similar goal. I see the book as a textual documentary drawing on in-depth interviews. It is based on 125 in-depth semi-structured interviews (two interviewees were interviewed twice) with 32 older homeowners, 46 social housing tenants, 32 private renters and four interviews with private renters whose rent was well below market value due to their dwelling being owned by a family member or friend. In addition, nine interviewees were able to talk about their experiences in the PRS and in social housing. The interviewees are profiled in Appendix B. Ninety of the interviewees were female and 30 were male. Three couples were interviewed. Ninety interviewees lived in Sydney and 33 in regional NSW. The main aim of the interviews was to establish how the housing situation of the interviewees had shaped and was shaping their lives. The interviews allowed me to get a sense of older people's lives in a range of situations. As Mansveldt (2008: 198) argues:

> Qualitative forms of interviewing are invaluable for highlighting the lived experience of elders, identity and place issues, focusing as they do on matters of exploration rather than extent, and emphasising the connections between the meanings of social settings and the individuals who inhabit them.

Of course, the dependence of this study primarily on in-depth interviewing means that I need to be circumspect about making generalised statements. Also, it is recognised that the recounts of interviewees are necessarily selective and partial: 'at different times and places there will be different and often contradictory interpretations of the same phenomena' (King and Horrocks 2012: 22). The constructionist position argues that we cannot presume that what the interviewee says in the interview necessarily reflects the interviewee's world. Thus, 'Respondents are not so much repositories of knowledge-treasuries of information awaiting excavation as they are constructors of knowledge in collaboration with interviewers' (Holstein and Gubrium 2003: 68). This argument presents the researcher with a dilemma. If the data cannot be accepted as reflecting the reality of the interviewee, how do we go about analysing the data collected? The constructionist approach argues that all we can do is analyse the interview itself: 'interviews merely report upon, or express, their own structures' (Rapley 2001: 307).

A compromise position is the interviewer approaching the interview material reflexively. The researcher needs to be aware of the interview as a co-construction. This position entails taking note of the talk of the interviewer and the interviewee, the argument being that the setting and interviewer play a central role in shaping the responses of the interviewee and that the interview itself is a particular kind of forum and interaction. In the interview, the interviewee may present recounts of their experiences and views that might be different to what they would present to friends, family or another interviewee. They will usually endeavour to present themselves in a favourable light or what Rapley (2001: 306) calls a 'morally adequate light'. This may involve highlighting some material and omitting content that may be too painful or revealing. This certainly does not mean that in-depth interviewing is a fruitless method, rather it means that when interviews are analysed, interviewee's answers should be contextualised. Ideally, the question that prompted the response needs to be taken into account.

There are certainly gaps in the study. There was limited input from interviewees who do not speak English at home and no Indigenous older people were interviewed. This was mainly a result of the mode of recruitment. Interviewees responded to advertisements placed in appropriate publications and websites or heard about the study through fellow residents. The latter was most evident in the case of social housing tenants. The study does not focus on older people in retirement villages or nursing homes, manufactured housing villages or on homeowners with a mortgage. Issues around gender are not given a prominent role. These are limitations of the current study and warrant future investigation.

Ethics permission for the study was obtained from the respective Ethics Offices at the University of New South Wales and the University of Technology, Sydney. All the interviews were audiotaped and transcribed. I conducted 109 of the 125 interviews. Six interviews were conducted by a Russian speaker with Russian public housing tenants in inner Sydney and 10 interviews were conducted by Geoffrey Brown with public housing tenants in Western Sydney. Geoffrey was a PhD student and living in Western Sydney at the time. Most of the interviews in Sydney were done face-to-face, but some were telephone interviews. Some interviewees were not enthusiastic about being interviewed at home and often they did not have the physical capacity or desire to travel to my office. An interview in a coffee shop is potentially difficult because of the possibility that it could be noisy. These interviewees felt comfortable and safe having a phone interview and these interviews were usually as productive and informative as interviews conducted face-to-face (see Sturges and Hanrahan 2004; Tausig and Freeman 1988). Most of the interviews with older people living outside of Sydney were phone interviews. A few travelled to Sydney for the interview.

All the interviews focused on the following themes:

- housing history
- the adequacy of the accommodation
- the cost of the accommodation and its impact
- finances/budgeting
- health and ageing in place
- the neighbourhood
- leisure and social connections
- social and family support

- housing options and policy
- the future

In the case of older renters, the landlord–tenant relationship and maintenance were additional themes.

A thematic approach was used to analyse the interviews. This approach is premised on the notion that what the interviewee says does reflect their world to a greater or lesser extent. Of course, as mentioned, interviewees will exaggerate certain aspects, omit important information and distort 'reality', but I sensed that in the main interviewees endeavoured to answer questions as honestly as their memory allowed. Analysis of the interviews involved identifying key themes and using NVivo software to organise the themes.

All of the names used are pseudonyms. In a few instances, I have changed small details in the quotes to avoid any possibility of identification.

Appendix B: profile of interviewees

Private renters interviewed

Year of interview	Pseudonym	Age	Weekly rent	In regular family contact	Number of years in *current* accommodation	Location
2005	Arieta	65	$140	Y	2	South-western Sydney
2014	Anthony*	86	$150	Y	60	South-western Sydney
2005	Barbara	72	$295	Y	2	Inner Sydney
2005	Beverley	70	$240	Y	3	Northern Sydney
2014	Bruce	71	$260	Y	9	Western Sydney
2015	Carmel	76	$343	Y	10	Hunter Valley
2013	Carol	70	$150	Y	6	Western NSW
2005	Chris	67	$220	Y	10	Northern Sydney
2008	David	70	$160	Y	1	Wollongong
2014	Eileen	64	$250	N	4 months	Western Sydney
2008	Elsie	71	$280	Y	2	Inner Sydney
2014	Faye	65	$250	Y	2	Mid-north coast
2015	Greg	74	$260	Y	14	Western Sydney
2015	James	68	$195	N	14	Inner Sydney
2008	June	77	$190	Y	4	South-western Sydney
2014	Leonie	66	$190	N	2	Western Sydney
2014	Lesley	68	$160	N	16	Hunter Valley
2005	Malcolm	66	$130	Y	8	Inner Sydney
2005	Marie	66	$150	Y	1	South-eastern Sydney
2015	Nellie	74	$125	Y	7	Central coast
2005	Pam	68	$150	Y	5	South-eastern Sydney
2005	Paul	74	$160	Y	1	Western Sydney
2015	Phyllis	66	$270	N	9 months	South-western Sydney
2013	Raelene	75	$330	Y	1	Wollongong
2015	Raymond*	69	$118	Y	7	South-western Sydney

The Australian Dream

Private renters interviewed (continued)

Year of interview	Pseudonym	Age	Weekly rent	In regular family contact	Number of years in current accommodation	Location
2008	Rhonda	78	$200	Y	7 months	South-western Sydney
2005	Richard*	66	$150	Y	10	Inner Sydney
2008	Robert	70	$175	Y	1	Western NSW
2008	Sophie	70	$165	Y	43	Central coast
2013	Thomas	66	$320	Y	10	Central coast
2005	Valerie	70	$200	Y	1	Inner Sydney
2015	Yvonne	71	$250	Y	3	South-eastern Sydney

*These interviewees were not quoted in the book.

Private renters with heavily subsidised rents*

Year of interview	Pseudonym	Age	Weekly rent	In regular family contact	Number of years in current accommodation	Location
2005	Julie **	74	$70	N	19	Northern Sydney
2013	Rosemary **	78	Not stated	Y	9	Wollongong
2006	William and Eleanor	85 (W); E (80)	$150	Y	4	North Sydney
2013	Wilma	78	$160	Y	16	Western Sydney

*The apartments of these interviewees were owned by family or friends and the rent charged was way below the market rate.
** These interviewees were not quoted in the book.

Social housing tenants interviewed

Year of interview	Pseudonym	Age	In regular family contact	Number of years in current accommodation	Location	Type of housing
2006	Alice	72	Y	Not stated	Western Sydney	Public
2008	Alina and Boris	69	Y	12	Inner Sydney	Public
2006	Ben	73	Y	11	Western Sydney	Public
2006	Betty	67	Y	24	Inner Sydney	Public
2005	Brian	80	Y	9 months	Northern Sydney	Community
2006	Catherine	70	Y	3 months	Inner Sydney	Public
2009	Daisy	80	Y	3	Western Sydney	Public
2006	Dan	75	Not stated	20	Inner Sydney	Public
2006	Doris	72	Y	20	Inner Sydney	Public

Appendix B: profile of interviewees

Social housing tenants interviewed *(continued)*

Year of interview	Pseudonym	Age	In regular family contact	Number of years in *current* accommodation	Location	Type of housing
2006	Dorothy	71	N	3	Inner Sydney	Public
2014	Ellen	66	Y	2	South-western Sydney	Public
2006	Evelyn	69	Y	23	Inner Sydney	Public
2014	Gaby	74	N	74	Inner Sydney	Public
2014	Gloria	70	N	1	Western Sydney	Community
2014	Gary*	76	Y	10	South-eastern Sydney	Public
2008	Glenys*	65	Y	10	Inner Sydney	Public
2006	Graham	73	Y	41	Western Sydney	Public
2006	Gwenda	70	Y	26	Inner Sydney	Public
2006	Hazel	71	Y	14	Western Sydney	Public
2014	Heather	68	N	48	Inner Sydney	Public
2014	Jean	81	Y	81	Inner Sydney	Public
2014	Jeanette	81	N	11	South-eastern Sydney	Community
2014	Joan	71	Y	36	South-eastern Sydney	Public
2014	Joanne	70	Y	35	South-eastern Sydney	Public
2006	John	72	Y	21	Inner Sydney	Public
2006	Joyce	85	Y	47	Inner Sydney	Public
2012	Kate	72	N	3	Hunter Valley	Community
2006	Kay	70	Y	15	Western Sydney	Public
2006	Kevin	75	N	12	Inner Sydney	Public
2009	Lada	69	Y	8	Inner Sydney	Public
2006	Louise	65	Y	21	Inner Sydney	Public
2009	Marina	77	N	20	Inner Sydney	Public
2006	Marion	68	Y	8	Western Sydney	Public
2006	Marjorie*	62	Y	27	Inner Sydney	Public
2014	Mavis	72	N	1	Western Sydney	Public
2014	Mildred	72	Y	17	South-western Sydney	Public
2015	Monica*	72	Y	46	Inner Sydney	Public
2014	Nina and Abram	79(N); 76(A)	Y	18	Inner Sydney	Public
2006	Norma	85	Y	22	Inner Sydney	Public
2009	Olga	75	Y	10	Inner Sydney	Public
2006	Patricia	70	Y	16	Inner Sydney	Public
2006	Pauline*	66	N	40	Inner Sydney	Public

Social housing tenants interviewed *(continued)*

Year of interview	Pseudonym	Age	In regular family contact	Number of years in *current* accommodation	Location	Type of housing
2009	Raisa	85	Y	17	Inner Sydney	Public
2005	Rita	82	Y	27	South-eastern Sydney	Community
2006	Roy	70	Y	3	Western Sydney	Public
2006	Valma	70	Y	2	Western Sydney	Public

* These interviewees were not quoted in the book

Interviewees who spoke about their private rental and social housing experience

Year of interview	Pseudonym	Age	In regular family contact?	Number of years in *current* accommodation	Location	Type of housing
2015	Anne	67	Y	4	South-eastern Sydney	Community
2005	Edna	74	N	8	Inner Sydney	Public
2014	George	73	Y	3	South-eastern Sydney	Public
2012 and 2014	Gloria*	70	N	16	Western Sydney	Community
2005	Jillian	92	N	9	Northern Sydney	Community
2005 and 2015	Judith*	67	Y	1	South-eastern Sydney	Community
2013	Lois	67	Y	9	Inner Sydney	Living with daughter
2006	Nancy	67	Y	1	Northern Sydney	Community
2008	Peter	70	N	1	Central NSW	Community

*Gloria and Judith were interviewed twice. In the first interview they were private renters in the second they were social housing tenants.
At the time of being interviewed Nancy and Anne had recently moved into social housing.

Appendix B: profile of interviewees

Homeowners interviewed

Year of interview	Pseudonym	Age	In regular family contact	Number of years in *current* accommodation	Location
2013	Barry*	74	N	30	Wollongong
2015	Beryl*	60	Y	2	Hunter Valley
2014	Christine	66	Y	22	Wollongong
2014	Coral*	65	Y	11	Hunter Valley
2015	Denise	75	Y	44	South-eastern Sydney
2013	Doreen	70	Y	31	Western NSW
2015	Doug	76	Y	9 months	Central coast
2015	Edward	84	Y	22	Northern Sydney
2013	Frances	76	N	34	Inner Sydney
2015	Francesca	70	Y	12	South-eastern Sydney
2015	Frank	74	Y	15	Western NSW
2013	Helen	69	Y	13	Wollongong
2015	Henry	67	Y	9	Central coast
2015	Ian	85	Y	26	Hunter Valley
2013	Irene	78	Y	39	Northern Sydney
2015	Jennifer	72	N	3	Western Sydney
2015	Joe	80	Y	18	Western NSW
2013	Joy	84	Y	45	Wollongong
2013	Julia	78	N	13	Inner Sydney
2015	Karen*	72	Y	2	Central coast
2015	Linda	87	Y	31	Northern Sydney
2015	Marlene	64	Y	24	Riverina
2015	Maureen	80	Y	15	Northern Sydney
2015	Paula	80	Y	25	Wollongong
2013	Roslyn	84	Y	53	Wollongong
2015	Shirley	77	Y	52	South-eastern Sydney
2015	Susan	66	Y	8	South-eastern Sydney
2015	Sylvia	70	Y	6	Northern Sydney
2015	Thelma	72	Y	5	Mid-north coast
2015	Tina	T (60) & 84	Y	12	Hunter Valley
2015	Val	82	Y	29	Northern Sydney
2015	Walter	80	Y	18	Inner Sydney

*These interviewees were not quoted in the book.

Endnotes

1. A gap in the study is older homeowners who have a mortgage. This grouping is not a focus of the current study. I was unable to interview a sufficient number of older mortgagees to draw meaningful insights. Further investment in this area is certainly warranted to gain a more complete understanding of the housing experiences of older Australians. In this study, 'homeowners' therefore refers to people who do not have a mortgage.

2. There was an important, albeit temporary, shift in housing policy in 2008 when, in response to the global financial crisis, the Australian Government allocated $5.638 billion to social housing over 3 years (2008–09 to 2011–12) and approximately 19 700 homes were built and another 12 000 dwellings that faced becoming uninhabitable were repaired (KPMG 2012).

3. Historically, housing built with funds provided by the Australian Government has been referred to as public housing. Public housing is administered by the housing authorities of the respective states and territories. Over the last two decades, the profile of government-subsidised housing has become more complex, with the increasing importance of community housing. Community housing is subsidised housing and is constituted mainly by public housing that has been handed over to CHPs. A small proportion of CHP stock has been built by the CHPs. The CHPs, which are non-government organisations or religious bodies, are responsible for the management and allocation of these homes. In regards to allocation, in NSW, the CHPs have to assess applicants using the government's common assessment tool for applicants to public and community housing (Pawson *et al.* 2013). In this study, when discussed in combination, public housing and community housing will be referred to as social housing. Social housing also incorporates public housing reserved for Indigenous households.

4. The Tenants' Union of NSW estimated that, at 30 June 2014, there were 400 to 600 protected tenants remaining in NSW. These tenants enjoy considerable security of tenure. Unlike the mainstream private renters who are covered by the provisions of the *Residential Tenancies Act 2010*, protected tenants fall under the provisions of the *Landlord and Tenant (Amendment) Act 1948 (Correspondence with Tenants' Union of NSW dated 23 February 2015).*

5. This figure was compiled from data supplied by Patrick Troy (see Troy 2012: 131, 141, 158, 180, 187 191).

6 Commonwealth Rent Assistance (CRA) is a subsidy given to low-income private renters. Community housing tenants are also eligible to apply. CRA is means tested. In order to qualify for CRA, an individual has to be dependent on a government benefit or receive more than the base rate of the Family Tax Benefit and their rent has to be above a certain level. In July 2015, the maximum CRA per fortnight for a single person was $64.29 a week and for a couple with no children, $60.40 per week. In June 2013, there were about 1.3 million recipients of CRA. The impact of CRA is significant. It is estimated that after receiving CRA, there was a 27% reduction in the in number of low-income households in rental stress (AIHW 2014: ix).
7 Karen Walsh, the general manager for housing services and renewal at St George community housing, helped ensure that my portrayal of community and affordable housing is precise.
8 The ABS Survey of Income and Housing of 14 569 households conducted in 2011–12 concluded that under 5% of older Australians were in social housing in 2011–12.
9 Residualisation refers to a significant increase in the concentration of seriously disadvantaged households (Jacobs *et al.* 2010).
10 Data from 1996 and 2011 Census, personal communication from Judy Yates, University of Sydney.
11 Data was supplied by Judy Yates, University of Sydney.
12 It is important to note that the interviews were done over a 10-year period starting in 2005 and ending in May 2015. Costs of accommodation obviously changed over time.
13 People who are dependent on Centrelink (the government's social security bureaucracy) for their income, can obtain interest-free loans from Centrelink for up to $1000.
14 Gloria moved into community housing in 2014 and her life was transformed; see Chapter 7.
15 If you earn an income while on the Age Pension, you receive a partial pension. The partial pension amount is determined by how much income you receive from other sources.
16 Bourdieu's concept of habitus refers to the 'system of durable and transposable *dispositions* through which we perceive, judge and act in the world' (Wacquant 2007: 267). These dispositions are acquired through individuals internalising their immediate social milieu. Although these dispositions or ways of seeing and acting in the world are changeable, they tend to be deep seated and mould individual's behaviour throughout their lifespan.
17 Judith was first interviewed in 2005 when she was a private renter. She was interviewed again in 2015 as a social housing tenant.

18. It is recognised that pets can play an important role in fostering wellbeing and good health (see McNicholas *et al.* 2005).
19. Unfortunately, I never asked Marie who she was referring to. I presume she was referring to the government.
20. Doris was interviewed in 2006 when the full Age Pension for a single person was $512.60 a fortnight. In June 2015 it was $860.20, an increase of $347.60, or 68%.
21. This was part of the government's stimulus package to counter the global financial crisis in 2008.
22. Utility bills refer to the gas and electricity bill. Some homes have only electricity.
23. The HILDA survey is a longitudinal study of over 10 000 Australian households. It began in 2001.
24. In an excellent review of existing research in the USA, Paula Span (2015) shows that ageing in place is not necessarily the best option. In the USA, it is estimated that close to 2 000 000 older people are now completely or mostly housebound. This can have dire consequences for the individuals concerned.
25. In many cases, at the start of a new lease, tenants have to pay up to 2 weeks rent in advance. In addition, they have to pay a 'bond' in case they breach the tenancy agreement. The bond can be equivalent to up to 4 weeks rent.
26. Glossodia and Freemans Reach are about 65 kilometres from Sydney.
27. About 3 years after this interview, Judith was offered a place in social housing. Perhaps the housing authority realised that Judith's mental health was deteriorating and that an urgent intervention was required. By the time she moved into social housing, she had spent all of her savings, ~$80 000, on basic living expenses. The cost of her accommodation meant that she constantly had to dip into her capital.
28. Chris was offered a place in community housing a few months after the interview.
29. The central coast is about 80 kilometres north of Sydney.
30. Gloria was offered a place in community housing about 2 years after the interview.
31. In NSW, a person who turns 85 has to undergo a medical review and a driving test if they want an unrestricted licence. Alternatively, a person can opt for a modified licence. In this case, no practical driving test is required but the person concerned will have restrictions put on their licence. They may be restricted in how far they can drive and may not be able to drive at night (New South Wales Government 2015b).
32. The New Deal for Communities areas are disadvantaged areas across the UK that were selected in 1998 and 1999 to be part of a 10-year program to reduce disadvantage.

33 This could certainly be a function of the way interviewees were recruited. It is probable that social housing tenants who are isolated would have been reluctant to volunteer for the study.
34 The Probus Club is a club for retirees. They hold regular events.
35 The issue of not having contact with children was a sensitive topic and I rarely pursued it in the interviews.
36 Medicare means that people on the Age Pension are able to see a general practitioner at no cost. They are what is called, bulk-billed. The practitioner accepts the agreed Medicare payment they receive from government as full payment for the service rendered and the patient does not have to pay anything for the consultation. The PBS means that, in 2016, people dependent on the Age Pension who had a Pensioner Concession card only had to pay $6.20 per script.
37 It is possible that social housing tenants who were highly stressed would not have agreed to be interviewed. Nevertheless, it is evident that their affordable rent and guaranteed security of occupancy meant that they would not be subject to the factors that precipitated so much stress among the private renters interviewed.
38 The insecurity of social housing tenants in Millers Point and its impacts is returned to in Chapter 8.
39 In 2007, the Australian Government introduced the Medicare Chronic Disease Dental Scheme (CDDS) that provided just over $4000 in Medicare benefits for people whose dental health was impacting on their general health. Recipients had to be referred by a general practitioner. Once referred, they could visit a dentist in the private health system. The scheme was abandoned after massive demand resulted in a cost blow-out.
40 I am not sure if Rob was being serious about the super glue.
41 Visioncare is a program run by the School of Optometry at the University of New South Wales. The program, which is funded by the state government, provides free spectacles once every 2 years to low-income applicants.
42 Very few of the social housing tenants appeared to have private health insurance.
43 Ann is referring to the gap between the bulk bill cost, which would be zero for the patient, and what she had to pay the specialist.
44 The Eye Hospital is a public hospital and treatment is free.
45 The waiting time for elective surgery in the public system in NSW can be extensive. It depends on the procedure. In 2013–14 the median waiting time was 49 days, but for a cataract operation it was 218 days (Gardiner 2014).
46 Most of the interviews with public housing tenants were conducted prior to the government's announcement that they intended to sell off public housing in Millers Point and they were thinking of extending the sell-off to other gentrified areas.

47 In the UK, Pawson and Gilmour (2010) found that the size of a housing association's stock did play a role in shaping tenant satisfaction. The smaller associations generally received higher ratings.
48 Prior to the state housing authority, the Maritime Services Board owned and managed the homes in Millers Point. Most of the male residents worked on the wharfs in the area.
49 Residualisation refers to a significant increase in the concentration of seriously disadvantaged households in an area (Jacobs *et al.* 2010).
50 All of the quotes in this chapter are from public housing residents.
51 This perception to a large extent does accord with the present profile of public housing. In NSW, ~60% of social housing residents are single and in public housing only 5% said that wages were their main source of income (New South Wales Government 2014).
52 The Richmond Report refers to the Inquiry into Health Services for the Psychiatrically Ill and Developmentally Disabled in New South Wales. It reported in 1983.
53 The figure of 100 000 is probably conservative. It is based on the 2011 Census data that established that there are approximately 115 000 older (65 plus) private renter households (see Table 2.2). If each household is constituted by 1.5 persons, there were 172 500 older private renters in June 2011. If 60% were in dire straits, this is equivalent to 103 500 people.
54 This projection is probably conservative. In the UK, which is facing a similar crisis to Australia around housing affordability but historically has had a far more substantial social housing sector, Steve Wilcox, a leading British housing scholar, has estimated that by 2040 a third of 60-year-olds will be renters (Eccles 2015).

References

ABC News (2012) 'Dental care 'disgrace' back under spotlight'. ABC, 2 May, <http://www.abc.net.au/news/2012-05-01/dental-care-disgrace-back-under-the-spotlight/3981822>.

Abrahamson V, Wolf J, Lorenzoni I, Fenn B, Kovats S, Wilkinson P, Adger WN, et al. (2008) Perceptions of heatwave risks to health: interview-based study of older people in London and Norwich, UK. *Journal of Public Health* **31**(1), 119–126. doi:10.1093/pubmed/fdn102

Adams RG, Torr R (1998) Factors underlying the structure of older adult friendship networks. *Social Networks* **20**, 51–61. doi:10.1016/S0378-8733(97)00004-X

Aldwin C (1991) Does age affect the stress and coping process? Implications of age difference in perceived control. *The Journals of Gerontology. Series B, Psychological Sciences and Social Sciences* **46**(4), 174–180.

Allen J (2008) *Older People and Wellbeing*. Institute for Policy Research, London, UK.

Anderson A (2015) 'Millers Point resale nets owner $590,000'. *Sydney Morning Herald*, 28 June, <http://www.domain.com.au/news/millers-point-resale-nets-owner-590000-20150628-ghzejc/>.

Apps P (1976) Home ownership – the Australian dream. *The Australian Quarterly* **48**(4), 64–75. doi:10.2307/20634876

Arthurson K, Jacobs K (2006) Housing and anti-social behaviour in Australia. In *Housing and Anti-social Behaviour*. (Ed. J Flint) pp. 259–280. Policy Press, Bristol, UK.

Arthurson K, Darcy M, Rogers D (2014) Televised territorial stigma: how social housing tenants experience the fictional media representation of estates in Australia. *Environment & Planning Environment A* **46**(6), 1334–1350. doi:10.1068/a46136

Atkinson R, Habidis D, Easthope H, Goss D (2007) *Sustaining Tenants with Demanding Behaviour: A Review of the Research Evidence, Positioning Paper, No. 97*. Australian Housing and Urban Research Institute, Melbourne.

Audit Office of New South Wales (2013) *Making the Best Use of Public Housing*. Auditor General New South Wales, Sydney, <https://www.audit.nsw.gov.au/ArticleDocuments/280/01_Public_Housing_Full_Report.pdf.aspx?Embed=Y>.

ABS (Australian Bureau of Statistics) (2007) *Census of Population and Housing: Media Releases and Fact Sheets, 2006*. Cat. no. 2914.0.55.002. ABS, Canberra, <http://www.abs.gov.au/ausstats/abs@.nsf/7d12b0f6763c78caca257061001cc588/578a29e8d156afdfca257306000d5799!OpenDocument>.

ABS (2009) *Housing Mobility and Conditions, 2007–08*. Cat. no. 4130.055.022. ABS, Canberra, <http://www.abs.gov.au/AUSSTATS/abs@.nsf/Latestproducts/4130.0.55.002Main%20Features22007-08?opendocument&tabname=Summary&prodno=4130.0.55.002&issue=2007-08&num=&view=>.

ABS (2011) *Australian Social Trends, Sep 2011, Housing Assistance for Renters*. Cat. no. 4102.0. ABS, Canberra, <http://www.abs.gov.au/AUSSTATS/abs@.nsf/Lookup/4102.0Main+Features10Sep+2011#INTRODUCTION>.

ABS (2012a) *Who are Australia's Older People? Reflecting a Nation: Stories from the 2011 Census*. Cat. No. 2071.0. ABS, Canberra, <http://www.abs.gov.au/ausstats/abs@.nsf/Lookup/2071.0main+features752012-2013>.

ABS (2012b) *Housing Tenure Data in the Census*. ABS, Canberra, <http://www.abs.gov.au/websitedbs/censushome.nsf/home/factsheetshtdc?opendocument&navpos=450>.

ABS (2012c) *Year Book Australia, 2012: Housing and Life Cycle Stages*. Cat. no. 1301.0. ABS, Canberra, <http://www.abs.gov.au/ausstats/abs@.nsf/Lookup/by%20Subject/1301.0~2012~Main%20Features~Housing%20and%20life%20cycle%20stages~132>.

ABS (2013a) *Housing Occupancy and Costs 2011–12*. Cat. no. 4130.0. ABS, Canberra, <http://www.abs.gov.au/AUSSTATS/abs@.nsf/DetailsPage/4130.02011-12?OpenDocument>.

ABS (2013b) *Population Projections, Australia, 2012 (Base) To 2101*. Cat. no. 32220. ABS, Canberra, <http://www.abs.gov.au/ausstats/abs@.nsf/Lookup/3222.0main+features52012%20(base)%20to%202101>.

ABS (2013c) *Disability, Ageing and Carers, Australia: Summary of Findings, 2012*. Cat. no. 4430.0. ABS, Canberra, <http://www.abs.gov.au/ausstats/abs@.nsf/Lookup/3A5561E876CDAC73CA257C210011AB9B?opendocument>.

ABS (2013d) *Where and How Do Australia's Older People Live? Reflecting a Nation: Stories from the 2011 Census*. Cat. No. 2071.0. ABS, Canberra, <http://www.abs.gov.au/ausstats/abs@.nsf/Lookup/2071.0main+features602012-2013>.

ABS (2014) *Australian Demographic Statistics, June 2014*. Cat. no. 3101.0. ABS, Canberra

ABS (2015) *Housing Occupancy and Costs, 2013–2014*. Cat. no. 4130.0. ABS, Canberra, <http://www.abs.gov.au/AUSSTATS/abs@.nsf/DetailsPage/4130.02013-14?OpenDocument>.

ACOSS (Australian Council of Social Service) (2002) *Public and Community Housing: A Rescue Package Needed*. ACOSS, Sydney.

Australian Government (2015) *Intergenerational Report, Australia in 2055*. Australian Government, Canberra.

AIHW (Australian Institute of Health and Welfare) (2007) *Older Australians at a Glance*. Cat. no. AGE 52. AIHW, Canberra.

AIHW (2013a) *Housing Assistance in Australia 2013*. Cat. no. HOU 271. AIHW, Canberra, <http://www.aihw.gov.au/WorkArea/DownloadAsset.aspx?id=60129545051>.

AIHW (2013b) *Australia's Welfare 2013*. Cat. no. AUS 174. AIHW, Canberra, <http://www.aihw.gov.au/WorkArea/DownloadAsset.aspx?id=60129544560>.

AIHW (2013c) *National Housing Survey: a Summary of National Results 2012*. Bulletin 117. Cat. no. AUS 172. AIHW, Canberra.

AIHW (2014) *Housing assistance in Australia 2014*. Cat. no. HOU 275. AIHW, Canberra, <http://www.aihw.gov.au/WorkArea/DownloadAsset.aspx?id=60129549033>.

Aylaz R, Akturk U, Erci B, Ozturk H, Asian H (2012) Relationship between depression and loneliness in elderly and examination of influential factors. *Archives of Gerontology and Geriatrics* **55**(3), 548–554. doi:10.1016/j.archger.2012.03.006

Barnes M, Blom A, Cox K, Lessof C (2006) *The Social Exclusion of Older People: Evidence from the First Wave of the English Longitudinal Study of Ageing (ELSA)*. Office of the Deputy Prime Minister, London, UK.

Bartlett H, Peel N (2005) Healthy ageing in the community. In *Ageing and Place*. (Eds GJ Andrews and DR Philips) pp. 98–109. Routledge, London, UK.

Beatty TKM, Blow L, Crossley TF (2009) *Is There a "Heat or Eat" Trade-off in the UK?* Institute for Fiscal Studies, University of Cambridge, Cambridge, UK.

Beck U (2009) *World at Risk*. Polity Press, Cambridge, UK.

Beer A (1993) A dream won, a crisis born? Home ownership and the housing market. In *Housing Australia*. (Ed. C Paris) pp. 147–172. Macmillan, Melbourne.

Beer A (1999) Housing investment and the private rental sector in Australia. *Urban Studies* **36**(2), 255–269. doi:10.1080/0042098993592

Bentley R, Baker E, Mason K (2012) Cumulative exposure to poor housing affordability and its association with mental health in men and women. *Journal of Epidemiology and Community Health* **66**(9), 761–766.

Bentley R, Baker E, Mason K, Subramanian SV, Kavanagh AM (2011) Association between housing affordability and mental health: a longitudinal analysis of a nationally representative household survey in Australia. *American Journal of Epidemiology* **174**(7), 753–760. doi:10.1093/aje/kwr161

Berkman LF (1995) The role of social relations in health promotion. *Psychosomatic Medicine* **57**(3), 245–254. doi:10.1097/00006842-199505000-00006

Biggs S, Phillipson C, Leach R (2007) Baby-boomers and adult ageing: issues for social and public policy. *Quality in Ageing and Older Adults* **8**(3), 32–40. doi:10.1108/14717794200700019

Biggs A, de Boer R, Jolly R, Thomas M (2008) *Parliament of Australia, Budget Review, 2008–09, Social Issues*. Parliamentary Library, Canberra, <http://www.aph.gov.au/library/pubs/RP/BudgetReview/Social_Issues.htm>.

Bounds M, Morris A (2005) High rise gentrification: the redevelopment of Pyrmont Ultimo. *Urban Design International* **10**(4), 179–188. doi:10.1057/palgrave.udi.9000152

Bourassa SC, Greig AW, Troy PN (1995) The limits of housing policy: home ownership in Australia. *Housing Studies* **10**(1), 83–104. doi:10.1080/02673039508720810

Bourdieu P (2002) *The Weight of the World: Social Suffering in Contemporary Society*. Polity Press, Cambridge, UK.

Bourdieu P (2003) *Fighting Back: Against the Tyranny of the Market 2*. Verso, London, UK.

Bowling A, Stafford M (2007) How do objective and subjective assessments of neighbourhood influence social and physical functioning in older age? Finding from a British survey of ageing. *Social Science & Medicine* **64**, 2533–2549. doi:10.1016/j.socscimed.2007.03.009

Brasche S, Bischof B (2005) Daily time spent indoors in German homes – baseline data for the assessment of indoor exposure of German occupants. *International Journal of Hygiene and Environmental Health* **208**(4), 247–253. doi:10.1016/j.ijheh.2005.03.003

Brownie S, Coutts R (2013) Older Australians perceptions and practices in relation to a healthy diet for old age. *The Journal of Nutrition, Health & Aging* **17**(2), 125–129. doi:10.1007/s12603-012-0371-y

Bruce J, McDermott S, Ramia I, Bullen J, Fisher KR (2012) 'Evaluation of the Housing and Accommodation Support Initiative (HASI) Final Report'.

NSW Health and Housing NSW, Social Policy Research Centre Report, Sydney.
Burchardt T, Le Grand J, Piachaud D (2002) Degrees of exclusion: developing a dynamic, multidimensional measure. In *Understanding Social Exclusion*. (Ed. P Agulnik) pp. 30–43. Oxford University Press, Oxford, UK.
Burke T, Ralston L (2004) *Measuring Housing Affordability*. AHURI Research and Policy Bulletin 45. AHURI, Melbourne.
Castles FG (1998) The really big trade-off: home ownership and the welfare state in the New World and the Old. *Acta Politica* **33**(1), 5–19.
Castles F (2005) The Kemeny thesis revisited. *Housing, Theory and Society* **22**(2), 84–86.
Chester L (2015) The privatisation of Australian electricity: claims, myths and facts. *Economic and Labour Relations Review* **26**(2), 218–240. doi:10.1177/1035304615574973
Chester L, Morris A (2011) A new form of energy poverty is the hallmark of liberalised electricity sectors. *The Australian Journal of Social Issues* **46**(4), 435–459.
Choi NG (1996) Older persons who move: reasons and health consequences. *Journal of Applied Gerontology* **15**, 325–344. doi:10.1177/073346489601500304
Chrisopoulis S, Beckwith K, Harford JE (2011) *Oral Health and Dental Care in Australia: Key Facts and Figures 2011*. Cat no. Den 214. AIHW, Canberra.
Colic-Peisker V, Ong R, Wood G (2015) Asset poverty, precarious housing and ontological security in older age: an Australian case study. *International Journal of Housing Policy* **15**(2), 167–186. doi:10.1080/14616718.2014.984827
Connolly S (2012) Housing tenure and older people. *Reviews in Clinical Gerontology* **22**(4), 286–292. doi:10.1017/S0959259812000123
Cook JT, Frank DA (2008) Food security, poverty and human development in the United States. *Annals of the New York Academy of Sciences* **1136**, 193–209. doi:10.1196/annals.1425.001
COTA (Council on the Ageing) (2012) *COTA Australia: Policy and Position Statements*. COTA, Canberra, <http://www.cota.org.au/lib/pdf/COTA_Australia/public_policy/policy_compendium_dec_2012.pdf>.
COTA (2014) *Submission into Inquiry into National Health Amendment (Pharmaceutical Benefits Bill)*. COTA, Canberra, <http://www.cota.org.au/lib/pdf/COTA_Australia/publications/submissions/submission_pbs_inquiry_july_2014.pdf Accessed 5 June 2015>.
Cox W, Pavletich H (2016) *12th Annual Demographia International Housing Affordability Survey: 2015: Rating Middle Income Housing Affordability*.

Wendell Cox Consultancy, Belleville IL, USA, <http://www.demographia.com/dhi.pdf>.

Cutcher N, Patterson Ross L (2014) *Affordable Housing and the New South Wales Rental Market.* Tenants Union of New South Wales, Sydney.

Dahlin-Ivanoff S, Haak M, Fange A, Iwarsson S (2007) The multiple meaning of home as experienced by very old Swedish people. *Scandinavian Journal of Occupational Therapy* **14**, 25–32. doi:10.1080/11038120601151714

Daley J, McGannon C, Savage J, Hunter A (2013) *Balancing Budgets: Tough Choices We Need.* Grattan Institute, Canberra.

Dalton T, Rowe J (2004) A wasting resource: public housing and drug use in inner-city Melbourne. *Housing Studies* **19**(2), 229–244. doi:10.1080/0267303032000168612

Danermark BD, Ekstrom ME, Bodin LL (1996) Effects of residential relocation on mortality and morbidity among elderly people. *European Journal of Public Health* **6**, 212–217. doi:10.1093/eurpub/6.3.212

Darab S, Hartman Y (2013) Understanding single older women's invisibility in housing issues in Australia. *Housing, Theory and Society* **30**(4), 348–367.

Darmon N, Drewnowski A (2008) Does social class predict diet quality? *The American Journal of Clinical Nutrition* **87**, 1107–1117.

Davey J (2007) Older people and transport; coping without a car. *Ageing and Society* **27**(1), 49–65. doi:10.1017/S0144686X06005332

de Jonge D, Jones A, Phillips R, Chung M (2011) Understanding the essence of home: older people's experience of home in Australia. *Occupational Therapy International* **18**(1), 39–47. doi:10.1002/oti.312

De Nardi M, French E, Bailey Jones J (2009) *Why Do the Elderly Save? The Role of Medical Expenses.* Federal Reserve Bank of Chicago, Chicago IL, USA.

de Quadros-Wander S, de McGillivary J, Broadbent J (2014) The influence of perceived control on subjective wellbeing in later life. *Social Indicators Research* **115**, 999–1010. doi:10.1007/s11205-013-0243-9

de Vries R, Blane D (2013) Fuel poverty and the health of older people: the role of local climate. *Journal of Public Health* **35**(3), 361–366. doi:10.1093/pubmed/fds094

Despres C, Lord S (2005) Growing older in postwar suburbs: the meanings and experiences of home. In *Home and Identity in Late Life: International Perspectives.* (Eds G Rawls and H Chaudhury) pp. 317–342. Springer, New York.

Doling J, Horsewood N (2011) Home ownership and pensions: causality and the really big trade-off. *Housing, Theory and Society* **28**(2), 166–182. doi:10.1080/14036096.2010.534269

Dreze J, Sen A (2002) *India: Development and Participation.* Oxford University Press, Oxford, UK.

Dupuis A, Thorns DC (1996) Meaning of home for older home owners. *Housing Studies* **11**(4), 485–501. doi:10.1080/02673039608720871

Dupuis A, Thorns DC (1998) Home, home ownership, and the search for ontological security. *The Sociological Review* **46**(1), 24–47. doi:10.1111/1467-954X.00088

Easterbrook L (2002) *Healthy Homes, Healthy Lives; Health Improvement Through Housing Related Initiatives and Services.* Care and Repair, London, UK.

Easthope H (2004) A place called home. *Housing, Theory and Society* **21**(3), 128–138.

Easthope H (2014) Making a rental property home. *Housing Studies* **29**(5), 579–596.

Eccles S (2015) 'One in three to face renting in retirement by 2040: millions of future pensioners face later years in properties they don't own'. *Daily Mail Australia*, 23 July, <http://www.dailymail.co.uk/news/article-3168885/One-three-face-renting-retirement-2040-Millions-future-pensioners-face-later-years-properties-don-t-levels-home-ownership-plummet.html>.

Elias N, Scotson JL (1994) *Established and the Outsiders.* Sage Publications, London, UK.

Ellen IG, Turner MA (1997) Does neighbourhood matter? Assessing recent evidence. *Housing Policy Debate* **8**(4), 833–866. doi:10.1080/10511482.1997.9521280

Elliot P, Wadley D (2013) Residents speak out: reappraising home ownership, property rights and place attachment in a risk society. *Housing, Theory and Society* **30**(2), 131–155.

Engelhardt GV, Eriksen MD, Greenlhalgh-Stanley N (2013) *A Profile of Housing and Health Among Older Americans.* Research Institute for Housing America, Macarthur Foundation, Chicago IL, USA.

Evans GW (2003) Housing and mental health: a review of the evidence and a methodological and conceptual critique. *The Journal of Social Issues* **59**(3), 475–500. doi:10.1111/1540-4560.00074

Fine M, Spencer R (2009) *Social Isolation: Development of an Assessment Tool for HACC services.* Centre for Research on Social Inclusion, Macquarie University, Sydney.

Fitzpatrick S, Pawson H (2014) Ending security of tenure for social renters: transitioning to 'ambulance service' social housing? *Housing Studies* **29**(5), 597–615. doi:10.1080/02673037.2013.803043

Flint J (2006) Maintaining an arm's length? Housing, community governance and the management of problematic populations. *Housing Studies* **21**(2), 171–186. doi:10.1080/02673030500484695

Furst T, Connors M, Bisogni CA, Sobal J, Winter L (1996) Food choice: a conceptual model of the process. *Appetite* **26**, 247–266. doi:10.1006/appe.1996.0019

Gardiner S (2014) 'NSW elective surgery waiting times remain the longest in Australia'. *Sydney Morning Herald*, 20 October.

Giddens A (1991) *Modernity and Self Identity*. Policy Press, Cambridge, UK.

Gilroy R (2005) The role of housing space in determining freedom and flourishing in older people. *Social Indicators Research* **74**(1), 141–158.

Giskes K, Turell G, Patterson C, Newman B (2002) Socio-economic differences in fruit and vegetable consumption among adolescents and adults. *Public Health Nutrition* **5**, 663–669. doi:10.1079/PHN2002339

Goward P (2014) 'No room for nostalgia in Millers Point debate'. *Sydney Morning Herald*, 2 April. <http://www.smh.com.au/comment/no-room-for-nostalgia-in-millers-point-debate-20140402-zqpn4.html#ixzz2xrWVPNvw>.

Harvey D (2007) Neoliberalism as creative destruction. *The Annals of the American Academy of Political and Social Science* **610**, 21–44. doi:10.1177/0002716206296780

Hasham N (2014) 'Government downplayed death warning at Millers Point'. *Sydney Morning Herald*, 11 August.

Hastings A (2004) Stigma and social housing estates: beyond pathological explanations. *Journal of Housing and the Built Environment* **19**, 233–254. doi:10.1007/s10901-004-0723-y

Hayward D (1996) The reluctant landlords? A history of public housing in Australia'. *Urban Policy and Research* **14**(1), 5–35. doi:10.1080/08111149608551610

Heywood F, Oldman C, Means R (2002) *Housing and Home in Later Life*. Open University Press, London, UK.

Higgs PF, Hyde M, Gilleard CJ, Victor CR, Wiggins RD, Jones IR (2009) From passive to active consumers? Later life consumption in the UK from 1968 to 2005. *The Sociological Review* **57**(1), 102–124. doi:10.1111/j.1467-954X.2008.01806.x

Hiscock R, Kearns A, Macintyre S, Ellaway A (2001) Ontological security and psychosocial benefits from the home: qualitative evidence on issues of tenure. *Housing, Theory and Society* **18**(1–2), 50–66. doi:10.1080/14036090120617

Holstein JA, Gubrium JF (2003) Active interviewing. In *Postmodern Interviewing*. (Eds JA Holstein and JF Gubrium) pp. 67–80. Sage, Thousand Oaks CA, USA.

Howden-Chapman P, Signal L, Crane J (1999) Housing and health in older people; ageing in place. *Social Policy Journal of New Zealand* **13**, 14–30.

Howden-Chapman PL, Chandola T, Stafford M, Marmot M (2011) The effect of housing on the mental health of older people: the impact of lifetime housing history in Whitehall 2. *BMC Public Health* **11**(682), 1–8.

HSBC (2007) *The Future of Retirement Study: the New Old Age*. Global Report. HSBC Insurance Holdings: London, UK, <http://www.hsbc.com/1/2/retirement/future-of-retirement/ future-of-retirement-2007>.

Hulse K, Milligan V (2014) Secure occupancy: a new framework for analysing security in rental housing. *Housing Studies* **29**(5), 638–656. doi:10.1080/02673037.2013.873116

Hulse K, Saugeres L (2008) 'Housing insecurity and precarious living: an Australian exploration'. Final Report No. 124. AHURI, Melbourne.

Hulse K, Milligan V, Easthope H (2011) 'Secure occupancy in rental housing: conceptual foundations and comparative perspectives'. Final Report No. 170. AHURI, Melbourne.

Hulse K, Burke T, Ralston L, Stone W (2012) 'The Australian private rental sector: changes and challenges'. Positioning paper No. 149. AHURI, Melbourne.

Izuhara M, Heywood F (2003) A life-time of inequality; a structural analysis of housing careers and issues facing older private renters. *Ageing and Society* **23**(2), 207–224. doi:10.1017/S0144686X02001125

Jacobs K, Atkinson R, Colic-Peisker V, Berry M, Dalton T (2010) 'What future for public housing'. Final Report No. 151. AHURI, Melbourne.

Jacobs K, Arthurson K, Cica N, Greenwood A, Hastings A (2011) 'The stigmatization of social housing: findings from a panel investigation'. Final Report No. 166. AHURI, Melbourne.

Janda M (2015) 'Australian housing near world's most expensive but forecast to rise further'. ABC News, Sydney, 15 January, <http://www.abc.net.au/news/2015-01-15/australian-housing-near-most-expensive-but-forecast-to-rise/6018696>.

Johnstone T (2014) 'Millers Point named the next prestige suburb as housing sell-off delivers record results'. *The Sydney Morning Herald*, 13 September, <http://smh.domain.com.au/real-estate-news/millers-point-named-the-next-prestige-suburb-as-housing-selloff-delivers-record-results-20140912-10ewnj.html>.

Johnstone MJ, Kanitsaki O (2009) Population ageing and the politics of demographic alarmism: implications for the nursing profession. *Journal of Advanced Nursing* **26**(3), 86–92.

Jones K (2015) 'Grey divorce'. *The Sun-Herald*, 31 May.

Jones A, Petersen M (2014) Older homeless people. In *Homelessness in Australia*. (Eds C Chamberlain, C Johnson, S Mallet and C Robinson) pp. 135–154. UNSW Press, Sydney.

Jones A, Bell M, Tilse C, Earl G (2007) 'Rental housing provision for lower-income older Australians'. Final report. AHURI, Melbourne.

Judd B, Olsberg D, Quinn J, Groenhart L, Demirbilek O (2010) 'Dwelling, land and neighbourhood use by older homeowners'. Final report No. 144. AHURI, Sydney.

Kearns A, Hiscock R, Ellaway A, Macintyre S (2000) 'Beyond four walls'. The psycho-social benefits of home. Evidence from West Central Scotland. *Housing Studies* **15**(3), 387–410. doi:10.1080/02673030050009249

Kemeny J (1977) A political sociology of home ownership in Australia. *Journal of Sociology* **13**(1), 47–52. doi:10.1177/144078337701300110

Kemeny J (1980) Home ownership and privatisation. *International Journal of Urban and Regional Research* **4**(3), 372–388. doi:10.1111/j.1468-2427.1980.tb00812.x

Kemeny J (2001) Comparative housing and welfare: theorising the relationship. *Journal of Housing and the Built Environment* **16**, 53–70. doi:10.1023/A:1011526416064

Kemeny J (2005) 'The really big trade-off' between home ownership and welfare: Castles' evaluation of the 1980 thesis, and a reformulation 25 years on. *Housing, Theory and Society* **22**(2), 59–75.

Kemeny J (2006) Corporatism and housing regimes. *Housing, Theory and Society* **23**(1), 1–18.

Kemp B, Paleologos Z, King S, Bellamy J (2016) *Rental Affordability Snapshot 2016. Greater Sydney & the Illawarra*. Anglicare, Sydney.

Kendig H, Bridge C (2007) Housing policy for a long-lived society. In *Ageing and Social Policy in Australia*. (Eds A Borowski, S Encel and E Ozanne) pp. 219–238. UNSW Press, Sydney.

King N, Horrocks C (2012) *Interviews in Qualitative Research*. Sage, London, UK.

Kneale D (2012) *Is Social Exclusion Still Important for Older People?* The International Longevity Centre, London, UK.

KPMG (2012) *Social Housing Initiative Review for Housing Ministers' Advisory Committee*. KPMG, Sydney.

Krieger J, Higgins DL (2002) Housing and health: time again for public health action. *Journal of Public Health* **92**(5), 758–768.

La Gory M, Ward R, Sherman S (1985) The ecology of aging: neighbourhood satisfaction in an older population. *The Sociological Quarterly* **26**(3), 405–418. doi:10.1111/j.1533-8525.1985.tb00235.x

Lawson J (2009) The transformation of social housing provision in Switzerland mediated by federalism, direct democracy and the urban/rural divide. *International Journal of Housing Policy* **9**(1), 45–67. doi:10.1080/14616710802693599

Lawton MP (1983) Environment and other determinants of well-being in older people. *The Gerontologist* **23**(4), 349–357. doi:10.1093/geront/23.4.349

Lawton MP (2000) Chance and choice make a good life. In *A History of Geropsychology in Autobiography*. (Eds JE Birren and JF Schroots) pp. 185–196. American Psychological Association, Washington DC.

Levenson R, Jeyasingham M, Joule N (2005) *Looking Forward to Care in Old Age; Expectations of the Next Generation*. King's Fund, London, UK, <http://www.kingsfund.org.uk/resources/publications/looking_forward.html>.

Libman K, Fields D, Saegert S (2012) Housing and health: a social ecological perspective on the US foreclosure crisis. *Housing, Theory and Society* **29**(1), 1–24.

Mallett S, Bentley R, Baker E, Mason K, Key D, Kolar V, Krnjacki L (2011) 'Precarious housing and health inequalities: what are the links?' Summary Report. Hanover Welfare Services, University of Melbourne, University of Adelaide, Melbourne Citymission, Melbourne.

Mansveldt J (2008) Ageing places – urban spaces: insights from interviews and focus groups into the spatiality of later life. In *Qualitative Urban Analysis: An International Perspective*. (Eds PJ Maginn, SM Thomson and M Tonts) pp. 197–212. Emerald Group, Bingley, UK, <http://www.emeraldinsight.com/doi/book/10.1016/S1042-3192%282008%299>.

Margetts BM, Thompson RL, Elia M, Jackson AA (2003) Prevalence of risk of undernutrition is associated with poor health status in older people in the UK. *European Journal of Clinical Nutrition* **57**, 69–74. doi:10.1038/sj.ejcn.1601499

Marston G (2004) *Social Policy and Discourse Analysis*. Ashgate, Aldershot, UK.

Mazzoldi R (2014) 'Millers Point: a long history'. *Tenant News* 108, November.

McEwen BS (2008) Central effects of stress hormones in health and disease: understanding the protective and damaging effects of stress and stress mediators. *European Journal of Pharmacology* **583**(2–3), 174–185. doi:10.1016/j.ejphar.2007.11.071

McIntosh G (1997) *Reforming Public Housing, Current Issues, Brief 31, 1996–97*. Parliament of Australia, Parliamentary Library, Canberra.

McNicholas J, Collis GM (2000) Dogs as catalysts for social interactions: robustness of the effect. *British Journal of Psychology* **91**, 61–70. doi:10.1348/000712600161673

McNicholas J, Gilbey A, Rennie A, Ahmedzai S, Dono J-A, Ormerod E (2005) Pet ownership and human health: a brief review of evidence and issues. *British Medical Journal* **331**(7527), 1252–1254. doi:10.1136/bmj.331.7527.1252

McPherson M, Smith-Lovin L, Cook JM (2001) Birds of a feather: homophily in social networks. *Annual Review of Sociology* **27**, 415–444. doi:10.1146/annurev.soc.27.1.415

Means R (2007) Safe as houses? Ageing in place and vulnerable older people in the UK. *Social Policy & Administration* **41**(1), 65–85.

Mee K (2007) 'I ain't been to heaven yet? Living here, this is heaven to me': public housing and the making of home in inner Newcastle. *Housing, Theory and Society* **24**(3), 207–228.

MIAESR (Melbourne Institute of Applied Economic and Social Research) (2012) *Poverty Lines: Australia – December Quarter*. MIAESR, The University of Melbourne, Melbourne, <https://melbourneinstitute.com/downloads/publications/Poverty%20Lines/Poverty-Lines-Australia-Dec-2011.pdf>.

MIAESR (2015) *Poverty Lines: Australia – December Quarter, 2014*. MIAESR, The University of Melbourne, Melbourne, <https://melbourneinstitute.com/downloads/publications/Poverty%20Lines/Poverty-lines-Australia_Dec2014.pdf>.

Morris A (2007) On the edge: the financial situation of older renters in the private rental market. *The Australian Journal of Social Issues* **42**(3), 337–350.

Morris A (2009) Living on the margins: comparing older private renters and older public housing tenants in Sydney, Australia. *Housing Studies* **24**(5), 693–707.

Morris A, Wilson S (2014) Struggling on unemployment benefits (Newstart) in Australia: the experience of a neoliberal form of employment assistance. *Economic and Labour Relations Review* **25**(2), 202–221. doi:10.1177/1035304614533462

Morris A, Judd B, Kavanagh K (2005) Marginality amidst plenty: pathways into homelessness for older Australians. *The Australian Journal of Social Issues* **40**(2), 241–251.

Motel A, Künemund H, Bode C (2000) Wohnen und Wohnumfeld älterer Menschen. [Housing and living arrangements of older adults.] In *Die zweite Lebenshälfte – Gesellschaftliche Lage und Partizipation im Spiegel des Alters-Survey [The Second Half of Life – Societal Stage and Participation in the Light of the 'Alters-Survey'.]* (Eds M Kohli and H Künemund) pp. 124–175. Leske & Budrich, Opladen, Germany.

Mowbray R (2010) Rough justice from the consumer, trader and tenancy tribunal. *Around the House* **81**, 7–8.

Mowbray R (2011) On retaliation. *Around the House* **85**, 12–13.

Mowbray R (2015a) When older people are forced to move. *Around the House* **101**, 18–23.

Mowbray R (2015b) The new face of poverty … older private renters. *Tenant News* **110**, 10–11.

Mowbray R, Boulton A (2011) Proposal to repeal landlord and tenant legislation: it's problematic. *Around the House* **87**, 13–15.

Muir K, Fisher K, Dadich A, Abelló D (2008) Challenging the exclusion of people with mental illness: the Mental Health and Accommodation Support Initiative. *The Australian Journal of Social Issues* **43**(2), 271–290.

Mullan P (2002) *The Imaginary Time Bomb: Why an Ageing Population Is Not a Social Problem*. I.B. Taurus, New York.

Naidoo Y, Morris A (2014) 'The centrality of housing tenure: further perspectives on the lives of older public and private renters in Australia'. Unpublished paper presented to the International Seminar on the Living Standard and Housing of the Elderly, comparing Australia and Japan. Tokyo [available from author].

New South Wales Government (2006) *Housing Assistance for Elderly Clients*. Housing NSW, Sydney, <http://www.housing.nsw.gov.au/Forms+Policies+and+Fact+Sheets/Policies/Housing+Assistance+for+Elderly+Clients+-+ALL0030D.htm>.

New South Wales Government (2010) *NSW Residential Tenancies Act 2010*, No. 42. NSW Government, Sydney, <http://www.legislation.nsw.gov.au/inforce/cfa8f374-676d-6eea-811e-95d70730f313/2010-42.pdf>.

New South Wales Government (2013) *NSW Affordable Housing Guidelines*. Family and Community Services, Housing NSW, Sydney.

New South Wales Government (2014) *Social Housing in NSW. A Discussion Paper for Input and Comment*. New South Wales Government, Family and Community Services, Sydney.

New South Wales Government (2015a) 'Rent and Sales Report No. 111'. Department of Family and Community Services, Sydney, <http://www.

housing.nsw.gov.au/NR/rdonlyres/F6A0E684-2BFE-4A1A-8309-75B0CB33A324/0/1Rent_SaleReport111.pdf>.
New South Wales Government (2015b) *Older Drivers*. Roads & Maritime, NSW Government, Sydney, <http://www.rms.nsw.gov.au/roads/licence/older-drivers/index.html>.
New South Wales Government (2016a) 'Rent and Sales Report No. 114'. Department of Family and Community Services, Sydney, <http://www.housing.nsw.gov.au/__data/assets/file/0003/361173/R-and-S-Report-114.pdf>.
New South Wales Government (2016b) *Unique Millers Point Property Sold*. Finances, Services & Innovation, Sydney, <https://www.finance.nsw.gov.au/about-us/media-releases/unique-millers-point-property-sold>.
Nussbaum M (2003) Capabilities as fundamental entitlements: Sen and social justice. *Feminist Economics* **9**(2), 33–59. doi:10.1080/1354570022000077926
O'Sullivan E, De Decker P (2007) Regulating the private rental housing market in Europe. *European Journal of Homelessness* **1**, 95–117.
Oswald F, Wahl H-W (2005) Dimensions of the meaning of home. In *Home and Identity in Late Life: International Perspectives.* (Eds GD Rowles and H Chaudhury) pp. 21–45. Springer, New York.
Oswald F, Wahl H-W, Schilling O, Nygren C, Fange A, Sixsmith A, *et al.* (2007) Relationships between housing and healthy aging in very old age. *The Gerontologist* **47**(1), 96–107. doi:10.1093/geront/47.1.96
Oswald F, Jopp D, Rott C, Wahl H-W (2011) Is ageing in place a resource for or risk to life satisfaction? *The Gerontologist* **51**(2), 238–250. doi:10.1093/geront/gnq096
Padgett DK (2007) There's no place like (a) home: ontological security among persons with serious mental illness in the United States. *Social Science & Medicine* **64**(9), 1925–1936. doi:10.1016/j.socscimed.2007.02.011
Palmer C, Ziersch A, Arthurson K, Baum F (2004) Challenging the stigma of public housing: preliminary findings from a qualitative study in South Australia. *Urban Policy and Research* **22**(4), 411–426. doi:10.1080/0811114042000296326
Palmer C, Ziersch A, Arthurson K, Baum F (2005) 'Danger lurks around every corner': fear of crime and its impact on opportunities for social interaction in stigmatized Australian suburbs. *Urban Policy and Research* **23**(4), 393–411. doi:10.1080/08111470500354216
Paris C (1993) *Housing Australia*. Macmillan, Melbourne.
Parliament of Australia (2007) *Measures to Increase Affordable Rental Housing*. Parliament of Australia, Canberra, <http://www.aph.gov.au/

Parliamentary_Business/Committees/Senate/Former_Committees/hsaf/report/c10>.

Parslow RA, Jorm AF, Christensen H, Rodgers B, Jacomb P (2005) Pet ownership and health in older adults: findings from a survey of 2551 community based Australians aged 60–64. *Gerontology* **51**, 40–47. doi:10.1159/000081433

Pawson H, Gilmour T (2010) Transforming Australia's social housing – pointers from the British stock transfer experience. *Urban Policy and Research* **28**(3), 241–260. doi:10.1080/08111146.2010.497135

Pawson H, Milligan V, Wiesel I, Hulse K (2013) 'Public housing transfers in Australia: past, present and prospective.' Final report No 215. AHURI, Sydney.

Petersen M, Parsell C, Phillips R, White G (2014) 'Preventing first time homelessness amongst older Australians.' Final report No. 222. AHURI, Brisbane.

Petersen M (2015) Addressing older women's homelessness: service and housing models. *Australian Journal of Social Issues* **50**(4), 419–438.

Petersen M, Parsell C (2015) Homeless for the first time in later life: an Australian study. *Housing Studies* **30**(3), 368–391. doi:10.1080/02673037.2014.963522

Phibbs P, Thompson S (2011) 'The health impacts of housing: towards a policy relevant research agenda'. Final report 173. AHURI, Melbourne.

Phillipson C (1998) *Reconstructing Old Age: New Agendas in Social Theory and Practice*. Sage, London, UK.

Phillipson C (2007) The 'elected' and the 'excluded': sociological perspectives on the experience of place and community in old age. *Ageing and Society* **27**, 321–342. doi:10.1017/S0144686X06005629

Phillipson C (2011) Developing age-friendly communities: new approaches to growing old in urban environments. In *Handbook of Sociology of Aging*. (Eds RA Settersten and JL Angel) pp. 279–293. Springer, New York.

Phillipson C, Baars J (2007) Social theory and social ageing. In *Ageing in Society*. (Eds J Bond, S Peace, F Dittmann-Kohl and G Westerhof) pp. 68–84. Sage, London, UK.

Pressman SD, Cohen S (2005) Does positive affect influence health? *Psychological Bulletin* **131**, 925–971. doi:10.1037/0033-2909.131.6.925

Productivity Commission (1993) *Public Housing, Volume 2*. Report No. 34. Australian Government, Canberra.

Productivity Commission (2013) *An Ageing Australia: Preparing for the Future*. Commission Research Paper Overview. Australian Government, Canberra.

Rapley TJ (2001) The art(fullness) of open-ended interviewing: some considerations on analysing interviews. *Qualitative Research* **1**(3), 303–323.

Ravetz A (2001) *Council Housing and Culture: A History of a Social Experiment.* Routledge, London, UK.

Ritzer G (2001) *Explorations in the Sociology of Consumption: Fast Foods, Credit Cards and Casinos.* Sage, London, UK.

Robb K (2015) 'Biggest jump in Sydney rents in five years: domain group'. *Sydney Morning Herald* 9 July, <http://news.domain.com.au/domain/real-estate-news/biggest-jump-in-sydney-rents-in-five-years-domain-group-20150708-gi7q92.html>.

Rose N (2001) Community citizenship and the third way. In *Citizenship and Cultural Policy.* (Eds D Merydyth and J Minson) pp. 1–17. Sage, London, UK.

Ross C (2000) Neighborhood disadvantage and adult depression. *Journal of Health and Social Behavior* **41**, 177–187. doi:10.2307/2676304

Rothbaum FM, Weisz JR, Snyder SS (1982) Changing the world and changing the self: A two-process model of perceived control. *Journal of Personality and Social Psychology* **42**, 5–37.

Rowles GD, Ravdal H (2002) Ageing, place, and meaning in the face of changing circumstances. In *Challenges of the Third Age: Meaning and Purpose in Later Life.* (Eds S Weiss and SA Bass) pp. 81–114. Oxford University Press, Oxford, UK.

Rubinstein RL (1989) The home environment of older people: a description of the psychosocial processes linking person to place. *Journal of Gerontology* **44**(2), 45–53.

Sampson G (2009) Weight loss and malnutrition in the elderly – the shared role of GPs and ADPs. *Australian Family Physician* **38**, 507–510.

Saunders P (1989) The meaning of home in contemporary English culture. *Housing Studies* **4**(3), 177–192. doi:10.1080/02673038908720658

Saunders P, Naidoo Y, Griffiths M (2007) Towards New Indicators of Disadvantage: Deprivation and Social Exclusion in Australia. Social Policy Research Centre, Sydney.

Saunders P (2011) *Down and Out: Poverty and Exclusion in Australia.* The Policy Press, Bristol, UK.

Scanlon K, Whitehead C, Arrigoita F (2014) Introduction. In *Social Housing in Europe.* (Eds K Scanlon, C Whitehead and F Arrigoita) pp. 1–20. Blackwell, Oxford, UK.

Scatigna M, Szemere R, Tsatsaronis K (2014) Residential property price statistics across the globe. Bank of International Settlements (BIS), Basel, Switzerland, <http://www.bis.org/publ/qtrpdf/r_qt1409h.htm>.

Scharf T, Phillipson C, Smith A, Kingston P (2002) *Growing Older in Socially Deprived Areas*. Help the Aged, London, UK.

Scheidt RJ, Norris-Baker C (2003) Many meanings of community. *Journal of Housing for the Elderly* **17**(1), 55–66. doi:10.1300/J081v17n01_05

Seelig T, Thompson A, Burke T, Pinnegar S, McNelis Morris A (2009) 'Understanding what motivates households to become and remain investors in the private rental market'. Final report 130. AHURI, Melbourne.

Sen A (1988) Freedom of choice. *European Economic Review* **32**(2–3), 269–294.

Sen A (1999) *Development as Freedom*. Oxford University Press, Oxford, UK.

Sen A (2000) *Social Exclusion: Concept, Application and Scrutiny*. Social Development Papers No. 1. Office of Environment and Social Development, Asian Development Bank, Manila, Philippines.

Sen A (2002) *Rationality and Freedom*. The Belknap Press of Harvard University Press, Cambridge, MA, USA.

Sen A (2009) Capability: reach and limits. In *Debating Global Society Reach and Limits of the Capability Approach*. (Ed. E Chippero-Martinetti) pp. 15–28. Fondazione Gingiacomo Feltrinelli, Milan, Italy.

Shon J-LPK (2007) Residents' perceptions of their neighbourhood: disentangling dissatisfaction, a French survey. *Urban Studies* **44**(11), 2231–2268. doi:10.1080/00420980701518966

Singh A, Misra N (2009) Loneliness, depression and sociability in old age. *Industrial Psychiatry Journal* **18**(1), 51–55. doi:10.4103/0972-6748.57861

Sixsmith A, Sixsmith J (2008) Ageing in place in the United Kingdom. *Ageing International* **32**(3), 219–235. doi:10.1007/s12126-008-9019-y

Slater T (2009) Missing Marcuse: on gentrification and displacement. *City: analysis of urban trends, culture, theory, policy, action* **13**(2–3), 292–311.

Smith SJ, Easterlow D, Munro M, Turner KM (2003) Housing as health capital: how health trajectories and housing paths are linked. *The Journal of Social Issues* **59**(3), 501–525. doi:10.1111/1540-4560.00075

Smith SK, Rayer S, Smith EA (2008) Aging and disability: implications for the housing industry and housing policy in the United States. *Journal of the American Planning Association* **74**(3), 289–306. doi:10.1080/01944360802197132

Somerville P (1992) Homelessness and the meaning of home: rooflessness or rootlessness? *International Journal of Urban and Regional Research* **16**(4), 529–539. doi:10.1111/j.1468-2427.1992.tb00194.x

Span P (2015) 'At home, many seniors are imprisoned by their independence'. *New York Times*, 19 June, <http://www.nytimes.com/2015/06/23/health/at-home-many-seniors-are-imprisoned-by-their-independence.html?rref=collection%2Fcolumn%2Fthe-new-old-age&_r=0>.

SCRGSP (Steering Committee for the Review of Government Service Provision) (2015) 'Report on Government Services 2015'. Productivity Commission, Commonwealth of Australia, Canberra.

Stone W, Burke T, Hulse K, Ralston L (2013) 'Long-term private rental in a changing Australian private rental sector'. Final Report No. 209. AHURI, Melbourne.

Sturges JE, Hanrahan KJ (2004) Comparing telephone and face-to-face qualitative interviewing; a research note. *Qualitative Research* **4**, 107–118. doi:10.1177/1468794104041110

Sweet E, Nandi A, Adam E, McDade TW (2013) The high price of debt: household financial debt and its impact on mental and physical health. *Social Science & Medicine* **91**, 94–100. doi:10.1016/j.socscimed.2013.05.009

Tausig JE, Freeman EW (1988) The next best thing to being there: conducting the clinical research interview by telephone. *The American Journal of Orthopsychiatry* **58**(3), 418–427. doi:10.1111/j.1939-0025.1988.tb01602.x

Taylor-Gooby P, Dean H, Munro M, Parker G (1999) Risk and the welfare state. *The British Journal of Sociology* **50**(2), 177–194. doi:10.1111/j.1468-4446.1999.00177.x

Tenants Union of New South Wales (2015) *Submission on the Discussion Paper 'Social Housing in NSW'*. Tenants Union of New South Wales, Sydney.

Thomas A, Garland R (1993) Supermarket shopping lists: their effect on consumer expenditure. *International Journal of Retail & Distribution Management* **21**(2), 8–14. doi:10.1108/09590559310028040

Torgersen U (1987) Housing: the wobbly pillar under the welfare state. In *Between State and Market: Housing in the Post-Industrial Era*. (Eds B Turner, J Kemeny and L Lundqvist) pp. 116–127. Almqvist and Wicksell International, Stockholm, Sweden.

Troy P (2012) *Accommodating Australians: Commonwealth Government Involvement in Housing*. The Federation Press, Sydney.

Tuan Y (1980) Rootedness versus sense of place. *Landscape* **24**, 3–8.

Twigg J, Majima S (2014) Consumption and the constitution of age: expenditure patterns on clothing, hair and cosmetics among post-war 'baby boomers'. *Journal of Aging Studies* **30**, 23–32. doi:10.1016/j.jaging.2014.03.003

Uchino BN (2009) Understanding the links between social support and physical health: a life-span perspective with emphasis on the separability of perceived and received support. *Perspectives on Psychological Science* **4**(3), 236–255. doi:10.1111/j.1745-6924.2009.01122.x

United Nations (1991) *The Right to Adequate Housing, Article 11 (1): CESCR General Comment 4*. United Nations, Office of the High Commissioner for Human Rights, Geneva, Switzerland.

United Nations (1997) *The Right to Adequate Housing, Article 11 (1): CESCR General Comment 7, Forced Evictions*. United Nations, Office of the High Commissioner for Human Rights, Geneva, Switzerland.

Victor C, Scambler SJ, Bowling A, Bond J (2005) The prevalence of, and risk factors for, loneliness in late life: a survey of older people in Great Britain. *Ageing and Society* **25**(3), 357–375. doi:10.1017/S0144686X04003332

Vincent JA (2006) Ageing contested: anti-ageing society and the cultural construction of old age. *Sociology* **40**(4), 681–698. doi:10.1177/0038038506065154

Wacquant L (2007) Pierre Bourdieu. In *Key Sociological Thinkers*. (Ed. R Stones) pp. 261–277. Palgrave Macmillan, New York.

Wacquant L (2008) *Urban Outcasts: A Comparative Sociology of Advanced Marginality*. Polity, Cambridge, UK.

Walker RB, Hillier JE (2007) Places and health: a qualitative study to explore how older women living alone perceive the social and physical dimensions of their neighbourhoods. *Social Science & Medicine* **65**(6), 1154–1165. doi:10.1016/j.socscimed.2007.04.031

Walker J, Mitchell R, Petticrew M, Platt S (2009) The effects on health of a publicly funded domestic heating programme: a prospective controlled study. *Journal of Epidemiology and Community Health* **63**(1), 12–17. doi:10.1136/jech.2008.074096

Waters A-M (2002) 'Do housing conditions make a difference to our health? Home ownership and renting in Australia'. AHURI Research and Policy Bulletin, Issue 6. AHURI, Melbourne.

Watson S (1988) *Accommodating Inequality: Gender and Housing*. Allen & Unwin, Sydney.

Watt P (2006) Respectability, roughness and 'race': neighbourhood place images and the making of working-class social distinctions in London. *International Journal of Urban and Regional Research* **30**(4), 776–797. doi:10.1111/j.1468-2427.2006.00688.x

Watt P (2013) 'It's not for us'. *City* **17**(1), 99–118. doi:10.1080/13604813.2012.754190

Wellman B, Leighton B (1979) Networks, neighbourhoods and communities: approaches to the study of the community question. *Urban Affairs Review* **14**(3), 363–390. doi:10.1177/107808747901400305

Wesley Mission (2015) 'The Wesley report: facing financial stress 2015'. Wesley Mission, Sydney.

Wiles JL, Allen RES, Palmer AJ, Hayman KJ, Keeling S, Ngaire K (2009) Older people and their social spaces: a study of well-being and attachment to place in Aotearoa New Zealand. *Social Science & Medicine* **68**(4), 664–671. doi:10.1016/j.socscimed.2008.11.030

Wiles JL, Leibing A, Guberman N, Reeve J, Allen RE (2012) The meaning of 'ageing in place' to older people. *The Gerontologist* **52**(3), 357–366. doi:10.1093/geront/gnr098

Wilkinson J (2005) *Affordable Housing in NSW: Past to Present, Briefing Paper 14/05*. New South Wales Parliament, Sydney. <http://www.parliament.nsw.gov.au/prod/parlment/publications.nsf/0/c43281eba16c7f36ca2570c40003081c/$FILE/Finalaffordable.pdf>.

Wilkinson P, Landon M, Armstrong B, Stevenson S, Pattenden S, Mckee M, *et al.* (2001) *Cold Comfort: the Social and Environmental Determinants of Excess Winter Deaths, 1986–1996*. Policy Press and Rowntree Foundation, Bristol, UK. <http://www.jrf.org.uk/sites/files/jrf/jr101-determinants-winter-deaths.pdf>.

Windle GS, Burholt V, Edwards RT (2006) Housing related difficulties, housing tenure and variations in health status: evidence from older people in Wales. *Health & Place* **12**, 267–278. doi:10.1016/j.healthplace.2004.08.010

Wood G, Chamberlain C, Babbacan A, Dockery M, Cullen G, Costello G, *et al.* (2008) 'The implications of loss of a partner for older private renters'. Final Report No. 116. AHURI, Canberra.

Wood G, Ong R, Cigdem M (2013) 'Housing affordability dynamics: new insights from the last decade'. Final Report No. 223. AHURI, Melbourne.

WHO (World Health Organization) (2007) *Global Age-Friendly Cities: A Guide*. WHO, Geneva, Switzerland.

Worsley A, Blasche R, Ball K, Crawford D (2003) Income differences in food consumption in the 1995 Australia national nutrition survey. *European Journal of Clinical Nutrition* **57**, 1198–1211. doi:10.1038/sj.ejcn.1601670

Wright F (2004) Old and cold: older people and policies failing to address fuel poverty. *Social Policy and Administration* **38**(5), 488–503. doi:10.1111/j.1467-9515.2004.00403.x

Wulff M (2000) 'The National Survey of Rent Assistance Recipients: a report on key findings'. Commonwealth Department of Family and Community Services, Canberra.

Wulff M, Reynolds M, Arunachalam D, Hulse K, Yates J (2011) 'Australia's private rental market: the supply of, the demand for, affordable dwellings.' Final Report, No. 168. AHURI, Melbourne.

Yates J, Bradbury B (2010) Home ownership as a (crumbling) fourth pillar of social insurance in Australia. *Journal of Housing and the Built Environment* **25**(2), 193–211. doi:10.1007/s10901-010-9187-4

Yeates C (2015) 'Rental growth slowdown signals property boom on borrowed time'. *Sydney Morning Herald,* 27 June, <http://www.smh.com.au/business/the-economy/rental-growth-slowdown-signals-residential-property-bust-on-the-way-20150626-ghxkdr.html>.

Young J (1999) *The Exclusive Society.* Sage, London, UK.

Wu Z, Schimmele CM (2006) Psychological disposition and self-reported health among the oldest-old in China. *Ageing and Society* **26**(1), 135–151. doi:10.1017/S0144686X0500423X

Ziersch A, Arthurson K (2005) Social networks in public and community housing: the impact on employment outcomes. *Urban Policy and Research* **23**(4), 429–445. doi:10.1080/08111470500354265

Ziersch A, Arthurson K (2007) Social capital and housing tenure in an Adelaide neighbourhood. *Urban Policy and Research* **25**(4), 409–431. doi:10.1080/08111140701665831

Index

accommodation costs   vii, 5, 27, 30
   Age Pension and   10, 82
   housing tenure and   29–45
   living costs and   47–83
   social housing tenants and   63–4
accommodation quality, health status and   85–115
accommodation searches
   cars and   61
   private renters and   94–5
activity levels, homeowners   114–15, 230
activity site, home as   108–9
adequacy of shelter   234
advanced urban marginality   223
affordable housing   23, 234
age-friendly environment, public housing tenants and   220, 224–5
ageing in place   85–6
   homeowners and   164–7
   United States of America   246
Age Pension   vi, 1, 2, 3, 4, 5, 6, 7–8, 15, 23, 24, 26, 29, 30, 31, 32, 52, 247
   accommodation costs and   47, 48, 49, 51
   dependence on   9–10
   diet and   55, 56
   expenditure reduction and   78
   health status and   148, 150, 177
   homeowners and   39, 74, 229
   house sale price and   111–12
   housing costs and   231
   housing tenure and   82, 93
   insurance costs and   42, 43–4
   mental health and   151–3
   other income and   245
   poverty line and   230
   private renters and   37, 45, 230
   rate of   8, 246
   rental costs and   33, 34, 35, 36–7, 228
   social housing tenants and   62, 158
   social isolation and   143, 144
   total dependency on   130, 131
   transport and   72
   women and   10
air conditioning, inadequacy of   79, 80
alcohol consumption   63, 221
American Institute of Nutrition   52–3
An Ageing Australia: Preparing for the Future   1
Anglicare   228

anti-social behaviour   125–6, 217–25
anxiety levels, social housing tenants   70–1
apartment blocks, maintenance failures   199
assets test   9
Australia, home ownership   29
Australian Bureau of Statistics (ABS)   30, 147, 231
Australian Council of Social Service (ACOSS)   22
Australian dream, home ownership and   18
Australian governments
   housing policy   17–27
   housing tenure and   5–6
Australian Institute of Health and Welfare (AIHW)   231
automatic pension withdrawals   70

bankruptcy declaration   52, 53
Barangaroo   205–6
basic necessities
   accommodation costs and   52–7
   deprivation of   14
   social housing tenants and   65
boarding house accommodation   90–2
bond money in advance   246
borrowings, medical expenses and   176
Bourdieu, Pierre   48, 235, 245
bowling clubs   132
British civil servants study   148
budgeting ability
   homeowners   74–8
   social housing tenants and   63, 71, 229
buffer savings levels, homeowners   230
bulk billing   247
   lack of   168, 171
   social housing tenants and   173

capabilities approach   13–15, 47–8, 62
capital gains tax   17
car ownership expenses   60–2
   accommodation quality and   87
   homeowners and   80–2, 110, 145
   insurance   61, 62, 73
   private rental tenants and   127, 130
   registration costs   72, 73
   single pension homeowners and   77
   social housing tenants and   72–4, 136–7
Castles, Frank   29
cataract operations   247

causality, health status and   148
Census 1996/2011   245
CentreLink   36, 40, 71, 112, 152, 168, 172, 245
Cessnock, median weekly rent   232
charity assistance
    dependence on   56, 57, 153
    homeowners and   176
    utility bills   69
cheap food, sources of   56–7
children
    estrangement from   137, 140
    homeowners and   75–6, 111, 140–1, 162
    private renters and   139–40, 152
    social housing tenants and   71, 72–3, 136–7, 158
    transport and   62
China, social housing tenants from   121
church activities
    private rental tenants and   126, 128, 129
    social ties and   119–20
cigarette smoking   63, 91
    private renters and   147
    social housing tenants and   68
Civil and Administrative Tribunal (NSW)   180, 192
clothes buying
    accommodation costs and   50, 64
    social housing tenants and   66
clubs and societies, social housing tenants and   124
Commonwealth Rent Assistance (CRA)   22, 23, 30, 231–2, 245
Commonwealth State Housing Agreement (CSHA)   21, 22
community bus service   121, 122, 123
community centres   121, 126, 144, 158, 200, 209, 224
    food distribution and   68
    public housing tenants and   223
community housing   71, 94, 96, 97, 160, 171
    advantages of   199, 201, 202
    Commonwealth Rent Assistance and   245
    consumption patterns and   50
    costs   45
    movement into   245
    older Australians and   40
    pet owners and   142
    rents   34, 38, 39
    social ties and   118–19
Community Housing Providers (CHPs)   22–4, 144, 196, 244
    maintenance levels   199–200, 201
    public housing sales and   204
community transport service   72

constructionist approach (interview method)   236
consumer price index (CPI), rent increases and   232
Consumer, Trader and Tenancy Tribunal   26
consumption patterns
    accommodation costs and   47–83
    housing availability and   12, 13
    private renters   52–7
    social housing tenants   62–74
contextualisation, in-depth interviews   236
control levels, health status and   148–9
cottage accommodation   154
Council on the Ageing (COTA)   150
council rates   44
    country towns   76
    single age pensioners and   76
couples (age pensioners)
    accommodation costs and   50–1, 83
    diet and   68
    homeowners   229
    lifestyle capacity and   74, 75
    private rental market and   37
    social housing tenants   66
credit cards   82
credit, social housing tenants and   64
critical gerontology   3

de facto security   194–5
deinstitutionalisation, public housing and   216
dental care costs   150, 168–9
    homeowners and   176–7
    public provision of   169, 177
    social housing tenants and   172–3
Department of Housing (NSW) (Housing NSW)   96, 98, 100, 103, 160, 201, 204, 208, 214–15
diet adequacy
    accommodation costs and   53–7, 59
    homeowners and   79
    private renters and   52–7, 67
    social housing tenants and   66–9
'difficult' public housing tenants   212, 213–14
disadvantaged people, social housing and   9, 25, 211, 212
disposable income
    consumption patterns and   48–57
    housing status and   30–1
    private renters and   35, 114
dispositions   245
divorce, retirement and   10
dog ownership, health benefits   142–3

domestic violence, public housing and   221
downsizing   20, 112–13, 115
driving licence, older persons and   246
drug taking and dealing, public housing   199, 214, 216, 221, 222
dualist rental market   230
dwelling size, social housing renters and   97–8, 99

Eastern suburbs (Sydney)   228
elective surgery waiting times   247
electrical maintenance, failure of   189
electricity prices
   homeowners and   79, 80
   increases   57, 59
   social housing tenants and   69–70
eligibility age, Age Pension   1, 2
emergency funds   70–1, 171
empathy, public housing tenants and   216, 225
energy poverty   57–9
energy supplement   9
ethics permissions   237
eviction, threat of   190
   Millers Point   206, 207–8
excursions, social housing tenants and   122–3, 125
expenditure planning, homeowners and   41–2, 78
extended family, neighbourhood ties as   120–1
Eye Hospital   174, 247

face-to-face interviews   237
family support   71, 72–3, 75
Family Tax Benefit   245
family ties   145
   homeowners and   12, 140–2
   private renters and   137–40
   social housing tenants and   135–7, 157
fear of the future, private renters and   152–4
feelings of shame, private renters and   153
financial restraints
   family ties and   138–9
   homeowners and   131, 132
   private renters and   137–8
   social activity limitations and   126, 127–8, 129–30
financial support
   children's   137–8
   medical expenses   167
fire alarms   193
first time home buyers' grants   18
fixed incomes   6, 29
food costs, medical expenses and   168

food shopping   48, 56–7
   disposable income and   48–57
   homeowners and   78–9
   private renters and   52–7, 59
   social housing tenants and   66–9
France, public housing   223, 224
fuel poverty   57
full-rate pension   9
functionings   14
funding cuts, federal government   197–8
Future of Retirement Study   2

gap fees   173
gardening activities
   homeowners and   108–9, 112, 166
   private renters and   193, 194
   social housing tenants and   203
gas bills   80
gender issues
   housing limitations and   10–11
   lack of coverage   237
generational habitus   48
Germany
   secure housing   7
   time spent at home   11
globalisation   3
global warming, housing temperatures and   9
'golden age' public housing   215
golfing   133
Goward, Pru   205
grammars of living   217
grandchildren
   homeowners and   141, 162
   private renters and   138
granny flat accommodation   87, 90, 103, 126, 192–3
Grattan Institute   1
green bans (1970s)   204
guarantees of occupancy   114

habitus   48, 245
head leases   103
Health and Retirement Study   148
health care, publicly funded   2
health insurance   43, 172, 247
   homeowners and   174–6
   private renters and   169
health status
   energy poverty and   58–9
   homeowners   74
   housing insecurity and   88, 89–90, 93–4
   housing quality and   8–9
   housing tenure and   vii, 85–115, 147–78

medical expenses and 167–8
pet ownership and 142
private renters 127, 154
social disorder and 126
social housing tenants 155–61
social ties and 117
heating inadequacy 58
homeowners and 79, 80
social housing tenants 69–70
high-rise apartments 100
holidays, homeowners and 65–6, 133–4, 145
home and contents insurance 43–4
homelessness 13
fear of 181
older Australians and 25–6
partner's death and 11
private rental tenants and 96, 98, 129
homeowners
accommodation costs and 39–45
Age Pension and 6, 229
family ties and 140–2
health status of 148, 161–7
housing tenure and 86
interviewees 243
lifestyle capacity 74–82
locational attachment 105–9
medical expenses and 174–7, 178
mortgages and 237
percentage decline of 231
private renters and 27
social ties 144, 117, 130–5
homeownership vii
Age Pension and 10
costs 40–2, 45, 108
Europe 7
importance of 11–12
increase in 18–19, 25
post World War 2 17–27
social class and 4
social housing tenants and 211
West Central Scotland study 161
homeowners without a mortgage, interviews with 244
home units 113
hotel gatherings, older homeowners 133
house block size 110–11
house deposits 18
Household Expenditure Survey (HES) 149
household improvements, homeowners and 109, 165, 166
Household, Income and Labour Dynamics in Australia (HILDA) survey 35, 70, 246
household maintenance, private renters and 187–92

households in greatest need (definition) 212
house maintenance failures 181
house rents, increases in 228
house sales, private renters and 181
housing affordability 2–3
United Kingdom 248
Housing and Accommodation Support Initiative (HASI) (NSW) 225–6
housing, as a human right 233
housing associations 119, 248
Housing Commission (NSW) 64, 95–6, 99, 100, 101, 102, 103, 155, 183, 184, 196
housing costs, Age Pension and 231
Housing Data Set (Australian Government) 231
housing finance 18
housing insecurity, mental health and 181–3, 184–5
housing longevity 131
Housing Ministers Council 23
Housing NSW, *see* Department of Housing (NSW)
housing policy, Australian governments 17–27
housing price increases, Sydney 232–3
housing resumptions, private renters and 184, 185
housing sell-offs, Millers Point 247
housing subsidies, right to 234
housing tenure 19, 118
accommodation costs and 29–45
health status and 85–115, 147–78
older Australians and 1–15, 26
private renters and 93–7
social housing and 101–2
social isolation and 120
human right, housing as a 233

impulse purchases, lack of 56
income additions, age pensioners and 40
income adequacy, social housing tenants 63
income percentage, social housing rents and 34–5
income restrictions
accommodation costs and 51
pet ownership and 143
in-depth interviews 235–8
Indigenous Australians, social housing and 24
individual freedoms, housing and 14
indoor temperature 9
Inquiry into Health Services for the Psychiatrically Ill and Developmentally Disabled (Richmond Report) 215–16, 248

insect infestations 90
insecurity of tenure, private renters 209, 227, 228
insurance costs
    homeowners and 42, 43, 229
    single pension homeowners and 77, 78
integrated rental market 230, 232
interest-free loans 245
International Covenant on Economic, Social and Cultural Rights (ICESCR), General Comment No 4 233
internet connection 65, 77
interview technique, limitations of 235, 236
interviewees
    profiles of 239–43
    recruitment method 236–7
intimidation, social housing tenants and 198
involuntary accommodation change 93–7

Kemeny's thesis 29, 45, 230

Landlord and Tenant (Amendment) Act 1948 244
landlord pastoral care, social housing tenants and 200–1, 209
landlord–tenant relations viii, 148, 179–209
large appliance expenses 81–2
large house properties, homeowners and 135
leaking taps maintenance 198
lease expiry 181, 184–5
leisure activities
    disruptions to 222–3
    homeowners' 163
    social housing tenants' 120
length of residence 11
liberated communities 117
life expectancy 156, 231
Lifeline 53, 152
life-long leases 180, 217
lifestyle capacity, homeowners and 74–82
lighting deprivation 58–9
living costs, accommodation costs and 34–5, 47–83
locality
    accommodation quality and 88–9, 104, 105
    homeowners and 105–9, 110
    housing insecurity and 94
    importance of 3
locational differences, median weekly rent 232
locational security, Millers Point 206
long-term leases 25, 194–5, 232
low-income households
    consumption patterns 48
    rental costs and 228
    social housing and 211, 214, 215
low-interest loans 17–18
lunchtime meetings, older homeowners 132–5

maintenance costs
    apartment blocks 199
    homeowners and 40–2, 43, 229
    Millers Point 207–8
    private renters and 208
    social housing tenants and 196–200, 209
maintenance of appliances 59, 60, 71, 82
maintenance support, social housing tenants and 203
major expenses
    homeowners and 80–2
    social housing tenants and 70–4
malnutrition 57, 59
malpractice, landlord 179
managing agents, supportive 191–2
Maritime Services Board 204, 206, 207, 208, 248
maximum pension supplement 9
Meals on Wheels 200
mechanical repair expenses, inability to pay 59–62
media image, public housing 223–4
median rents 31–2, 232
medical crises
    accommodation costs and 153
    transport availability and 73–4
medical expenses
    homeowners and 174–7, 178
    private renters and 167–71, 178
    social housing tenants and 171–4, 178
Medicare 149, 171, 173, 228, 247
Medicare Chronic Disease Dental Scheme (CDDS), abandonment of 247
medication expenses
    income capacity and 68, 148, 149
    private renters and 228
Melbourne Institute of Applied Economic and Social Research (MIAESR) 31, 32
mental health status
    accommodation status and 147, 148–9, 151, 152–4
    Age Pension and 177
    housing sell-offs and 205
    maintenance difficulties and 190
    public housing tenants and 215, 216, 219, 224
micro-locales 218
Millers Point, Dawes Point and the Rocks 104–5, 180, 200, 202, 248

'difficult' public housing tenants and   213–14
  housing sell-offs   204–8, 209, 247
  public housing tenants at   229, 247
minor repairs, social housing tenants and   197
mobile phone ownership   51–2, 65
mobility limitations   118
'morally adequate light'   236
mortality rates, public housing tenants   205
mortgage holders   18, 19, 20

National Health Survey (NHS)   147
neighbourhood support
  age-friendly   212–13
  homeowners and   131, 134–5, 165, 166
  social housing tenants and   118, 120–2, 123–4, 144
neoliberal ethos, housing tenure and   5
Netherlands, secure housing   7
net overseas migration   231
New Deal for Communities (UK)   246
New South Wales (NSW)   vii, 37, 44, 170, 179, 180, 217, 225
  community housing providers of   244
  electricity price increases   57
  hospital system   247
  periodic agreements   26
  regional   99
  social housing decline in   24
noise excess, public housing tenants and   220–1
Norfolk Island   134
notice to vacate   180
nursing homes   165, 237

older Australians   vii, vii
  definition   5
  demographic shift   1
  government housing policy and   17–27
  home ownership and   39–45
  housing tenure and   19
  private rental sector and   24, 25–7, 33, 34, 35–9
  social housing rents and   31, 33–5
older homeowners, *see* homeowners
older private renters, *see* private rental tenants
older public housing tenants, *see* public housing tenants
older social housing tenants, *see* social housing tenants
ontological security   181
optometrists
  private renters and   170
  social housing tenants and   173

Orange, council rates   44
osteopathy expenses   177
outright house ownership   19–20
owner-occupiers   30

partner loss
  homelessness and   11
  income disadvantage and   37–8, 40
pathologising discourse, public health tenants   215
Pensioner Concession Card   247
pensioner rebates (council rates)   44
periodic agreements   26
personal fragility, house maintenance and   187–8
personal grooming, poverty and   50
personal insecurity, public housing tenants and   218–20
personal security   13
  homeowners and   111, 113
  public housing tenants and   99–100, 218–19, 224
  social housing tenants and   123
personal space, invasion of   218–19
personal stress, private renters and   227
pet ownership   142
  homeowners and   81, 108
  mental health and   246
  private renters and   54
Pharmaceutical Benefit Scheme (PBS)   149, 168, 247
pharmaceutical expenses
  medical expenses and   168, 172
  private renters and   94
  social housing tenants and   171–2, 173
physical environment degradation, public housing   221–2
physiotherapy expenses   150, 170
place attachment
  homeowners and   109–12
  public housing tenants and   224–5
political engagement, housing and   12
population composition, public housing tenants   213–17
poverty line   9, 10, 14
  Age Pension and   230
  private renters and   19, 31–2, 35
  social housing tenants and   65
principal residence   17
privacy invasions, public housing tenants and   220–1
private rental sector (PRS)   vi, vii
  disposable income and   30–1
  failure of   231
  social housing tenancy and   158–9, 160, 162, 163, 164

social impacts of 7, 13
    variations in 232
private rental tenants
    accommodation costs and 98, 156
    accommodation quality and 86–93
    Age Pension and 228, 230
    consumption patterns 50
    diet and 52–7
    government policy and 18, 22
    health status 147, 148, 151–5, 177
    homeowners and 142
    income inadequacy 83
    interviewees 239–40, 242
    lack of primary control 148
    living difficulties and 45
    medical expenses and 149–50, 167–71, 178
    mobility 118
    older people as 25–7, 33, 34, 35–9, 40
    public housing and 100
    security of tenure/occupancy 5–6, 93–7, 113–14, 180–7, 208, 231
    social activities and 117, 126–30
    social isolation and 143–4, 149, 227
private renters with heavily subsidised rents, interviewees 240
Probus Club 133, 247
Productivity Commission 1
profiles, interviewees' 239–43
property status, landlord–tenant relationship and 191, 192
protected tenants 244
pub accommodation 91
public housing 114
    decline of 22
    definition 244
    government commitment to 21
    maintenance of 198–9
    Millers Point 204–8, 229
    personal security concerns 99–100
    public spaces in 221, 223
    security of tenure 24, 120
    sell-offs 159–61, 180, 196, 204–8, 209
    social housing tenants and 121, 122
    social isolation and 119
    Western Sydney 237
public housing tenants
    changing composition of 212–17
    pet ownership and 143
    private renters and 225
    residualisation and 211–26
public transport 72
    homeowners and 110, 112
    inadequacy of 61, 80, 81
    private renters and 128
    social isolation and 154–5

qualifying age, Age Pension 5
qualitative interviewing technique 235
quality of life, accommodation costs and 47–83

real estate agents, private renters and 188
recurring expenses, homeowners and 135
regional New South Wales
    Age Pension and 74–5
    location of interviewees 235
removal costs 93, 111, 114
removal resistance 103–5, 110
rental accommodation, lack of 17
rental rates
    community housing providers and 23
    increases 20, 21, 22, 26, 180, 190, 193
    maintenance and 189–90
    mental health status and 153
    private renters and 13, 36, 114, 181, 183, 208–9, 227, 232
    security of occupancy and 7
rent assistance 21, 51, 130
renter maintenance responsibility 189–90
rent in advance 246
rent pegging 24, 25, 196, 201
rent security, private renters and 186–7
residential longevity, social housing tenants 120, 123
Residential Tenancies Act 2010 (NSW) 179, 187, 189, 244
residualisation, social housing 211–26, 245, 248
retirement provisions, housing security and 29–30
retirement villages 113, 162, 237
Ritzer, George vi
rootedness, social housing tenants 195
Russian-speaking public housing tenants 124
    family ties and 135–6
    interview method 237
    social housing and 200

Salvation Army 56, 59
satisfaction levels, homeowners 161–3
savings dependency 13, 246
    homeowners 39–40, 175
security of occupancy 4, 7, 24, 25, 26, 27, 86
    homeowners and 161–3, 167
    housing adequacy and 234
    private renters 36, 180–7, 194–5, 227, 228, 231, 232
    public housing tenants and 120
    social housing tenants 156–7, 158–9, 178, 195–6, 201–8, 209

security problems
   accommodation and   88, 89, 90–1, 92
   social housing tenants and   102–3, 104–5, 199
self-deprivation, private renters and   49
Sen, Amartya   13–15
sense of ownership, social housing tenants and   201–3
serviced room accommodation   89
shared accommodation   90–1, 92–3
shopping expeditions   144, 200
   private rental tenants   126
   social housing tenants   122
short-term leases, public housing   217
siblings
   homeowners and   141
   private renters and   138
single person households
   accommodation quality and   87–93
   homeowners   106–7
   house maintenance and   41–2, 43
   lifestyle capacity as   74, 76–8
   private rental market and   20, 33, 36, 37–8, 50, 52
   social activity and   125
small investor landlords
   housing maintenance and   188–9
   political power   232
social activities
   homeowners and   133
   private rental tenants and   126–30
   social housing tenants and   156, 157, 158, 159
social class, housing tenure and   3–4
social exclusion   12–13
   public housing tenants and   222–3
social housing
   Australian Government and   244
   construction of   233
   definition   244
   housing tenure and   91, 93
   inadequacy of   231
   private renters' changeover to   160
   quality of   97–100
   reduction of   5, 6, 19, 23, 24, 27
   regulation of   230
   rents and   45
   residualisation   211–26
   urban design and   124
   waiting lists   vii, 95–6, 97
social housing tenants   114
   accommodation advantages   101–3
   Age Pension and   229
   consumption capacity of   62–74
   health status of   155–61
   income adequacy   82–3

interviewees   237, 240–2, 247
landlord pastoral care and   200–1
maintenance and   196–200
medical expenses and   171–4
mobility and   118
private renters and   245
profile   248
rents 31, 33–5
rights   180
security of occupancy   86, 195–6, 201–8
sense of ownership   201–3
social ties and   117, 119–26, 144
social inclusion   12, 13, 164
social isolation
   factors   120
   homeowners and   166–7
   levels of   143–4
   mental health status and   149
   private rental tenants and   126–30, 154–5
   public housing tenants and   119
   social housing tenants and   137
social security, home ownership and   30
social ties   104
   accommodation options and   vii, 117–45
   homeowners and   130–5
   private renters and   227
   social housing tenants and   120, 196, 229
social wellbeing
   housing and   12–13
   primary control and   149
sociology, uses of   vi
sole accommodation costs, women and   10–11
sole homeowners, social activities   131
spare accommodation   107–8, 141–2
spatial control
   homeowners   108, 163–4
   private renters and   192–5
   social housing tenants and   201–4
   tenant–landlord relationship and   185–6
specialists' fees   150, 168, 171, 173
special needs, social housing tenants   211–12
spectacles
   costs   150, 168, 170
   free provision of   247
standard of living, housing and   233–4
stigmatisation, public housing tenants and   217, 223–4, 226
strata titles   6, 39, 44–5, 113
street markets   57
stress levels
   private renters   151–2, 153–4
   social housing tenants   155, 158–9
structural unemployment   224
studio apartments   98–9, 193

study methodology (description) 235–8
subsidised housing 244
subsidised medications 150
substance abuse, public housing tenants and 218
superannuation 74
support facilities, public housing tenants and 196, 216–17, 225–6
surgery expenses, homeowners and 175, 176
Survey of Income and Housing (ABS) 245
Switzerland, secure housing 7
Sydney vii, 78, 99, 101, 113, 114, 121, 141, 151, 160, 180, 196, 205, 206, 237, 246
   council rates 44
   location of interviewees 235
   median weekly rent 31–2, 232
   private rental market 37, 38, 39, 98, 227, 228, 232–3
   serviced room accommodation 89

telephone contact 137, 164
telephone interviews 237
tenants' associations vii, 122, 123, 144, 157
   anti-social behaviour and 222
   Millers Point sell-offs and 206
   social housing tenants and 197, 198, 201
tenants' rights, landlords and 179–209
Tenants' Union (NSW) 179, 180, 215, 244
tenure access, social housing 211
ten-year lease
   private renters and 186–7
   social housing tenants and 180
textual documentary 235
theatre-going, homeowners and 132–3
thematic approach, in-depth interviews 237–8
threatening behaviour, public housing tenants and 218
time spent at home 11–12
total fertility rate (TFR) 231
travelling expenses, homeowners 74–5
trust development, social housing tenants 123

unemployment 13
   social housing tenants and 211, 212, 224
United Kingdom (UK) 246
   public housing 215, 224, 248
   social exclusion in 12
United Nations 11
United States of America (USA)
   ageing in place 246
   home ownership 29
   public housing 215, 223, 224
Universal Declaration of Human Rights, housing and 233
University of New South Wales 237, 247
urban precinct, Sydney wharves area 206
utility bills 57–9, 164
   homeowners and 79–80
   single age pensioners and 76
   social housing tenants and 69–70

vandalism, public housing 199, 214, 218, 222
village life, homeowners and 166–7
Visioncare 170, 247
visiting relations, private renters and 139
volunteer activities
   mental health and 157
   private rental tenants and 129, 130
   social housing tenants and 136

waiting lists
   dental services 150, 169
   social housing tenants 96, 97, 173, 184, 211
water heating maintenance 198
Weight of the World, The (Bourdieu) 235
welfare state, weakening of 2, 29
Western Sydney 237
white goods renting 71
Winston Parva study 216–17
women, pension limitations and 10–11
working class
   home ownership and 4, 18
   private renters and 25

www.ingramcontent.com/pod-product-compliance
Lightning Source LLC
Chambersburg PA
CBHW020454030426
42337CB00011B/116